Car

Titles in the *Objekt* series explore a range of types – buildings, products, artefacts – that have captured the imagination of modernist designers, makers and theorists. The objects selected for the series are by no means all modern inventions, but they have in common the fact that they acquired a particular significance in the last 100 years.

Car

Gregory Votolato

REAKTION BOOKS

For Arthur and Max

Published by Reaktion Books Ltd
33 Great Sutton Street
London EC1V 0DX, UK

www.reaktionbooks.co.uk

First published 2015

Printed and bound in China

A catalogue record for this book is available from the British Library

ISBN 978 1 78023 452 6

Contents

Preface

While visiting the bankrupt city of Detroit in the summer of 2013, I saw vividly the long trajectory of the American automobile, from its rise, presented as a heroic historical narrative at the Henry Ford museum and Greenfield Village, to its decline, revealed in the vast ruin of the architect Albert Kahn's astounding Packard factory. Few people live or work downtown any more. Yet evidence of the city's heyday is still detectible in a few lavish remnants, such as the Art Deco Fisher Building and the Detroit Art Institute, where Diego Rivera's murals of the Ford factory elegantly survey the wonders and horrors of the entire system of mass car production.

Those affluent decades of the Motor City's past are now echoed in nearby Dearborn. There, in present-day Ford country (home to Ford's Product Development Center, the Henry Ford museum and Greenfield Village), all appears secure and fresh, a picture-postcard suburb reminiscent of 1950s America, where the whole population seems to drive either a new Mustang or a classic Mustang, lovingly tended and displayed with pride on the driveway in front of each tidy Colonial or Ranch-style house.

The fall of Detroit came about for many complex reasons to do with labour relations, immigration, race, corporate complacency, political shenanigans and prejudicial zoning, to mention but a few.

The windscreen view familiar to almost everyone in the motoring world also served as inspiration to artists, who saw landscapes framed in a new, kinetic way that altered their relation with outdoor subjects, the car often becoming a mobile studio.

In the calm centre of it all, however, remains an image of that compelling object, the car, forever revolving on a turntable, its gleaming body draped with a lightly clad, pulchritudinous model. In reality, at this end of its 130-year history, the car itself remains much as it was when it first appeared, a private transportation vehicle with four wheels and an internal combustion engine for power. It still accommodates, typically, between two and eight people. It represents the owner's wealth, values and status in society. It continues to be one of the most desirable objects available commercially to billions of people throughout the world. And it still has a significant carbon footprint from its manufacture, and contributes increasingly to environmental pollution and global warming owing to its ever-expanding use and from its disposal.

Albert Kahn's pioneering Packard plant, opened in 1903, was the prototype for early 20th-century mass car-production factories. Since the decline of Detroit it has housed small manufacturing, storage and rave parties. A Spanish developer plans its restoration and return to mixed use.

Back at home in England, I see the cars that pass along the busy coastal road below my window as either sanctuaries or solitary prison cells, magic carpets or mobile fortifications, attractive examples of hollow rolling sculpture, instruments of mass destruction and totems of irrational consumer choice; in other words, bundles of contradictions that defy easy interpretation. In the face of a vast literature about the car, I hope this book will communicate a balanced sense of the personal values and the practical reality of this inscrutable, magnetic, appalling and unavoidable object, central to modern life and yet threatening to its survival.

As a North American male growing up in a pleasant, pavement- and bus-free suburb in the 1950s, I worshipped cars. The Tomorrow Land motorway, with its miniature petrol-driven sports cars, at Disneyland in Los Angeles was my first driving experience, as an eleven-year-old, and it held out a promise of freedom and independence that I never fully recaptured as an adult on US Interstates or even on the German Autobahn. Yet in keeping with counter-cultural attitudes of the 1960s and the nascent Green movement of the '70s, I came to dismiss that love for cars as a bourgeois affliction dispensable in the European metropolitan culture I embraced. Lately, however, I think about cars more earnestly, and I realize their significance more acutely with each passing year. I see their many charms balanced against the immense harm they do, environmentally and psychologically. And yet I maintain a degree of optimism about the many directions in which their design may move to provide pleasure, to serve changing needs, and to do less harm in cities and within the global context of twenty-first-century personal mobility.

Regardless of how green we may wish to be in our travel behaviour, if we need or want to go to another continent, there is no practical alternative to flying. Increasingly in the developed world, high-speed trains are providing an excellent alternative to short flights or to long drives. Commuters travelling regularly from far-flung suburbs to city centres are also packing on to trains in order to avoid parking problems and traffic jams. Yet millions of drivers still prefer to sit alone in their cars, creeping towards their destination, than to share space with strangers in a train carriage. And there remains the pleasure of a road trip. British byways and twisting Alpine roads still evoke a certain delight that is achievable only in a car.

Many people today consider an automobile their most cherished possession, that which makes their lives rich and satisfying. Others may not be in love with their car, but cannot imagine how they would function without it. Some of those who live in cities with good public transport have given up owning a car altogether. Many more around the world, however, are looking forward to having a car of their own for the first time. And therein lies the problem. The desire for automobiles is still growing, at a time when the dangers of their proliferation are increasingly clear. Today, more than a billion car owners see the private automobile as the ultimate transport vehicle, disregarding its inefficiency, and will use no other form of transport unless forced to do so. Others, in professions from engineering to psychology, who recognize its limitations, are attempting to re-define the car for the future. Nevertheless, the general public seems to be enraptured by the emotive advertising and styling calculated to appeal to our most irrational, distasteful and even sociopathic tendencies.

Once upon a time, the automobile was seen as a plaything for rich sportsmen and adventuresome, competitive women. Early endorsements of the car defined it in terms familiar to people of means and leisure, its first user group. In 1903 *Automobile Review* published 'What the Automobile Can Do':

The automobile is a most prominent factor in modern education and travel and a pleasant form of transportation that appeals more potently, and widely, to the intelligence of the man or woman, than any other form of enjoyment. People are more stimulated by the automobile than by any other sport . . . [It] will outstrip ordinary mail trains, or move as gently through the streets as a hansom cab; a machine that will take its owner across the continent as easily as it will take him down to his office from his suburban home.[1]

Those early cars provided the first motorists with distinctly new pleasures, and it was in this respect, as much as from practicality, that the automobile evolved from a sporting luxury into an object of mass desire, promoted relentlessly by design and advertising. And it soon generated changes to the built environment that created a

By the time this illustration was published in 1910, the car's path of destruction was visible to all, but few could resist its mesmeric charms. Albert Levering, 'The God of Their Idolatry – Sacrifice Offerings to the Gasoline Chuggernaut', *Puck* magazine.

closed cycle of desire and dependency. By offering young people an escape from the strictures of the post-Victorian home and family, it became a social necessity, as Facebook is today. Even now, it offers relief for those whose homes are more prison than retreat. And it is in itself a haven; a place to be alone while enjoying a private view of the public realm populated by people, who may be interesting to watch, but with whom the motorist need have no unwanted contact. And in such sprawling cities as Los Angeles or Melbourne, the car – that icon of freedom, adulthood, success and personality – is perceived by many as a necessity for every journey, no matter how short.

Affectionate portrayals of the car appear regularly in film – *Cars* (2006), the various *Herbie* movies – and television, emanating prominently from North America, where the role of the automobile in everyday life goes largely unquestioned. Nostalgia for earlier days of the open road appears persistently in the arena of entertainment, while antique, classic and custom car meetings in all established motoring countries reflect a deep reverence for collectible vehicles, focusing on the car body as a fetish. Typically, the annual Paris Retromobile event attracts hundreds of exhibitors, restorers and auctioneers, plus tens of thousands of visitors celebrating the finest historic automobiles and automobilia, confirming the car as the pre-eminent exemplar of twentieth-century industrial art.

Car lovers tend to take the universal appeal of the automobile for granted, and avoid considering it in any larger context than its attractiveness to them personally. Even within diverse communities from Africa to the Australian outback, as the anthropologist Daniel Miller noted, cars have resisted serious analysis, perhaps more than any other major product of industrial society. Miller wrote that among scholars the car was not 'legitimate as a topic to focus upon'.[2] Such an aversion is symptomatic of the mesmeric effect the car has, almost paralysing serious attempts to investigate its grasp on lives and minds.

Alternatively, the sociologist John Urry called the car 'the quintessential manufactured object, the major object of individual consumption, the predominant global form of quasi-private mobility [that] . . . constitutes the good life . . . and which provides potent literary and artistic images and symbols, the single most important cause of environmental resource-use . . . pollution and wars', confirming the car as the central object within a huge matrix of big ideas and even bigger issues.[3]

Polarized arguments arising ever since its invention have either celebrated or vilified the car. Yet they seldom examine its relationship to the lives of motorists living in conditions where cars serve distinctive purposes, and where they are understood differently from the cars of stereotypical suburbanites in the developed world.[4] Those alternative uses are, however, helpful as indicators of how the car may evolve throughout the world in the near future in response to newly perceived needs and conditions, such as those of the elderly, the homeless or the millions of new drivers, with no experience of cars, flooding suddenly on to recently built roads in rapidly motorizing countries.

It is commonly understood that the car functions intimately as an extension of our bodies and as an expressive means of negotiating the rules of society, a role also fulfilled by fashionable clothing, long recognized as an influence in automotive design. Our cars tell the world who we think we are and act as our proxies in the public realm. Much automotive literature and media attention concentrates on style and performance, with typical celebratory publicity presenting the car as an ever-improving product, increasingly efficient, safe and satisfying to the owner/user with every technological and aesthetic advance. A short drive in any modern car would support this view, but underlying every advance, there is and has always been a subtext that the hype does not disclose.

In the 1920s the Russian Futurist Ilya Ehrenburg portrayed the car in terms of dehumanizing production systems (mining, rubber extraction, the assembly line), a grotesque accident toll and, most interestingly, its antisocial influence on drivers.[5] Critics continue to investigate how basic automotive technology and styling have related to the class structures associated with motoring and the primary activities of work and leisure. The historian David Gartman commented sharply that the immense effort of designing meaning into cars as a replacement for genuine meaning in life and work has cost humanity

The glamour of the European-style luxury car penetrates deeply into the less developed world, where the real thing only reaches the richest and often the most corrupt members of society. Man's embroidered tunic with Rolls-Royce motif, c. 1970, Nigeria.

millions of lives, trillions of dollars, and immeasurable damage to the landscape and environment. Perhaps it would be better to put meaning back into . . . jobs, families, and communities than to continue to burden a transportation machine with the task of saving souls.[6]

Recent systematic approaches to understanding the car include attempts to audit its various expenses beyond the purchase price and running overheads. They include its incalculable ecological 'costs', the development and upkeep of the automotive infrastructure, the value of time spent driving, the treatment of car-related illnesses and injuries, the cost borne by taxpayers in countries that fund a public health service or by private insurers' premiums elsewhere. Now, a torrent of statistical evidence has proved today's car to be the primary agent of global environmental degradation.[7] This realization has prompted critiques – predominantly metropolitan in focus and lacking empathy with drivers – to promote only existing alternatives, train, bus, bicycle and foot, while preaching: 'Thou Shalt Not Drive.' In the face of such bluntly anti-car sentiment, it seems that there is need for a more nuanced, realistic and creative approach to the automobile, that problem child of the industrial world, recognizing its compelling personal attraction while confronting its corrosive influences and looking towards its future.

Although widening understanding of the automobile and its effects could move pro- and anti-car debates forwards, such big contexts may obscure the object itself and neglect the personal relationship between ourselves and our cars, which can be seen as addiction, the 'right' to drive or the favourite mantra of twenty-first-century car advertising, 'emotional involvement'. Without a close-up view of the car and a finer understanding of why its use is so contagious, any proposed solutions to its problems are of limited value.

Whereas the stereotypical automobile enthusiast is interested in the car primarily as a vessel of excitement, other users prioritize economy and sustainability. Some do both. In the 1930s the 'comprehensive' designer Buckminster Fuller boasted that his attention-grabbing Dymaxion Car was capable of 100 mph (160 km/h) thanks to its lightness and streamlined, aeronautically inspired body, and he loved to 'demonstrate' it. In addition to its extraordinary appearance, it was elegantly engineered to provide economical private transportation for the whole population with minimum impact on world resources. The car achieved 30 mpg, and the 'carbon footprint' of its proposed mass manufacture would be low, since Fuller, like Ford, intended his car to be upgradeable and to last a lifetime.

The architect Norman Foster, an admirer of Fuller and sometime collaborator with him, commissioned a re-creation of the Dymaxion Car in connection with an exhibition he curated in 2010 of Fuller's work. Foster said of the car's relevance to automobiles today:

> The maxim of doing more with less is more urgent and imperative today than it's ever been. In a way the Dymaxion was the classic people-mover before its time . . . and [it] demonstrates . . [Fuller's] belief in friendly clean technology that would enable the species to survive if they used their intelligence.[8]

Particularly since the Second World War, the words 'economy' and 'car' have been linked only in the most spartan automobiles. Nevertheless, some of the tiniest and most efficient 'people's cars' have also been fun to use, and are deeply admired. Examples include the original models of the Volkswagen Beetle, Austin Mini, Citroën 2CV and Fiat 500. In the twenty-first century the innovative Smart city car has taken up the baton of the minimal car, but it is alone in its segment.

The typical car remains large and powerful, accommodating between two and eight times the number of people it usually carries, which is only one. Its lack of fundamental innovation combined with massively expanding car ownership in countries including Brazil, India and China challenge the industry to develop designs for personal mobility that will ameliorate rising numbers by improving economy in use, reducing congestion, devouring less energy in production, occupying less space when parked and, most controversially, prioritizing longevity over disposability. With China alone producing over 18 million cars in 2013 (more than twice as many as Japan and four times the number produced in the USA), and its market for first-time buyers barely scratched, a new automotive paradigm is urgently needed.[9]

The Smart citycar was originally developed by fashion-watch manufacturers Swatch, in collaboration with Daimler-Benz, and launched in 1998. Its small size and cheeky character attract large measures of either affection or hostility, but it is softening the ground for future designs.

Even such a new model of thinking may not be enough to stem the impact of car use on the global environment, but – barring the unfeasible abandonment of private transportation around the world – it may be our best hope. And while that demand may not be filled by a universal Chinese people's car, several specialized types of private vehicle will more likely fill that colossal demand.

Despite the growth of global automobile use, the USA remains a huge market and the most entrenched car culture. Since 1970, its car registrations and vehicle miles travelled have greatly exceeded population growth. Americans' love affair with big vehicles has also deepened in recent decades, to the extent that the average family car is now a 3-ton, 160+-km/h (100+-mph) four-door pick-up truck, a multi-purpose vehicle (MPV) seating seven, or a four-wheel-drive sports-utility vehicle (SUV) dressed in chrome, leather and shiny faux walnut. This brings me to the question of what can reasonably be described as a 'car', a significant one now, when the types of vehicle we use to get around on public roads have the potential to spawn new segments for the industry, such as low-speed electric vehicles (EVs) and various kinds of quadricycle and tricycle. Today's 'cars', as we know them, make up about three-quarters of the total motor vehicles in the world.[10]

The size of cars ranges roughly from the 400-kg Renault Twizy electric microcar to the American Presidential Cadillac One, estimated to weigh over 6,400 kg (more than 7 tons). Larger or smaller vehicles at present belong to other species. Car classification systems are used to distinguish one body type or size from another for various purposes including registration, marketing and taxation, as defined by such agencies as the European New Car Assessment Programme (NCAP), the US Environmental Protection Agency (EPA) and the Society of Indian Automobile Manufacturers (SIAM). Typical classes, also known as segments, include Microcars (A-segment), MPVs

(M-segment), Heavy-Duty Pick-up Trucks (J-segment) and the largest, Special Purpose Vehicles (SPVs). New cars also carry various star or letter ratings for energy efficiency or carbon emissions, but these can be of dubious integrity unless certified by the respective government or validated by the Geneva-based International Organization for Standardization (ISO).

As with labelling, other initiatives to promote cars with energy-saving characteristics have proved unreliable. The ecological advantages of the benign-sounding 'flexi-fuel' vehicles, capable of running on either biofuel or gasoline, came into question as a result of their legal coverage by manufacturers' US tax bonuses. Such cars remained thirsty and continued to consume ordinary gasoline as their main or only fuel (biofuel-dispensing stations are

North America's most popular vehicle, Ford's F-series pick-up truck has become typical of the standard family car in a land of truck-driving moms and dads. A leather- and walnut-trimmed, upscale 2015 Ford Raptor is seen here in its natural habitat, the suburban driveway.

few and far between) in spite of their privileged tax status. Thus their 'green' credentials turned out to be somewhat of a myth.[11]

On the other hand, hybrid technology, developed in the 1990s by relatively progressive Japanese car makers, became a commercial success and allowed significant fuel savings. Before 1900, Ferdinand Porsche and the Belgian Henri Pieper constructed hybrid gasoline-electric vehicles. Subsequently other hybrid cars appeared. Among them, the Woods Dual Power is notable, as about 600 were produced in Chicago between 1916 and 1918. This car's electric motor powered the car at speeds of up to 24 km/h (15 mph), when a conventional four-cylinder internal combustion engine (ICE) took over to propel the vehicle to its top speed of 56 km/h (35 mph). Despite its innovative propulsion system, the Woods Dual Power was slow in comparison with gasoline cars in its high price class, and so it failed commercially.

In the early 1970s General Motors supported the scientist Victor Wouk, known as the 'grandfather' of hybrid vehicles in the USA, to develop a gasoline-electric hybrid as a direct response to the abortive

The Woods Dual Power was an early petrol-electric hybrid car, produced in its hundreds from 1916 to 1918. It is a forerunner of the modern Prius.

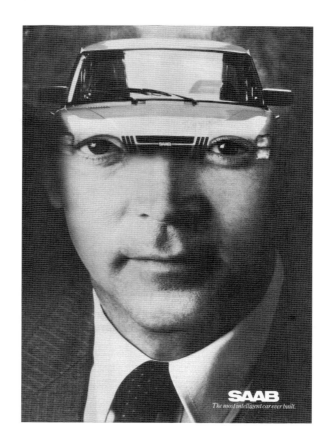

US Clean Car Incentive Program (CCIP) of 1970, but GM withdrew support when CCIP was cancelled. Audi and Volvo also produced hybrid prototypes between 1989 and 1992 but did not pursue production, while Daimler-Benz experimented with fuel-cell technology, which has not yet become a significant factor in the car industry. Toyota made the initial breakthrough, launching the first mass-produced hybrid car, the Prius, in 1997 and significantly improved models in 2003 and 2009. That 'engineering marvel' won many automotive awards and became a popular success, acquiring the cachet of an 'intelligent' car once conferred upon Saab.[12]

Alongside conventional appeals to status, sex and speed in most car advertising, some manufacturers have appealed to the motorist's intelligence in ads such as this one for the 1965 Saab 99, designed by Sixten Sason.

Even the Prius, however, remains a standard twentieth-century car in most respects, a direct descendent of the Woods Dual Power. The twenty-first-century car could become a significantly more diverse range of machines, as recent thinking suggests a plurality of car types in response to possible mobility needs in the future, and convergent technology. Credible scenarios link future cars with urban transit developments, intelligent vehicle infrastructures, evolving communications systems and mixed renewable fuels, as well as new body types and sizes to address a global motoring context – urban, suburban, rural, shared, personal, local, long-distance, luxury, economy, work, sport, leisure and so on.

Past futurologists mistakenly predicted the ubiquity of flying cars by the end of the twentieth century, whereas GM's Futurama of the 1950s more accurately foresaw a world of autonomous cars as the culmination of that trend towards ease, comfort and laziness in driving.[13] They also envisioned road-trains, proposed as linked autonomous cars that would benefit from the safety and economy of riding in tandem on motorways with electronically controlled lanes into which vehicles would flow according to speed and pre-planned routes, somewhat like the logged flight paths of aircraft. Yet such blue-sky thinking remained in the realm of science fiction until the necessary enabling technology developed sufficiently to be joined up. With that union of technology, the seemingly fanciful ideas of the past could be realized both to meet twenty-first-century demand for sustainability and to suit an information-age lifestyle.

In the midst of an increasingly overwrought consumer culture, there arises also the question of ownership. According to the sustainability guru John Thackara,

the principle of 'use, not own' can apply to all kinds of hardware: buildings, roads, vehicles, offices. For anything big, heavy and fixed,

we don't have to own it – just know how and where to find it when we need it.[14]

Such a view has considerable merit in a rational world of useful products and environments. However, it is debatable what position the car has in a rational world, when the strong emotional bond between motorists and automobiles is constantly reinforced by seductive styling, toy-like control mechanisms and manipulative advertising. Yet other forces are at work, too.

Today's cars are controlled more by electronics than they are by the driver. From closing the boot lid to starting the engine and

This superhighway of the future, as envisioned around 1959 in the US, was a bit off the mark in relation to later automotive styling trends, but it did present a tempting view inside the autonomous car, technically possible today.

adjusting the mirrors or seat, almost every action we perform is handled by microprocessor-based electronic control units (ECUs) throughout the car. And that is before it has even left the garage. An average car now contains between 50 and 100 ECUs, which represent between 30 and 50 per cent of the retail price of an internal combustion engine (ICE) car and more for a hybrid vehicle. Such devices rely on millions of lines of software code to function, suggesting that today's automobile is more electronic than mechanical.

It is now almost fully equipped to drive itself, and the Department of Motor Vehicles in the state of California is currently mandated to legislate for the routine use of autonomous vehicles on public roads. Such a law has the potential to enhance car-sharing schemes, road pricing, parking and electronic traffic control, and could relocate the car within a product-service system, like mobile phones, standing alongside the current dominant system of private ownership. Above all, such new legislation should increase safety and convenience.

California has suffered more than just about any place on the planet from its addiction to driving. Automotive smog was born in Los Angeles, and examples set there have not always been good, as when Governor Arnold Schwarzenegger conspicuously ran a fleet of gargantuan Hummers in the 1990s. Yet it is also a fount of automotive innovation, and arguably the world's leading trendsetter in automotive taste. California was the first American state to pass air-pollution legislation in the 1940s, and it was in the Los Angeles celebrity culture that the Prius achieved star status. The state legislature moved towards regulating such ride-sharing car app companies as Sidecar and Lyft, effectively sanctioning web-based hitchhiking. Hybrids are commonplace, and charging stations are plentiful by comparison with other North American car towns. Today, Elon Musk's California-built electric Tesla has the highest possible prestige among the state's smart and affluent. Therefore it is not surprising that California, the home of Google, led in testing autonomous cars on public roads and is leading in legislation to enable their common use. Watch automotive trends in Los Angeles, and before long they are likely to appear everywhere.

1 Design

Origins

Today's concerns about the proliferation of car use across the globe have evoked parallels with fears mooted around the turn of the twentieth century over the growing number of horses in such cities as London and New York. By 1900 London had more than 200,000 working horses, and Manhattan 130,000, not including animals from country farms delivering fresh food daily.[1] Horses outstripped even humans in terms of population increase in the world's greatest centre of immigration, Manhattan Island, its streets becoming foetid swamps in wet weather and sending up clouds of toxic dust in the summer.[2]

The cost of stabling and feed also rose, while the cash value of manure was deflated by new phosphate fertilizers, a problem for companies that owned thousands of horses and offset their costs by selling manure to farmers.[3] Meanwhile, residents, who recognized rotting piles of dung as breeding grounds for disease-carrying insects, demanded improved sanitation.

And so, in the last decades of the nineteenth century the problems and limitations of the horse became obvious: they were too slow to keep pace with modern life, and their endurance was limited by their need to rest and eat. They were expensive to feed, to groom,

The interior layout and appointments of high-performance coupés such as the Ferrari 365GT 2+2 provided a model for mass-produced vehicles branded as 'personal cars' in contrast to the prevailing family cars of the mid-20th century. As lone drivers now make up a high percentage of all journeys, that label seems prescient.

to treat for illnesses and to stable, and they threatened public health and hygiene in cities. The quest was on for a mechanical successor. This chapter highlights some of the trends that led to the architecture and technology of the modern car, and reveals clues planted in the early years of the automobile to the ways cars may now evolve.

Potential alternatives to horse power had appeared throughout the nineteenth century: first steam, then electricity and internal combustion engines propelling light vehicles. Of those early experiments, Henry Ford wrote: 'They were received with interest rather than enthusiasm and I do not recall any one who thought that the internal combustion engine could ever have more than a limited use', an opinion often expressed today about electric and hydrogen fuel-cell vehicles.[4]

Many claims were made to the 'invention' of the automobile. Early precursors included a three-wheeled artillery carriage built by the French military engineer Nicolas-Joseph Cugnot in 1769, arguably the first motorized road vehicle. In 1878 the French inventor Amédée Bollée Sr built La Mancelle, a steam-powered car designed for standardized production. Yet it required an operating crew of two and a tender to carry its water and coal, making it more of a road locomotive than a car.

Early inventors who built cars driven by internal combustion engines include the Belgian Etienne Lenoir (1863), Edouard Delamare-Deboutteville in France (1884) and Albert Hammel in Copenhagen (1888).[5] During the final quarter of the nineteenth century, electricity also entered the picture, beginning with a battery-powered car shown by Gustave Trouvé at the Paris International Exposition of Electricity in 1881.

In the 1870s George B. Selden made a controversial US patent application for a 'road engine' that was finally granted in 1895 after many amendments, effectively confirming him as the inventor of the automobile. The historian James Flink called this 'probably the most absurd action in the history of patent law'.[6] A group of car manufacturers, led by Henry Ford, finally overturned Selden's patent after a long legal battle.[7]

While all claims to be 'first' at anything should be treated cautiously, the design and construction of that first true automobile are generally credited to the German Karl Benz. He demonstrated his first successful car, a three-wheeled vehicle, in Mannheim in 1885, patented it in 1886 and began producing it for sale two years later. A single-cylinder engine powered the car, which was steered by a tiller and had leaf-spring suspension in the rear and a mechanical transmission brake. What distinguished the Benz was its ground-up design, with a bicycle-style tubular steel frame. Benz sold a standardized four-wheel version, the Velo, under licence, first in Germany and France, then around the world – 67 of them in 1894 and twice as many the following year. Its 1-litre engine produced 3.5 hp, giving a top speed of 19 km/h (12 mph). By the end of the nineteenth century, Benz had become Europe's leading car maker, completing 572 vehicles in 1899.

Other German inventors who contributed to the development of the motor car included Siegfried Marcus and Wilhelm Maybach and his long-time partner, Gottlieb Daimler, who developed their own lightweight, high-speed internal combustion engine (ICE) suitable for use in cars, small boats and aircraft. Between 1890 and 1895 they built and sold about 30 cars and larger road vehicles. Like the Benz motor, Daimler's engine was sold under licence abroad.

In France, Émile Levassor and René Panhard used Daimler engines in a series of about 30 cars they began building in 1890, cars that established the conventional automobile layout. The 'Système Panhard' featured a four-wheel chassis, a front-mounted engine and a sliding-gear transmission driving the rear wheels.

Panhard and Levassor were among a group of French automotive pioneers who set that country on course to become the leading motoring nation in the 1890s.

Britain was slower to start building cars, partly because of the Locomotives Act of 1865, which required an escort waving a red flag to walk ahead of any self-propelled vehicle on a public highway.[8] The so-called Red Flag Law was finally repealed in 1896, liberating aspiring British car makers to begin production. Among the first was the dubious Harry J. Lawson, collaborating with an upright Anglo-German engineer, Frederick R. Simms, who promoted the terms 'petrol' and 'motor car' in British usage and who co-founded the Royal Automobile Club. With Simms's help, Lawson manufactured Daimler engines in Britain from 1897, forming the pioneer British automobile brand and establishing the city of Coventry as the centre of British motor manufacturing. In 1900 Daimler's status was cemented by royal patronage, when one of its models was the first car purchased by the Prince of Wales.

Massachusetts brothers Charles and Frank Duryea demonstrated the first successful gasoline-powered American car in 1893. Starting out as bicycle makers and mechanics, the brothers turned to the construction of an automobile for everyday use, the Duryea Motor Wagon, a four-wheel horse buggy retrofitted with a 4-hp, four-stroke, single-cylinder, water-cooled petrol engine of Frank's design, a friction transmission, a low-tension ignition with crank-starting in the rear, and a spray carburettor. Frank was the engineering talent, while Charles styled himself the 'inventor', promoting Duryea cars and seeking investment.

A Duryea car won an automobile race sponsored by the *Chicago Times Herald* in 1895, and the following year competed successfully in the London to Brighton 'Emancipation Run', celebrating the repeal of the Locomotives Act. Following those successes, Duryea

Motor Wagons sold as fast as they could be made. Although some of the company's models were expensive – such as the phaeton bought as a gift for the Chinese dowager empress – Charles Duryea's objective was to produce a car for motorists of ordinary means. His innovative two-passenger, two-cylinder, air-cooled Buggyaut of 1907 sold for $650, but appeared only in time to be overshadowed by the superior Ford Model T, which soon became the first universal people's car.

The royal motorist Edward VII is seen here in a Daimler belonging to Lord Montagu of Beaulieu in 1902. Edward already had his own 1900 model Daimler Tonneau.

The critical factor in determining the most significant contributions to the early development of the automobile was the suitability of those prototypes to batch or series production. Inventors like Benz and Duryea, who designed and built standardized automobiles first in their tens and, by the turn of the twentieth century, in their hundreds per year, became the accepted originators of the modern car.

Brothers Charles and Frank Duryea quarrelled furiously and publicly, each claiming credit for designing, selling and winning a race in America's first successful car. Charles is pictured here in the Duryea Motor Wagon of 1895.

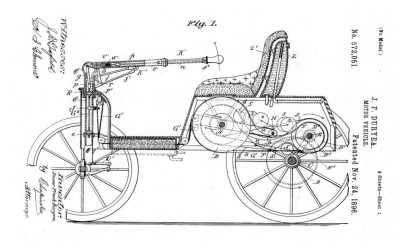

(No Model.)

No. 572,051.

J. F. DURYEA.
MOTOR VEHICLE.

Patented Nov. 24, 1896.

6 Sheets—Sheet 1.

Fig. 1.

Standardization

Histories of the early car often distinguish between elite hand-built European automobiles and standardized American cars, suggesting that only American industry could produce high-tolerance, interchangeable parts in large quantities.[9] Yet British and French bicycle manufacturers had demonstrated just such capabilities in the early 1890s, while Léon Bollée and De Dion-Bouton manufactured engine parts to 'Swiss watch' tolerances.[10] Nevertheless, history repeats the story of three Cadillacs, demonstrated famously at London's Royal Automobile Club in 1908: they were dismantled and their 2,000 parts were mixed before being reassembled to run in an 800-km (500-mile) endurance trial at Brooklands race circuit. For this the club awarded Cadillac the prestigious Dewar Trophy for the year's most outstanding automotive achievement, interchangeability. According to the automotive historian Malcolm Jeal, 'if in 1900–1901 three De Dion-Bouton motor cars had been

Patent drawing for the 'Duryea Road Vehicle', 1895, showing its very simple, light buggy design, typical of the American-type horseless carriage.

submitted to a similar test . . . the outcome would have been exactly the same.'[11] Yet the American determination to produce relatively low-cost cars in great quantities truly set its car makers apart.

The large North American consumer market and the greater distances of rural communities from public transport had encouraged efficient large-scale manufacturing of horse-drawn vehicles since the mid-nineteenth century. By 1900 American carriage factories were turning out nearly 1 million vehicles annually. Half of those were light, owner-driven buggies, a specifically American type of vehicle suitable for standardization and systematic production. The buggy became a primary model for the American automobile.

Many US car makers were from relatively humble backgrounds, and several, including the Duryeas, were cycle mechanics. Ransom E. Olds, the son of a blacksmith, aimed to build cars for the large middle class. His first success was the simply designed Curved Dash Oldsmobile of 1901, constructed on an early assembly line and priced at a reasonable $650.[12] Following Olds's example, Henry Ford, who disappointed his father by not taking over the family farm, improved the assembly line as the central feature of the modern mass-production system.

Bicycles and carriages were not the only models for car manufacturers. Waltham Manufacturing Company was an offshoot of the Massachusetts-based Waltham Watch Company, the world's largest maker of precision timepieces, a company experienced in the economic advantages of standardized products. Its offshoot, Waltham Manufacturing, founded by Charles Metz, initially made Orient bicycles, then motorcycles, but also started building steam, electric and petrol cars in 1898. In 1903 it launched the simple Orient Buckboard, at $350 advertised as the world's cheapest automobile. In the same decade there were many modestly priced American cars between $400 and $600, including the Stearns, the Locomobile and the Sears Motor Buggy, sold by mail order. At the time $600 reflected approximately four months' earnings for a senior (male) city high-school teacher or a mid-ranking government administrator.[13]

Early motor cars quickly became popular with daily travellers, such as doctors and salesmen. The Oldsmobile was advertised as 'as indispensable to business as the telephone'. Car registrations in the USA rose from 8,000 in 1900 to a million in 1912.[14] There were upwards of 23,000 cars on Britain's roads by the end of 1904, and that figure more than quadrupled to over 100,000 by 1910.[15] France, the world's largest automobile manufacturing country in the early twentieth century, produced 32,000 cars in 1904 alone; it remained the world's top exporter of cars until the First World War, and Europe's leading manufacturer until the 1930s.[16]

The most famously low-priced car of the century, Ford's Model T, was initially not cheap, starting at $825 for a roadster when it launched in 1908. Its conventional design, attributed to Ford's production team including Childe Harold Wills and Joseph Galamb, was cleverly engineered to be easy to drive, while its up-to-date appearance compared well with other similarly priced light cars. It was also available in a range of colours until 1913, when black became standard owing to its low cost and rapid-drying properties.[17] What distinguished the Model T from its Ford predecessors and from its competitors in the industry was its rigorous standardization.

The Model T's 20-hp four-cylinder motor was connected by a drive shaft to a live rear axle controlled by a planetary gearbox with two forward speeds and reverse, requiring little gear-changing. The chassis was high enough to clear the worst roads or even rutted fields, while its left-hand steering was one of many up-to-date features of this all-purpose car. It weighed only 545 kg (1,200 lb) thanks to the use of light, strong vanadium steel, which Ford produced in his factory. All its main features had been tested in earlier models, ensuring reliability. It was economical to run (achieving 35 mpg), simple to drive and easily repaired.

According to Ford, 'the important feature of the new model . . . was its simplicity, the fewest number of standardized parts and a single model.'[18] Those who still saw the car only as a luxury were not impressed, inciting Ford to provocative statements, such as the notorious quip: 'Any customer can have a car painted any colour that he wants, so long as it is black.'[19] While standardization was a central principle of Ford's system, his advertising emphasized that this was not a cheap car, but rather a 'fine car' sold at a low price through the economy of his orderly production system and his efficient business model.[20]

Ford also had the commercial advantage of an established chain of dealers offering servicing and parts. With the success of the Model T, he could concentrate on how to increase output, decrease the cost of unit production, cut his profit margin per car and sell for ever lower prices. In this way he would tap a huge market of first-time car buyers.

The German historian Sigfried Giedion dated the theory of production, which became known as Fordism, back to the division of labour employed to manufacture pins in eighteenth-century Europe. Giedion also found antecedents in the USA, in the interchangeable parts of mid-nineteenth-century locks patented by Linus Yale Jr, in the continuous production line used by Oliver Evans in his mechanized flour mills of the late eighteenth century, and in overhead rail systems used to transport pig carcasses through the stages of processing in the Cincinnati meat-packing houses of the 1860s.[21] In the late 1850s the Austrian chair maker Thonet also began using a simple production line and knock-down shipping methods in its global furniture enterprise, making nearly 2 million chairs per year by 1913. Above all, Giedion credited Frederick Winslow Taylor with establishing the principles of 'scientific management' and time-motion efficiency during the late nineteenth century, principles so commonly accepted that Ford presented them simply as common sense.[22] Ironically, Taylor died in 1915, the same year that Ford achieved an electrified moving assembly line for the production of the Model T, yet Ford's autobiography (1922) never mentions him.

However, Ford described in detail the application of a rational process, such as that encouraged by Taylor, to construct his car economically:

> In our first assembling we simply started to put a car together at a spot on the floor, and workmen brought to it the parts as they were needed in exactly the same way that one builds a house . . . The first step forward in assembly came when we began taking the work to the men instead of the men to the work . . . Along about April 1, 1913 we first tried the experiment of an assembly line . . . Then we raised the height of the line eight inches – this was in 1914 – We had adopted the policy of 'man-high' work . . . The speed of the moving work had to be carefully tried out . . . Every piece of work in the shops moves; it may move on hooks on overhead chains going to assembly in the exact order in which the parts are required; it may travel on a moving plat-form, or it may go by gravity, but the point is that there is no lifting or trucking of anything other than materials.[23]

My Life and Work reveals that Ford's interest lay in the manufactur-ing process, the economic aims of industry, and how their evolution would shape the car. It also reveals how the great strengths and the fatal limitations of the Model T were products of Ford's view of the manufacturing process, of the ethics of the automobile industry and of capitalism itself. In describing how and why he devised his single-model concept, he wrote:

> My associates were not convinced that it was possible to restrict our cars to a single model . . . It is extraordinary how firmly rooted is the notion that business – continuous selling – depends not on satisfying the customer once and for all, but on first getting his money for one article and then persuading him he ought to buy a new and different one.[24]

By 1908 several manufacturers were using some form of production line. Currier, Cameron & Company used such an assembly line when they built bodies for the Duryea of 1898. Ransom Olds used the same method to build the Curved Dash Oldsmobile of 1901–7, a single model of simple design, constructed of interchangeable parts.[25] Yet that car became an object of desire, one of the most elegant of all horseless carriages, demonstrating persuasively that a mass-produced vehicle could be beautiful.[26]

The Curved Dash runabout was an important and memorable design, and 18,508 of them were made. It had a 5-hp engine and a planetary gearbox, like the later Model T, with a reverse and two forward gears for easy driving; it could reach 32 km/h (20 mph). The simple assembly line used by Olds to build the car employed the same method that carriage makers had been using since about 1850. A cart would start at one end of the factory, carrying the car's frame. As it passed each department, parts would be attached until the finished vehicle reached the end of the line.

Although the scale, speed and efficiency of mass production were increased dramatically by Henry Ford and his production team led by Charles Sorensen, no further step-change occurred until the introduction of robots and the application of Japanese thinking to

car making after half a century, the latter incorporating Ford's hatred of waste and the traditional Japanese respect for economy and thrift. 'Lean manufacturing', as it has become known, is the management philosophy derived primarily from Toyota's production system, optimizing flow throughout the process.

Ford chassis being transported to final assembly on a recently electrified assembly line, c. 1917.

Toyota identified several areas in which waste should be eliminated or reduced to achieve maximum efficiency, including overproduction, waiting time, transportation and defects. Kiichiro Toyoda, founder of Toyota Motors, introduced such ideas into his system of 'just in time' production, inspired by his study of supermarkets as well as by his admiration for Henry Ford's sense of economy. The Toyota philosophy propelled that company to become the world's largest car producer in 2007.

The Curved Dash Oldsmobile (1901–7) was a simple yet elegant machine. Art Nouveau-inspired ornament on its carefully finished bodywork set it apart from many of the crude prototype vehicles of its time. But the real differences were its standardized construction and production on a rudimentary assembly line.

Ingredients

'Find out all about this, I told him. That is the kind of material we ought to have in our cars.' After picking up a shard of very light metal from the wreckage of a French racing car, Henry Ford's eureka moment was his 'discovery' in 1905 of vanadium steel, the material that made the Model T lighter and stronger than its early competitors. 'Until then', Ford explained in his autobiography,

> we had been forced to be satisfied with steel running between 60,000 and 70,000 pounds tensile strength. With vanadium, the strength went up to 170,000 pounds . . . Having vanadium in hand I pulled apart our models and tested in detail to determine what kind of steel was best for every part – whether we wanted a hard steel, a tough steel or an elastic steel. We, for the first time I think, in the history of any large construction, determined scientifically the exact quality of the steel.[27]

General Motors (GM) soon followed with its own research units, led from 1920 by Charles F. Kettering and eventually consolidated in the GM Technical Center.

Developing alongside the materials from which cars are made was the material that fuels them. If coal had powered the nineteenth century, oil and its refined form, petroleum, powered the twentieth. Before the First World War, the British engine designer Harry Ricardo undertook research into the physics of internal combustion, leading to the development of fuel octane ratings and higher-octane petrol. After the First World War Ricardo's American counterpart, Kettering, and his colleague Thomas Midgley at GM experimented to find a cure for engine knock and to achieve higher compression, reduce wear on the motor and improve economy. In response to post-war fears of oil shortages they sought an alcohol-based fuel, which was renewable and non-polluting and cured knock. However, the cheaper and more available solution they found in 1922 (as alcohol production was restricted in the USA during Prohibition) was the gasoline additive tetraethyl lead, quickly identified as a major health hazard but not banned from car fuel until the 1980s because of resistance within the industry.[28]

Whereas the consolidated power of the Detroit Big Three manufacturers (GM, Ford and Chrysler), US Steel and the major oil companies resisted any significant advances in the internal combustion engine to improve efficiency and lower emissions, even in the face of growing public concern over air pollution in the 1950s, some politicians and activists in those areas worst affected by smog persuaded local and federal legislators to pass a sequence of Acts and control measures to force car makers to clean up emissions. Michigan and California led the way, and the result was the passage of the federal Clean Air Act of 1970, which concentrated the minds of Detroit for the first time on developing cleaner engines and cleaner fuels for their cars.

Drivers, too, even those in the most heavily polluted American cities, resisted any suggestion that they use their cars less, citing the freedom to drive as an inalienable right. Their bond with their cars proved to be stronger than their desire for clean air, clean water or clean soil. The answer to automotive pollution, when it was finally recognized as a factor equivalent to carcinogens in cigarettes, would have to be a technological fix.

Unlike managers at Ford and Chrysler, the president of GM, Edward Cole, promoted emissions to a high corporate priority, creating a Catalytic Converter Task Force in 1969 to perfect and apply that new technology to the problem of emissions. He went on to tackle the even more substantial challenge of removing lead from petrol, which GM itself had introduced to it in the 1920s. Despite intense resistance from automotive engineers, who feared the effects of the catalytic converter on performance, and oil men, who resisted the investment required to convert their production and distribution to high-octane unleaded fuel, Cole pushed the industry towards substantially lowering smog-causing emissions from cars. According to the historian Tom McCarthy, 'Cole's efforts showed just how much an industry-leading company could do when its leader decided to tackle a problem.' Yet it was legislation in the form of the Clean Air Act amendments of 1970 that gave the industry 'a sharp prod that forced it to adopt the catalytic converter . . . that took the biggest bite out of smog-causing emissions'.[29]

If there were invisible material changes under the bonnet, the composition of car bodies was also changing in subtle ways. Plastics became familiar to drivers at the most intimate level of contact with the car – through the steering wheel. In 1912 the Celluloid Corporation had devised a thermoplastic named Lumarith, a powder that could be injected into a mould and instantly be turned out as a finished steering-wheel rim in smooth, durable plastic. Lumarith became a standard material for interior components by the mid-1930s, but few drivers gave much thought to the nature of the material they were handling.

The earliest plastic car bodies were constructed for exhibitions and to announce new models, such as the Olympia, built by GM's German subsidiary, Opel. A unique prototype was unveiled at the Berlin Motor Show in 1935; its streamlined, transparent Plexiglas body, designed by the engineer Russell Begg, revealed the car's unitary construction to the delight of visitors. This was the first new Opel model to be created under the influence of GM's Art and Color Section, and it anticipated another transparent show car built in Plexiglas, for Norman Bel Geddes's Highways and Horizons Pavilion at the New York World's Fair of 1939. That 'ghost car' was a Pontiac sedan created to promote GM's new all-steel, 'turret-top' bodies while illustrating the potential of Plexiglas (poly-methyl methacrylate), produced from 1936 by the German-American chemical company Rohm and Hass. The car dazzled 25 million viewers at the fair with a thrilling surrealism that promised an amazing crystalline future.[30]

Henry Ford, meanwhile, was experimenting with *growing* new synthetic materials in an attempt to link car manufacturing with American domestic agriculture. He had been experimenting with a plastic derived from soybeans since the 1920s, and in 1941 displayed a prototype car featuring a streamlined, all-plastic, pontoon body styled by E. T. Gregorie.[31] Lowell E. Overly, working in Ford's soybean laboratory at Greenfield Village, executed the design and made the body moulds. He described the plastic from which the car was made as soybean fibre impregnated with formaldehyde in a phenolic resin.[32] The soybean laboratory was one of many Ford initiatives aimed at the use of farm surpluses, to ensure American self-sufficiency in raw materials and to reduce the polluting effect of manufacturing. But as with producing alcohol fuel, devoting agricultural land to crops for car production was anathema to many stakeholders and to the general public.

The Pontiac 'ghost car', a transparent Plexiglas-bodied vehicle exhibited at the New York World's Fair of 1939–40, was a surreal object displaying the latest in materials and constructional technology. It exerted a magical effect on a massive audience.

As a result of steel shortages during the Korean War in the early 1950s, GM chose fibreglass for the lightweight body of their flashy new Corvette sports car (1954), which, along with the spartan East German Zwickau and Trabant, became the pioneer plastic-bodied production car.[33] The Zwickau P70 (1955–9), predecessor of the more famous Trabant, featured a steel unitary structure clad in panels of Duroplast, made from recycled Soviet cotton and waste phenolic resin from East Germany's dyeing industry, making it by far the first mass-produced car to use recycled plastic for body panels. Unfortunately, Duroplast is not itself recyclable, a fact that has resulted in thousands of indestructible Trabant bodies ending up in landfill.

Since 2000 cars have on average contained nearly 10 per cent plastic and plastic composite materials increasingly derived from

The East German AWZ P70 Zwickau Coupé, built between 1955 and 1958, sported one of the earliest plastic-production bodies and the first made from recycled material. It was the direct predecessor of the more famous Trabant.

grasses, soy, corn and other crops.[34] Today's soy-reinforced plastic body panels and soy-derived foams recall such innovative products of the 1920s as the wood substitute 'Fordite'.[35] And they continue the debate over traditional materials versus renewables. Other materials from which cars were built by 2010 included aluminium, zinc, magnesium, copper, lead, iron, glass and rubber, and various types of steel. Although steel remained the most important material, because of its strength and durability, its weight has demanded that its use be reduced. Any benefits from that reduction, however, have been more than offset by the increasing size of standard private cars, now typically massive SUVs, continually bigger in every automobile segment and widely loved for their brawn, especially in North America.

That love for big cars is the greatest barrier against controlling the use and weight of materials. Daimler's French-built Smart car, which employed the usual proportions of steel for its cellular safety frame, floor panels, reinforced seat structures and mechanics, saved weight and reduced its carbon footprint simply by requiring far less of all materials and production energy than a full-sized car.[36] Although the Smart has spawned few competitors and failed to establish a clear market segment, the impact of its radical architecture is seen widely in city car concepts.

Systematic, Hydromatic, Ultramatic[37]

Whereas the Smart car demonstrated the ease of driving a very small car in town, progressive refinements have made all production cars ever more attractive, restful and undemanding places. Yet for early internal combustion engines, simply starting up took a major effort. According to the motoring journalist L.J.K. Setright, in the early days of the car, 'quite frequently the main criterion applied in the choice of a chauffeur would be his physical strength, in view of the effort visibly required for starting the engine.'[38]

> One might have to check the presence of fuel in the tank, pump up air pressure within it to deliver fuel to the carburettor, open the main fuel tank, adjust the hand throttle, retard the ignition, engage any half-compression device such as had become popular in big engines, adjust the rich-mixture control or alternatively make use of priming cocks, turn on the main oil supply tap beneath the tank of lubricant, adjust any drip feeds downstream of that tap, check that the handbrake was engaged and the gearbox in neutral position, and finally switch on the ignition circuit. Then one might address the starting handle.[39]

It took strength to turn the crankshaft manually, using a handle fixed directly to it. And should the engine backfire, the crank could be thrown back with violence capable of breaking the operator's arm. All this could make the ICE car as difficult to start as a steamer, which normally took several laborious minutes building sufficient boiler pressure to drive off.

The main alternative to cranking the internal combustion engine or waiting for steam pressure was to drive an electric vehicle (EV), which started instantly at the touch of a button. When paved roads reached only to the city limits and the majority of motor trips were short, the limited range of electric cars suited many private users, and fleets of electric commercial vehicles were used in London and other cities around 1900 for deliveries and as taxis.

At the Paris and New York automobile shows of 1900, many cars on display were either electric or steam-powered. Of automobiles registered that year in the USA, steam powered 40 per cent, electricity 38 per cent and petrol 22 per cent. Nearly 34,000 electric cars were registered in North America in 1900. Meanwhile, the Lohner-Porsche

Elektromobil and its variant, the original petrol-electric hybrid car, dazzled the Paris Exposition Universelle.

Electric cars were easy to start, free from vibration, silent and clean, and accelerated without gears. Because they ran smoothly and travelled mainly over paved city streets, they could be built with luxuriously upholstered closed bodies, which featured refinements including curved window glass and electric lighting, earning them a reputation as 'the aristocrats of motordom', the motto of the Baker Electric Motor Vehicle Company. Famous owners of such gracious automobiles included Thomas Edison, who manufactured nickel-iron batteries for them, William Howard Taft, the first American president to own and drive a car, and Clara Ford, wife of Henry (although Ford tired of having to collect Clara and tow the car home when it ran out of charge).

Not all electric cars were the dignified models popular with ladies and doctors. The Belgian racing driver Camille Jenatzy's torpedo-shaped Jamais Contente broke the land-speed record in 1899, exceeding 1 mile/minute (100 km/h). Open-top sports models built by Bailey of Massachusetts also set speed and endurance records, including a 1,600-km (1,000-mile) trial through New England in 1910 to prove the Edison battery, which the *New York Times* described as 'no longer a myth, but an accomplished fact, not to be scoffed at, but to be regarded with awe and serious interest'.[40] These were the ancestors of today's high-performance California-built Tesla electric cars, designed by Franz von Holzhausen, with a 320-km (200-mile) range and top speed electronically limited to 200 km/h (125 mph). Because of the superior torque of electric vehicles, Teslas accelerate from 0 to 60 mph in a neck-snapping 4.2 seconds, satisfying even the most ardent gearheads.

The engineer and historian Gijs Mom argued convincingly in 2002 that the electric car had always failed in its promise to become an all-purpose vehicle, rather than simply a city car. However, with the establishment of car-sharing companies such as Uber, increasingly stringent restrictions on parking and speed within cities, and reductions in urban motorway construction, the low speed, high-tech, electric-powered city car is showing new potential to fill an important role in urban mobility. Its low CO_2 footprint, silent operation and the greater manoeuvrability provided by hub motors will guarantee its efficiency and appropriateness. Meanwhile, extended range, high-performance motorway cruisers such as the Tesla Model S have proven the potential of EVs as all-purpose cars.[41]

EVs reached the peak of their popularity in 1912, the year the electric self-starter was introduced to ICE cars, but they stayed in commercial use as milk floats, because their silent operation suited early-morning deliveries in residential neighbourhoods. With sustained oil shortages in Japan after the Second World War, the Prince Motor Company (later Nissan) produced the Tama electric car, ancestor of the Nissan Leaf. With a range of 100 km (60 miles) and a top speed of 35 km/h (22 mph), it was used until the early 1950s, mainly as a city taxi.

Also rooted in problems associated with oil, the current resurgence of interest in EVs stems additionally from new uses for low-speed vehicles, such as golf carts, which have been increasingly popular since the mid-1950s. EZGO, Cushman and Yamaha built them, while Sears Roebuck sold them by mail order. They provided the pattern for Neighbourhood Electric Vehicles (NEV) such as those designed by Dan Sturges and built today for various purposes by Global Electric Motorcars (GEM). These small crossover vehicles bear comparison with earlier cycle cars, the microcars of the 1950s and current city car prototypes for use where speed limits are low. Future expansion of this automotive segment will depend on better safety design and revised licensing regulations and road layouts that enable such cars to share roads comfortably with bigger, faster vehicles.

New EVs address both sustainability and the trend towards ease of operation, spawning design initiatives that aim to provide a new personal transportation culture for the twenty-first century. Designers, scientists, urbanists, entrepreneurs and politicians realize that conditions are ripe for the increased production of electric-powered, computer-controlled vehicles that will do less environmental damage while being safer and more easily operated. Media interest in Google's self-driving cars also suggests a growing public curiosity about forthcoming developments in automotive technology (see p. 289).

The creation of practical autonomous cars began in the 1980s with the pioneering work of the German aeronautical and aerospace scientist Ernst Dickmanns to devise a series of driverless vehicles controlled by visual reference, using saccadic vision (rapid-eye movement), probabilistic logic (a system that perceives its environment and takes appropriate action) and linked computers. In 1994–5 Dickmanns's autonomous Mercedes performed, by visual referencing alone, two significant public demonstrations with observers on board, first near Paris and then on a 1,758-km (1,092-mile) trip through Germany and Denmark.[42]

Another initiative, launched in 2003 by William Mitchell of the Media Laboratory at Massachusetts Institute of Technology, was sponsored by GM with the architect Frank O. Gehry as an adviser. Their research resulted in a reconceptualization of the small car, employing existing technology to produce a practical autonomous vehicle that could drive independently or be linked in a chain, eliminating the normal car-to-car safety distance. Media Lab's William Lark led the design of CityCar, which was intended to function like a smartphone on wheels, was designed with 'high consumer appeal

[and] a new automotive DNA', and aimed to enrich the user's experience by being linked to the road infrastructure and other road users.[43]

Designs emerging from the project include gyroscopically balanced two-wheel Segway vehicles and Lark's four-wheel CityCar, incorporating a folding mechanism to reduce its parking footprint. Electric hub motors in each fully steerable wheel enable it to rotate 360 degrees and move sideways as well as forwards and backwards while eliminating the necessity for mechanical brakes and suspension assemblies. CityCar measures 2.5 m (8 ft 2 in.) long when extended for driving, and 1.5 m (4 ft 11 in.) when folded for parking, recalling a prototype collapsible three-wheeled car built in 1929 by Engelbert Zaschka to ease the parking problems of Weimar-era Berliners. A final prototype, the Hiriko car, designed for car-sharing schemes, was announced in 2013 and built in the Basque area of

Designed by Californian transport visionary Dan Sturges, GEM neighbourhood electric vehicles are built for short journeys at low speed. With city speed limits widely reduced to less than 40 km/h (25 mph), such cars have a promising future.

Spain. It was scheduled for use in Berlin at Deutsche Bahn's main terminus, but lack of finance stalled its production.

That is nothing new. Finance has always been behind or against every significant development in automotive engineering and design. Early investors in car manufacturing were also connected with related industries including steel, oil, rubber, glass, chemicals, paint and timber. Car making expanded those industries (and blocked others), while raising government tax revenues by stimulating the building of roads and the development of land.[44] Thus, particularly in North America, the aim of industry and government was to increase the pool of drivers and expand the automobile market by putting everyone behind the wheel of a car. Cranking the internal combustion engine was the first hurdle.

The German electrical engineer Robert Bosch took the earliest steps by developing an improved magneto and, with his colleague Gottlob Honold, an effective spark plug. Then, in 1903, Clyde J. Coleman sold

Hiriko, the Basque word for 'urban', was the name given to the production version of MIT Media Lab's CityCar project, developed in the Basque country of northern Spain. Because of its folding mechanism and very small parking footprint, the Hiriko is ideal for car-sharing programmes and crowded parking environments.

his patent for an electric automobile starter to the founder of Dayton Engineering Laboratories (Delco), Charles Kettering, who soon joined Henry Leland at Cadillac. There, Kettering's group of engineers, the 'Barn Gang', perfected the electric self-starter, which appeared on the Cadillac Model 30 (1912), advertised as the 'Car without a Crank'. Kettering's battery-generator system not only facilitated starting, but also powered the lights and provided spare electrical capacity for accessories that would enhance all future cars' comfort and desirability.

Another impediment to universal driving was gear shifting. A hydraulic automatic gearshift had been patented in the USA as early as 1908 by Clarence Hollister, and used in a four-cylinder light car built in about 1914 by Philo Remington, owner of the Remington arms and typewriter companies. The Owen Magnetic car of 1915–21, designed by Thomas Edison's protégé, Justus Entz, featured an electromagnetic transmission that controlled the acceleration of this large luxury car, advertised as the 'Car of a Thousand Speeds' and designed for owner-drivers. In Britain, too, such luxury makers as Armstrong Siddeley and Daimler were fitting Wilson pre-selector gearboxes and semi-automatic clutches by the late 1920s. Yet for many new drivers with little training, the manual gearbox was recognized as a commercial hindrance, one that GM addressed in 1928 with a fully synchronized transmission, designed by Earl A. Thompson for Cadillac. But such improvements were only interim measures in the quest for an automatic car.

Thompson and his staff experimented throughout the 1930s with 'shiftless' transmissions, finally launching Hydra-Matic Drive on the Oldsmobile of 1940. GM sold over 200,000 of these costly options from their launch in late 1939 until the halt of civilian car production in early 1942. By then the US War Department wanted automatic gearboxes for a new generation of tanks, to prevent

.

stalling on the battlefield and to ease the operation of their double tracks. According to Alfred Sloan of GM,

> for the passenger car driver, the automatic transmission is of value because of its convenience and simplicity in operation – there is one less thing about driving a car he has to think about. When it comes to ... the huge vehicles of modern warfare, automatic transmissions are needed for smooth functioning.[45]

After the war GM advertised those automatic gearboxes in its new cars as tested in 'hard usage on the battlefield'. Their popularity contributed to the increased percentage of Americans who drove. In 1949 some 40 per cent held driving licences. By 1960 nearly half drove, and by 2000 that percentage had risen to two-thirds, most of them using automatics.[46]

Whereas American cars capitalized on insulating the driver from any sense of driving as work, a different attitude prevailed in Europe. There, the three-pedal manual transmission remained the preference of most motorists, who enjoy demonstrating their skill by the manipulation of gear stick and clutch pedal. Such a view could also be found in America, the home of the automatic; *Car and Driver*'s critic Tony Swan compared Volkswagen's manual and automatic transmissions in 2013:

> The more compelling advantages of a manual transmission are the sensations that go with enhanced command of the machinery . . . As good as the VW DSG [automatic] is – with or without paddles – it doesn't deliver the sense of involvement that goes with dancing on three pedals. It's a major component in the driving enjoyment of any vehicle, amplifying the partnership of car and driver . . . when a driver is more closely engaged with driving, he or she is far less likely to be

The C A R
THAT HAS NO CRANK

Game changer. The 1912 Cadillac Model 30 solved the problem of crank-starting the internal combustion engine. It signalled the end of the first generation of electric cars, and its battery's spare capacity subsequently powered all the electrical automotive accessories that today's motorists take for granted.

Automatic transmission made driving sufficiently easy for even the least technically minded individuals to master. It also reduced stalling, which made driving on the world's battlefields considerably safer for the crew.

texting, eating or anything else. That in itself makes the case for three-pedal driving.[47]

Such affection for the antiquated stick shift is related, then, to feelings and sensations rather than actual control, economy or safety; and many drivers eat, steer and text *while* shifting gears.

Setright presented a British counter-argument when he wrote in 2003: 'People feel obliged to drive three-pedal cars to prove themselves members of an elite, though the skills [to shift] nowadays required are absurdly trivial.' He praised the brilliance of several innovative automatics, and lamented that 'still people choose to trample a clutch pedal, to heave a lever around, to waste time with every shift and waste energy through being too often in the wrong gear.'[48] Setright recognizes that the manual gear lever in an otherwise fully automated twenty-first-century car functions essentially as play equipment.

While the mechanics of driving became simpler, the spare electrical capacity of the Kettering system encouraged the development of accessories for comfort and entertainment, despite their adverse effect on weight and fuel economy. In 1940 electric windows were standard on the Lincoln Continental, while by 1950 power steering, power brakes, electrically adjustable seats, automatic headlight dimming, station-seeking radios, electrically operated convertible roofs and powered radio aerials were all commonly available on American cars at all price levels.

As cars became heavier, manufacturers increasingly sought a way to lighten their steering, especially for parking. Inspired by innovations in the steering of ships, the engineer Francis Davis, working for the car maker Pierce-Arrow in the 1920s, devised a hydraulic power-steering system for automobiles, but it was not exploited commercially. War production stimulated the implementation of a practical power-steering unit installed on armoured cars built by Chevrolet in 1940 for export to Britain. By 1945 more than 10,000 heavy military vehicles had been equipped with power steering. Finally, Chrysler revived Davis's expired patents and employed a hydraulic power-steering unit, Hydraguide, on its Imperial of 1951, setting a trend that subsequently encouraged almost unrestricted automotive weight gain.

Although power steering is now taken for granted, even the latest electric power steering is criticized for reducing the driver's feeling of control. Tony Swan described the handling of the Toyota Camry (2012) as 'competent in everything, just right for a driver who doesn't want to be involved any more than is absolutely necessary'.[49] The Camry's status as a popular favourite in the USA suggests that many drivers prefer ease to involvement.

Just as the increasing size and complexity of modern buildings demanded mechanical heating, ventilation and air conditioning to improve habitability, the closed cars dominant from the mid-1920s required new means of introducing fresh air, heated, filtered and eventually cooled and dehumidified to keep motorists comfortable in all weathers.[50] In early cars, makeshift arrangements derived from horse-drawn carriages were used to warm the feet. In about 1920 Rickenbacker, National and other manufacturers installed pipe systems in their closed cars that circulated hot exhaust gases to warm the interior, and in 1923 Studebaker boasted: 'Every Studebaker Sedan is completely equipped including a heater.' Yet they were all ineffective.

The breakthrough was made in 1938 by Nils Eric Wahlberg, who developed a flow-through heating and ventilation system that became the standard. Wahlberg's Nash Weather Eye drew fresh air into the car's fan-assisted, thermostatically controlled heater; the air was filtered and circulated to warm the cabin and directed to clear condensation from the windscreen. It also equalized the air pressure outside and inside the moving car, reducing draughts. The addition of refrigeration and humidity control provided full air conditioning, introduced as an expensive and cumbersome option by Packard in 1940.

With the advent of affordable and reliable air conditioners by the 1960s, motoring in hot weather became more comfortable than remaining at home. When houses and offices finally caught up with the air-conditioned comforts of the car, together they generated a seamlessly cooled environment, where motorists seldom had to feel the outside temperature during their daily activities.

Carchitecture

While technical advances made cars more comfortable and effortless, their size and shape evolved with similar aims. Climbing up on to an early Edwardian car was a physical manoeuvre that demanded agility and specialized clothing, especially for women in corsets and trailing skirts. The large wheels necessary to clear rutted country roads were connected by beam axles on which sat full or semi-elliptical springs supporting the frame to which the body was bolted. That vertical stacking of elements, aggravated by placing the engine under the seat, elevated the driver and passengers high in the air, a position familiar to those accustomed to sitting on a horse.

A lower driving position was facilitated by the general adoption by about 1905 of the Système Panhard, in which the engine was moved to the front. The advantage of a lower vehicle in convenience, handling and stability was demonstrated in 1908 by Ettore Bugatti's Type 10 Petit Pur-Sang (Little Thoroughbred). This tiny prototype and its immediate successors, built for racing and road use, challenged the equation of quality and speed with size, initiating the interwar European-style roadster. The Bugatti was small, light and low, riding on 25-in. (63.5-cm) wheels when a comparably priced Fiat roadster used 37-in. (94-cm) rims. Following the First World War, improvements to roads made smaller wheels acceptable, reducing to an average 15 in. (38 cm) by the 1950s and 10 in. (25.5 cm) on the Austin Mini of 1959.

When Vincenzo Lancia designed a structural monocoque/unibody for his Lambda of 1922, he enhanced the lightness and rigidity of the car while dramatically reducing its height compared with its tall, body-on-frame contemporaries. In a monocoque structure the body and chassis are integrated to form a single rigid unit, like an eggshell. The Lancia Lambda's skiff-like open body was stabilized by its transmission tunnel, which ran down the middle of the floor like the keel of a boat, further lowering the centre of gravity.

Unlike true monocoque structures, most cars are built with unitized bodies using a framework of tubes, box sections and bulkheads that give the combined body and frame its integrity, their stressed skin providing some additional strength. One of the first unitized sedans, the Citroën Traction Avant of 1934, established the proportions of the modern closed car, so low as to eliminate the need for running boards. Such low-built cars remained the norm until the tall SUVs of the 1990s once again necessitated running boards.

The evolving exterior proportions and the interior spatial characteristics of the automobile were naturally related. The concept of 'organic' architecture, promoted in the later nineteenth century by the American architect Louis Sullivan, declared that the exterior form of a building should be determined by its structure, function and interior arrangement, as opposed to the Beaux Arts approach, which prioritized the facade, behind which interior spaces were made to fit.[51] In car design there existed a similar tension between fitting

the occupants within a pre-determined form or designing the body shape around them.

As the practice of ergonomics developed in the 1930s, manufacturers employed seating bucks, mock-ups used to study the interiors of their early streamlined cars, testing visibility, dimensions, accessibility and the arrangement of the controls. The shift from box-like wooden frames to unitized all-metal bodies presented new challenges. Carl Breer's design for the Chrysler Airflow (1934) altered the car's architecture by placing the engine over the front axle and moving passengers forward within the wheelbase, providing a smoother ride and improved handling. More radical experiments in streamlining, such as William Stout's Scarab (1932–), featured flexible seating plans that anticipated later minivans, including the Fiat Multipla of 1956 and the Renault Espace of 1984.

Meanwhile, seats themselves evolved from thinly padded wooden benches to the electronically personalized driver's chair of today, and led other types of furniture in technical innovation while following popular taste. Edwardian touring cars featured individual bucket seats, like contemporaneous tub chairs, wrapping

The steel unibody structure combined with front-wheel drive in the Citroën Traction Avant of 1934 made possible the car's low centre of gravity, fine handling and sleek proportions typical of the modern car.

around each occupant to help keep them on board; their upholstery conformed to domestic types, deeply tufted and buttoned, in leather to resist the elements.[52]

At about the time of the First World War, full-width bench seats appeared in sleek new torpedo touring cars, while in post-war sedans, typically seating five, front seats were movable forward and back on tracks to accommodate drivers of different heights and reaches. By the mid-1930s, two-door models carrying four or five people featured front seats with hinged squabs, each folding forward independently to ease access to the rear seat. This simple innovation led to the increasing popularity of coupés and cabriolets and to the demise of four-door convertible sedans and of uncovered 'rumble seats' (uncovered folding seats to the rear).

Interior design also contributed to the image of the car as a 'bedroom on wheels' and all that entailed. In the late 1930s, when motels were still relatively rare, Nash Motors patented a fully reclining seat-back that enabled motorists to convert their car into a full-length double bed. Nash continued to promote its Pullman-style

The multi-purpose vehicle has many precedents, but this cutaway view of the 1956 Fiat Multipla shows the type in a very pure form and at the beginning of its extraordinary rise to ubiquity.

interiors until the 1960s, by which time camper vans and motels had made them redundant.

A more sophisticated interior layout originated in European 'gran turismo' sport coupés, such as the Ferrari 250 Europa with its 2+2 seating configuration featuring a central console flanked by individual bucket seats at the front and a contoured bench behind. Americans soon discovered the pleasures of these stylish grand tourers, and developed their own less expensive and temperamental versions. The four-passenger Ford Thunderbird of 1958 was the popular pioneer of this type.

While the exterior was extravagantly styled under the direction of George Walker and Joseph Oros, the T-Bird's most influential feature was its sporty interior. Like the Ferrari, its cabin was bisected by a bulky transmission tunnel, a consequence of the car's very low profile. To disguise that incursion into the cabin space, the designers created a console incorporating radio speaker, heating controls,

Bucket seats helped to keep early motorists on the car, but their elaborately buttoned leather upholstery and overall shape conform to the familiar aesthetics of the upper-class Edwardian home and office – decor familiar to this 1906 Brasier's occupants.

ashtrays and electric-window switches, transforming an intrusive mechanical element into a trendsetting feature.[53] That individualistic seating plan distinguished this 'personal car' from standard six-passenger family cars, such as the short-lived Edsel, launched in the same year. While the Edsel sank without trace, the T-Bird sold briskly and signalled the trend towards solo motoring for personal pleasure. It spawned Ford's later Mustang and Capri, both best-selling 2+2 coupés.

When the singular bucket seat replaced communal benches as the norm, its shape evolved, with headrests added to avert whiplash injuries. Motorized or manually operated mechanisms controlling height, rake and horizontal position further tailored the driver's experience. By 1998 Biomechanics Corporation of America (BCAM) International's 'intelligent' car seats, housing a computer in the squab (seat back) to control the contour of the entire surface, automatically custom-fitted any occupant with personalized lumbar, thigh and back

The Ford Thunderbird was the first mass-market 'personal car'. Its sporty 2+2 interior layout was a rejection of the standard six-passenger family car.

support while frequently checking the comfort of the occupant and adjusting if necessary.[54]

As early as 1940, the industrial designer Walter Dorwin Teague wrote: 'Automobile manufacturers have made, in the past few years, a greater contribution to the art of comfortable seating than chair builders in all preceding history.'[55] The modern car seat progressed significantly beyond domestic and office seating in providing comfort and also protection. Yet equally important was the illusion these seats created of the mass-produced car as a bespoke product, fitted to the driver as carefully as a custom-made shoe.

In contrast to these incremental improvements, the architecture of the car took a quantum leap with the British Motor Corporation (BMC) chairman Leonard Lord's radical Austin Mini of 1959, which represented a fundamental reconsideration of automotive space. Setting the front-mounted engine transversely above the front-wheel drive transmission, and moving the wheels to the corners of the chassis, the car's designer, Alec Issigonis, freed enough space to create a comfortable four-seater within an overall length of 3.05 m (10 ft). Such a tiny car, however, highlighted questions about safety that were bubbling up in Europe and North America, as accident statistics rose throughout the 1950s with expanding car ownership and higher speeds on new superhighways.[56]

Safety catch

In March 1965 American car design entered the political arena when Senator Abraham Ribicoff opened congressional hearings summoning Detroit's top executives to explain their manufacturing priorities on the subject of quality, value and safety. Later that year, Ribicoff's adviser, the crusading lawyer Ralph Nader, published his indictment of American car manufacturers' values, *Unsafe at*

Any Speed, a book that became a best-seller because almost the whole population was involved in the unwholesome pact between motorists and manufacturers based on the car's pre-eminent appeal to identity and status.

Nader argued that Detroit ignored research into the lethal effects of 'stiletto' styling, and condemned engineers and stylists alongside corporate executives for the callous neglect of safety.[57] His efforts contributed to the passage in 1966 of the US National Highway Traffic Safety Act. Yet the thrill of speed and the drug of styling had spiked a cocktail that long overshadowed sobriety in car design. When in 1956 Ford attempted to sell safer automobiles with William Burnett's 'Lifeguard Design', featuring 'deep-dish' steering wheels, foam-padded dashboards, laminated window glass and optional seat belts, buyers were unimpressed. Meanwhile, accident statistics for both motorists and pedestrians surged, prompting experimentation outside the industry.

In the early 1950s John O. Moore of Cornell University's Automotive Crash Injury Research project began conducting experimental crash tests, initially using corpses (soon replaced by dummies), and found that the cause of most injuries was lack of passenger restraint. These findings resulted in the design and construction of the Cornell-Liberty Safety Car, designed by the engineer Frank J. Crandell as an 'ideas vehicle' conceived to promote car safety.[58] The body incorporated full-perimeter bumpers, anti-burst accordion doors and an impact-absorbing frame, while the fully padded interior featured inertia-reel seat belts, recessed handles and controls, and six bucket seats with head restraints to reduce whiplash. The driver occupied the centre of the front row, with passenger seats set slightly back to the right and left, so as not to obstruct side views. Despite a sleek initial concept sketch by Raymond Loewy, the completed C-L car was an awkward reworking of a 1956 Ford. Yet as an intelligent

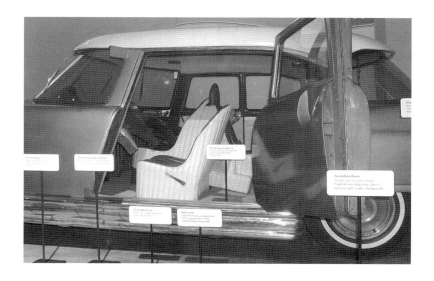

and ethical design it provided a refreshing alternative to Detroit's futuristic 'dream cars'.

Meanwhile, in Europe, Mercedes quietly prioritized safety, continually implementing such devices as the compressed-air safety cushion, patented in 1953 in the USA by the engineer John Hetrick but ignored by the car maker for which he worked. In 1963 the Japanese inventor Yasuzaburou Kobori filed patents in fourteen countries for the design of the airbag on which current types are based, but it was not produced either. GM offered an airbag and two-point lap seat belt as an option in the 1970s, but it was Mercedes that finally developed the modern airbag in 1981, used in combination with three-point shoulder belts, pre-tensioned to reduce the risk of injury from the airbag itself.

The car makers best known for safety design were Scandinavian. The Swedish firms Volvo and Saab pioneered the passenger safety cage, effective crumple zones, impact-absorbing bumpers, the

An antidote to the Walter Mitty spaceship aesthetic of auto industry concept cars at mid-century, the independently built Cornell-Liberty Safety Car of 1958 addressed the terrible post-war rise in auto accident fatalities and injuries, when major manufacturers were uninterested in safety design, as it 'didn't sell'.

collapsible steering wheel, the rear-facing child seat, head restraints, multiple airbags and inflatable side-impact curtains, earning a reputation for above-average performance in crashes. Their resulting popularity around the world pushed reluctant, style-obsessed competitors to prioritize safety, and demonstrated that design reform *can* precede regulation, although it seldom does.[59]

The history of safety innovation is entangled with improvements in performance, comfort and body design, and the lack of allure in this aspect of a car's specifications also relegated it to a low priority in advertising, as most buyers ignore the quality of an airbag or crumple zone, opting instead to buy bigger, heavier, more defensive cars. Nevertheless, accidents have declined since the beginning of safety regulation in the 1960s, and particularly since the passage of seat-belt laws governing motorists themselves.

While the car interior is now a more protective space, the street too has become less threatening to anyone not encased in 2 tons of armour. Efforts to reduce pedestrian injuries began in the first decades of motoring. Early patented devices included various 'pedestrian catchers', intended to scoop up safely in a net attached to the front of the car any unlucky pedestrian who got in its way. Now electronic sensors trigger an airbag to lift the bonnet, adjusting its angle to reduce the effect of hitting a pedestrian. Mark Shane Howard of Ford patented such a system in 1999, but Jaguar was the first manufacturer to use it with pyrotechnic deployment in 2006. Such devices followed EU standards set to reduce pedestrian injuries also by reconfiguring the frontal contours and materials of modern cars.

Despite genuine improvements in safety, some corporations still appear to show a disdain for the security of their customers. In 2014 the GM chief executive and other top managers once again appeared before the US Congress following the recall of about 28 million cars, mainly American models alleged to have caused deaths and injuries from crashes in which airbags did not inflate because of defective ignition switches. GM managers were aware of the problem and withheld information about it for nearly ten years before a private lawsuit on behalf of a victim sparked the recall and the ensuing scandal.

The World Health Organization's report on road safety (2014) listed 1.3 million road deaths for the previous year, and projected an increase of 144 per cent in Southeast Asia over the period 2000–2020 and of 83 per cent in middle- and low-income countries generally by 2020. Only in high-income countries, it predicts, will this toll be slightly offset by an estimated 27 per cent decrease, largely resulting from strict traffic rules.[60] And despite the dubious practices and faulty products of major manufacturers, the overwhelming cause of minor 'fender benders' and fatal crashes alike is driver error, inattention, incapacity or recklessness. The only cure is advanced technology backed by appropriate regulation. According to the electrical engineering professor Thomas Little,

> the goals to save energy, reduce [emissions] and improve safety have driven the specialization and adoption of electronics in particular . . . We are giving up little pieces of control in exchange for safety. The interesting question is, at what point will you and I be willing to say, 'Okay. I am not going to drive the car; it is going to drive me.'[61]

Design or styling

Historians identify and mythologize the work of individuals they deem to be automotive auteurs, such singular individuals as Ferdinand Porsche or Horacio Pagani.[62] Other significant figures are managerial overseers of design teams who developed new types of car, such individuals as BMC's Leonard Lord or Pierre-Jules Boulanger at Citroën.

Among the most influential design managers, however, was Harley Earl, who initiated symbolic car styling at GM and, as vice president of the corporation, led the styling division from 1937 to 1959. Earl's ideas, baroque taste, forceful personality and corporate position ensured his reputation as the ultimate promoter of styling and as the designer of many memorable GM cars. His hierarchical and systematically branded use of symbolism required teams of skilled draughtsmen and clay modellers to develop and refine new ideas for each car in the company's product line: Silver Streak speed lines decorating the Pontiac, porthole vents for Buick, tail fins on the Cadillac. Earl's successor as vice president of styling, William Mitchell, described Earl's aim: 'To make a car look as big and as powerful and as glamorous as possible, and decorated all to hell'.[63]

The process of styling began with thematic sketches, which Earl and his divisional chiefs would select for development into scale drawings: side, front, rear. The historian C. Edson Armi described the process as 'highly schematic and totally flat in its formative and creative stages'.[64] Even today's designers call those ornamental lines, bulges or intaglio scoops that distinguish one model from another 'graphics'. Clay modellers, a type of craftsman that Earl introduced to the corporate design process, then sculpted 3/8-scale and full-scale models of the finished car using industrial plasticine to translate the designers' ideas into three dimensions. They finished the form with a coloured plastic film, Dinoc, to simulate paint, chromium and glass. This remains the standard design method in the age of computer-aided design. Today, however, the techniques of drawing and modelling have become more flexible and faster with advanced technology such as 3-D digital printing of sketch models.

When the only really important question in automotive design seemed to be, 'Is it sexy?', styling was an obvious solution. The Silver Streak motif devised under Harley Earl's overall leadership at GM was a typical means of sexing up the generic car body and gave the Pontiac brand its identity.

Who really deserves credit for designing a production car? Armi asserted that the 'creator' is unquestionably the chief of the design department, who coordinates the work of others and accepts or rejects their input. By his definition, Frank Hershey designed the original Ford Thunderbird. Yet Hershey acknowledged his team, including stylists Bill Boyer and Chase Morsey, who introduced one of the more significant ideas in automotive marketing history, to define the Thunderbird as a 'personal car', recognizing a new and rapidly growing desire for an individualistic vehicle designed to be driven primarily for pleasure.[65] Yet Hershey also spoke of how and why the credit for that successful design went to Ford vice president George Walker:

> In his contract it was stipulated that he and only he was to get credit for any designs that came out of Ford and that only he was to figure

Harley Earl introduced clay modelling as a means of developing unified car bodies in the era of streamlining. This BMW 1-Series coupé in clay mock-up reflects the sculptor's skill still necessary to the automotive design process today. It is in the sculptural quality of the car body that its allure is formed.

in any publicity concerning design . . . As long as I was there, Walker did not figure in any way in the designs of the Ford cars.[66]

Walker was an industrial designer, an automotive-industry outsider and brilliant coordinator of talent. He brought to car design his broad fine-art background and experience as an illustrator, typical of the first generation of industrial designers, but unusual among industry car stylists. His talent was as a marketeer occupying centre stage at Ford, just as Raymond Loewy or Henry Dreyfuss did in their multidisciplinary practices.[67] The historian David Gartman argued that this confuses creativity with power and organizational position, declaring that 'the creator in auto design is always the group.'[68] For this reason, there is often disagreement when the authorship of a particular design is ascribed to an individual, and members of design teams have famously contested that credit.

Throughout its history, car design has formed a separate activity from other design fields. Early car designers were typically trained on the job, in the great custom body builders' workshops, in tightly controlled styling studios or within corporate-sponsored automotive design courses, practising exclusively in that field, as did Sergio Pininfarina and Giovanni Michelotti. More recently, however, that picture has broadened. Giorgetto Giugiaro's talent was recognized early in art school, but his automotive design skills were acquired through an apprenticeship at Fiat. Later, having created significant designs for nearly every manufacturer from Alfa Romeo to Zastava, he founded Ital Design, an industrial design practice applying his personal aesthetics to home and office furniture, Seiko watches and Nikon cameras, among a wide range of product types.

Beyond car design's relatively hermetic world, some notable outsiders created memorable vehicles or developed new concepts. Those exceptions include a radical concept by the Italian architect Mario

Bellini, the Kar-a-Sutra (1972), a 'mobile environment' created for the exhibition *Italy: The New Domestic Landscape* at the Museum of Modern Art in New York in 1972. A lime-green fibreglass van, its interior furnished with beanbag-type seating for ultimate flexibility, Kar-a-Sutra was reminiscent of the Citroën Mehari (1968), a plastic-bodied utility sports car based on the 2CV/Dyane, designed by the plastics pioneer Roland de la Poype. Yet the larger Kar-a-Sutra had long-term implications for the design of the next decade's minivans, and particularly the Renault Espace of 1984. It remains a rare union of architectural thinking and automotive design.

Industrial designers such as Raymond Loewy and Brooks Stevens successfully led teams of auto stylists designing for independent manufacturers, including Studebaker and Willys in the USA. But their ideas and the cars they created were typically out of step with the aesthetics of the major Detroit manufacturers, and their status as consultants limited their influence within corporations. Today's styling studios divide their design teams among specialist interior designers, exterior designers and detail artists concentrating, for example, on headlights. And the design studios of nearly all the major manufacturers are led and staffed by graduates of a few world-renowned vehicle-design courses.

That relatively closed shop of automotive design generally excluded women, who entered the profession in small numbers. An early exception was the daughter of an Arrol-Johnston manager, Dorothée Pullinger, who trained as a body draughtsman in the company's Scottish works. Continuing the wartime practices of working women in the early 1920s, Pullinger contributed significantly to the design and manufacture of the Arrol Galloway car. She adapted the vehicle specifically for female drivers, reducing the car's size and weight, repositioning and miniaturizing controls, and raising the driver's seat to improve vision. She also managed the factory where it was built by an all-woman workforce from 1920 to 1925.[69] Pullinger's approach to creating a genuine 'woman's car' contrasts with the later, market-driven activities of female automotive designers.

In Detroit styling studios, women were employed more for publicity than for design. Typically, during the 1950s GM appointed a group of young women, dubbed the Damsels of Design, to 'feminize' their cars. Assigned to a special subsection of the interior-design department, their highly publicized innovations included glove-compartment vanity mirrors and make-up holders, fur-look upholstery and dramatic colour schemes such as hot pink, black and gold. Publications in which they appeared looked like fashion or home-decoration spreads, and they also worked in the Frigidaire Production Studio styling appliances and furniture for the company's 'Kitchen of the Future'.

Women such as GM CEO Mary Bara have risen to the highest management positions, while women designers have also achieved greater influence within some companies. The former Volvo designer Cynthia Charwick-Bland described how management accepted a challenge by two of the company's women employees to build a concept car designed from the perspective of female designers. The resulting YCC concept (2004) aimed to ease maintenance and increase security; it featured easy-to-reach fuel and windscreen-washer reservoirs, run-flat tyres, keyless entry and self-parking, which further research showed were features as attractive to men as to women, although results showed women's expectations to be higher overall. Charwick-Bland wrote: 'It's a subtle thing but huge in the mind of women and women designers. We created and designed a car that fulfilled the greater expectations of women and met the expectations of men.'[70]

Outside the auto industry, Coqueline Courrèges, wife of the Paris fashion designer André Courrèges, brought a couture sensibility to the image of electric automobiles, designing a series of 'bubble cars' in collaboration with AC Propulsion of California, which supplied mechanical platforms powered by lithium-ion batteries. Beginning with La Bulle in 2003, the futuristic styling of these cars recalled the Space Age fashions for which the House of Courrèges was known in the 1960s. In 2006 Coqueline demonstrated the three-seater 180-km/h (112-mph) ZOOOP, which featured a gold-tinted transparent dome reminiscent of the astronauts' helmets she and her husband popularized as part of their Moongirl fashion line in 1968. The ultra-light 690-kg (1,520-lb) ZOOOP combined performance with style in a way no other motor-industry product did, meeting the road with bright yellow tyres and creating a jaunty effect, like automotive go-go boots.[71]

2 | Driver

Bonding

While returning home recently on a late-night train from London, I overheard the conversation of two young overseas students discussing their hopes and plans for the future. The elder and more worldly of them advised the other, with passion: 'You *must* get a car. With a car you're king of your own country.' I was reminded of stately Minervas, Hispano-Suizas and Rolls-Royces. Historically, that kingliness was denoted by the size, power and elegance of those cars, which became prime exemplars of regal transport, owned and driven conspicuously by royalty in their countries of manufacture. Nevertheless, what the South American student argued was that any car could confer on its driver kingly status through the absolute autonomy it provides.

F. Scott Fitzgerald, peripatetic king of the Jazz Age, described the car as an escape from 'the dullness and the tears and disillusion of all the stationary world', while the novelist Sinclair Lewis, also writing in the 1920s, described one of his characters' feelings for his car as 'poetry and tragedy, love and heroism'.[1] Such lyrical observations about the relationships we develop with cars are rehearsed widely in settings ranging from online gearhead blogs, such as the popular *Jalopnik*, to the critical journal *Culture Change*, founded in 1988 by the Sustainable Energy Institute in California. This chapter considers the components of the intense or addictive relationship many of us form with cars, and reflects on how it might be channelled more fruitfully in response to impending developments in the technology, system and culture of automobility.

The obvious question is: why and how do people love cars? Yet the answers are many and varied, and that deep connection between drivers and their cars shows up as a standard feature of popular culture, mythologized most grandly in films. Marlene Dietrich's boat-tailed Auburn Speedster in the heist drama *Desire* (1936) perfectly complements that actress's classic beauty and demonstrates her character's glamour and independence. Similarly, in *Bullitt* (1968) Steve McQueen's Mustang GT, the star of a highly memorable and influential cinema car chase, revealed his character's determination and daring. McLaren and Ferrari Formula One racing cars were the mechanical embodiments of masculine rivalry in *Rush* (2013), while an aged Thunderbird forever bonded Thelma and Louise on their final flight from male oppression in 1991. Through their mechanistic choreography, Michael Caine's fleet of Mini Coopers in *The Italian Job* (1969) rendered vividly the charismatic dodging and weaving of that ultimate cockney gangster. And Marty McFly's DeLorean transformed the ordinary high-school kid into an intrepid time-traveller in *Back to the Future* (1985). These portrayals of the alliance between drivers and their cars dramatized the central reality and mythology of the automobile era and furnished background images with which many ordinary drivers slip behind the wheel on their daily commute.

The car industry is always on the alert for new ways to enhance that alliance. To divine the requirements for vehicles in 2025–30, an interdisciplinary research team composed of experts from design, engineering and development departments at BMW was recently

set the task of exploring such issues with individuals and institutions around the world. Their aim was to shed a more nuanced light on how major shifts in technology could bring about new forms of human interaction via the automobile, how motorists would want to experience the interiors of future cars, and what sort of culture might develop alongside fundamental changes in the car itself. While style, speed and mechanical control were the essential qualities that linked cinema heroes with their cars in the last century, the BMW team sought deeper haptic and cognitive interaction that could be fostered between motorist and machine.[2]

Yet many motorists succumb directly to the aesthetic seduction of the car, worshipped as a fetish object. The sculptural forms, colours and ornamental details of cars all captivate and entertain us with their magic. That attraction to form, symbolism and finish is exploited psychologically and commercially by sophisticated design and

Ultimate glamour in the streamline era: Marlene Dietrich at the wheel of a Gordon Buehrig-designed Auburn 851 boat-tailed Speedster in the heist film *Desire* (1936).

marketing in the service of the brand, which offers us access to a club that we feel represents best who we think we are and what image we want to present on the street. The difference is illustrated by comparing the Citroën DS3 of 2010, very French in its quirky rebelliousness, with German products in the same market segment. The Citroën, styled under the direction of Mark Lloyd, conspicuously challenges current automotive fashion with a distinctive set of expressive forms and glittering ornament, emphasizing the company's tradition of nonconformity. Meanwhile, the competing Audi A1, styled by Stefan Sielaff, is fastidiously rational in appearance, reminding prospective purchasers that technology leads design in the Audi stable. Another popular competitor in the segment, the BMW Mini, has its roots firmly planted in the Austin Morris legend of British creativity and uniqueness, and determinedly evokes the impudent spirit of *The Italian Job*.

In the James Bond films of the 1960s, the spy's silver Aston Martin, perfectly tailored to the character's covert needs, told us instantly much of what we as an audience needed to know about him, and much about his fantastic world of action and glamour. Even more than 50 years later that link between the image of the British super-spy and the Aston Martin brand has remained credible thanks to carefully controlled product continuity. The spy, his colleagues Q and M, the deranged villains, fabulous locations and Bond's girls are all linked through that testosteronic silver coupé. The Bond franchise turned for some years to BMW for their star cars, but that image never quite suited the British spy; it was too forthright, too Germanic. One of the biggest questions now facing researchers in the BMW team is how to adapt the forms and user experience of 'the ultimate driving machine' to new robotic technologies and new automotive architectures while retaining their brand's carefully cultivated image.

Yet beyond its totemic value, perhaps the most immediate and compelling aspect of any automobile's appeal today is its promise of connectedness – to people, places and experiences – achieved partly through the physical act of moving but also from the connections made en route through the electronic media and information technology accessed through the car and designed into it. Whereas knobs, levers and push-buttons controlled most of the functions of the car in the past, today the touch screen and voice command are primary links between the driver and the automobile. Thus the mechanics of control are being replaced by more flexible and personal commands. The benefits of such systems are found in their apparent ease and their capacity to upgrade via new software. However, the tactile advantages of the older methods are lost, and the complexity of the many features combined in an electronic system may contribute to driver confusion and possibly to alienation.

Emancipation

It was a deeply involved woman who made the first ever long-distance drive in an automobile. In August 1888 Bertha Benz, wife of Karl Benz and a staunch supporter in the development of his first experimental cars, decided to prove to the doubtful inventor (and to the world) that his new Patent Motorwagen was good enough to be sold commercially. To do this she and her sons, aged thirteen and fifteen, embarked on the 100-km (60-mile) drive from Mannheim to her mother's home in Pforzheim. The trip there and back revealed some of the car's faults, such as its inability to climb hills, up which she and the elder boy pushed it. Along the way she also had to find an apothecary shop to buy fuel, clear a blocked fuel line with her hatpin, and insulate an ignition wire with her garter. By nightfall she had arrived safely, and she cabled her husband to advise

him that he must include a low gear in his next car's transmission to improve its uphill performance.[3] Despite the subsequent male-orientated history of the car, Bertha Benz defined it as a woman's machine right from the start.

Around the turn of the twentieth century other women drivers confronted the noxious stereotype of the helpless female motorist that arose soon after the birth of the car. Londoner Dorothy Levitt became a successful competitor in early British and French speed competitions, hill-climbs and endurance trials in the first decade of

Early star of British motoring Dorothy Levitt demonstrates running repairs dressed in overall and large hat for her 1905 booklet of advice for aspiring lady motorists, *The Woman and the Motor Car*. She raced cars and boats powered by Napier engines and promoted motoring as a sport for women..

the twentieth century. She wrote a column for women on motoring (1903–8) for the illustrated weekly newspaper *The Graphic*, and published a booklet for aspiring women drivers, *The Woman and the Car* (1907). She also demonstrated the technique of driving to Queen Alexandra and her daughters, appeared in advertisements for the Napier car, and set records in automobiles and speedboats powered by Napier engines, considered 'the Stradivarius' of early motors.[4] She was the first English woman to have driven officially in motor races, from 1903, preceded only by the French women Baroness Hélène van Zuylen and Camille du Gast, who competed in European road races in 1898 and 1901 respectively.

Levitt's glamorous appearance in specialized motoring millinery and elegant duster coats helped to establish an attractive public image of the female driver in contrast with critical portrayals of the time, which characterized female motorists as 'mannish', which some were. The extraordinary French driver Violette Morris underwent a double mastectomy ostensibly to make her more comfortable behind the wheel of her racing cars. By contrast, the coquettish Levitt wrote on motoring fashions and automobile body styles in an attempt to integrate the sporting attractions of motoring with the usual aesthetic concerns of upper-class women.

An accomplished horsewoman, Levitt compared driving with riding, since many potential female motorists at that time were also competitive horsewomen. She wrote: 'The hardest thing is to keep in the car . . . It is far harder work to sit in the car than to ride a galloping horse over the jumps in a steeplechase.'[5] She also provided advice about the most useful composition of a tool kit, and included photographs taken by Horace Nicholls, to illustrate her instructions and to demonstrate her direct engagement with the gritty, mechanical aspects of motoring. They convincingly portray the modern woman, emancipated by the automobile.

The First World War dramatically accelerated the independent status of women, not least through their assumption of various jobs behind the wheel in cars, ambulances and trucks, and on motorcycles.[6] To aid in the war effort, the American expatriate writer Gertrude Stein imported to France from the USA a new Model T Ford in order to drive for the American Fund for French Wounded. In words attributed to Alice B. Toklas, Stein became quite a proficient driver in all respects, except 'backing', and was 'ready to drive the car anywhere, to crank the car as often as there was nobody else to do it, to repair the car. I must say she was very good at it.'[7]

The role of the car in the growing independence of women cannot be overestimated, and it extended to their campaign for universal suffrage in the first quarter of the twentieth century. While it also featured as a dais in the campaigning of male politicians at the time,[8] the historian Julie Wosk describes how

> female suffragists capitalized on the automobile as an iconic object, decorating the machine with banners, slogans and symbolic colours: in England, the automobiles wore the suffrage colours purple, white and green, and in the United States, they were painted 'suffrage yellow'.

Automobiles featured in processions, rallies and demonstrations as a symbol of women's self-sufficiency, worldliness, competence and modernity. Wherever suffragettes lectured publicly out of doors, at meetings and parades, their cars provided an impressive and specifically modern podium, frequently decorated with bunting, emblazoned with symbols and painted with slogans in the colours of their particular branch of the movement. The car as a commanding object drew attention to the power of women's suffrage, while as a practical instrument of mobility it helped to spread their ideas to the widest possible constituency.[9]

The seduction of style

If some women had proven that they were fully capable of operating even the most challenging of early automobiles, manufacturers quickly saw the advantage in making the passenger car more comfortable, easier to operate and increasingly appealing to both male and female buyers by providing alluring interiors and enhancing the appearance of the body.

In the years before the First World War – when the great majority of passenger cars were open types ranging from the lightest cycle cars to massive, powerful touring cars – closed automobiles were also being built in small numbers, providing models of what car travel could offer in comfort and even luxury. Electric broughams are the type of early car for which the majority of closed bodies were constructed, offering every refinement then available for the relaxation of drivers and passengers, including the novelty of electric lighting inside and out, when most homes did not yet have it. Their convivial interiors typically provided bench seating for three abreast, facing forwards, with an additional bucket seat, mounted on a pedestal, which could swivel around from a forward-looking position at the front to face the other occupants at the rear of the cabin. Plush broadcloth upholstery and thick carpeting covered all internal surfaces, while crystal bud vases attached to the window pillars were a typical nicety. A conservatory of glass surrounded the passengers in a mobile observation lounge, which was also a conspicuous enclave of privilege, where one could be seen.

In its amenity and configuration, the electric brougham set a standard to which all luxurious, owner-driven, closed vehicles would aspire in later years. As a mobile social space, such interiors have rarely been surpassed in a standard production automobile, although such concept cars as the Toyota/Sony Pod of 2001 and Mario Bellini's

The Detroit electric car of 1914 was among the finest and most popular of its luxurious breed of city car. Its tall roof provided plenty of space for exotic feathered hats – pity the snowy egret.

Kar-a-Sutra of 1972 attempted to redefine the car interior as a more actively social space, emphasizing loosely configured or flexible face-to-face seating, in contrast with the rigidly forward-facing layouts of most cars. Like their horse-drawn Victorian predecessors, Edwardian electric broughams, devised as mobile salons, aped the style of upper-class drawing rooms through their finishes, colour and decor, although from the earliest days they were often more tastefully executed than typical homes of the time.

Most commentators on the history of car design agree that automotive styling began when GM supremos Lawrence Fisher and Alfred Sloan appointed the California coachbuilder Harley Earl (see below) to form an Art and Colour Section (renamed Styling Section in 1937), intended to carry out an annual update of their cars' appearance and develop a long-term strategy of aesthetic

Inside a Detroit electric brougham, all was familiar and comfortable. Like a little drawing room on wheels, the car's convivial layout, curved window glass, thick carpets, silent operation and 'deep Turkish cushions' made city motoring pleasurable.

evolution by brand. And while it is true that the purely cosmetic annual model change increased the commercial significance of appearance and profoundly influenced the design techniques of the automobile industry, the accepted view of Earl's importance generally ignores the previous history of that aspect of car design which in earlier years would have been described simply as 'beauty'.

The ancient Vitruvian triad of 'firmness, commodity and delight', used since antiquity to assess quality in architecture, has also been invoked to describe the qualities of cars – from the first motor carriages to the present day. 'Firmness' may be translated as power or durability. 'Commodity' can be defined as comfort or amenity. The charmingly slippery notion of 'delight' has been interpreted as character, style or beauty. Loosely echoing Vitruvius, an advertisement for the Winton Motor Carriage published in *The Horseless Age* on 4 April 1900 described the car's significant qualities, bordering a picture of the machine – 'Strength, Speed, Durability, Beauty'.

While nearly all the articles in *The Horseless Age* focused on technical developments, new patents, insurance matters and comparisons of the various forms of propulsion then vying for acceptance, advertisements increasingly featured appearance as a significant consideration for the potential buyer. By 1902 the 12-hp Packard touring car was advertised with the claim: 'No machine in this or any other country is more graceful.'[10] That claim reflects the established aesthetic appreciation of horse-drawn carriages, still the customary vehicles of the wealthy. An advertisement of 1914 maintained that link with carriage design, declaring that the Rauch & Lang electric brougham 'presents a quiet richness of design and finish that outrivals that of any monarch's conveyance . . . in master-productions that embody the genius of the artist and the skill of the finished craftsman'.[11] Such a claim is consistent with the previous 60-year history of Rauch & Lang as society coachbuilders.

The transference of aesthetic concerns from carriage builders to car makers was natural to the upper end of the market, and typically involved the buyer purchasing a chassis from the motor manufacturer and then having a custom body fitted to it by a separate coachbuilding firm. For those companies that were attempting to target a mass market, product engineering and manufacturing technology far exceeded appearance in importance well into the 1920s. O. E. Hunt, director of Chevrolet in the early 1920s, later wrote: 'Even comfort, initially, was a secondary matter, and appearance, economy, etc., got scant, if any, attention . . . Engineering was the all-absorbing activity and the engineer was usually the dominant personality.'[12] It was also the abiding area of concern for owner-drivers, who had to understand the mechanics of their cars in order to keep them going.

The problem for mass producers was to transfer that pride in appearance from coachbuilt cars to those for the many, while changing the nature of the bond between driver and car from the challenge of mechanics to the easy appreciation of style. GM president Alfred Sloan believed that the ascendancy of closed cars during the 1920s demanded a new emphasis on styling, as their high roof structures presented visual problems that had largely been absent from the previously dominant open touring cars. That change in the car body, from open to closed, plus the development of a coordinated corporate structure, new production technology and materials, and a competitive market, encouraged a more calculated exploitation of appearance that resulted in styling becoming the highest priority for the firm.

Sloan's interest in visual branding was shared by Lawrence Fisher, whose family coachbuilding firm had made high-class carriages and custom car bodies. In 1926, as head of the Cadillac division of GM, Fisher met the young Californian Harley Earl, whose family was also in the custom car business. Earl's Los Angeles clientele included such top Hollywood celebrities as the director Erich von Stroheim, the actress Mary Pickford ('America's Sweetheart') and the cowboy-film star Tom Mix. For such clients Earl integrated the various elements of the car's body into a more streamlined whole that appeared longer and lower than the competition, and it was this effect that Fisher sought in a new companion car for the exclusive Cadillac.

That car was named LaSalle, and Earl was brought to Detroit to style it. He borrowed its lines from the sophisticated French-built Hispano-Suiza – an established form of plagiarism in American car design, but henceforth established as corporate policy. Inseparable from styling was the annual model change, created specifically to make buyers unhappy with their old car, which, according to the writers Bianca Mugyenyi and Yves Engler, 'quickly became undesirable and even embarrassing'. They cite Sloan, who freely admitted the rationale for annual models: 'The reason is simple . . . we want to make you dissatisfied with your current car so you will buy a new one, you who can afford it.'[13] Such unashamed opportunism was common in the fashion industry and among manufacturers of many kinds of consumer product, but the plot thickened with the rise of GM styling, the annual model change and research-based advertising. Although the age of a car had previously been designated by its year of manufacture, the new model year ran from September rather than from January, with revised styling prematurely and artificially ageing the current model, which then remained only stylish enough to appeal in the used-car market.

Another characteristic of Earl's Los Angeles custom car designs had been the embellishment of his clients' vehicles with personalizing details, such as the saddle bolted to the body of Tom Mix's Cadillac. This quality became Earl's major contribution to the mass-produced car, and it encouraged buyers to select a vehicle distinguished by multicoloured paint combinations and superficial trim details from among all the essentially identical vehicles rolling off the assembly lines. In theory, motorists then bonded with their own car as a personal badge of identity.

What is generally overlooked, however, is that a more authentic bond had already formed between motorists and even the most plain, standardized automobile of its day, the Model T Ford. Gertrude Stein and Alice B. Toklas had named their first two Fords Auntie and Godiva, and decorated the second with a variety of 'gifts' provided by friends to adorn the car in her nudity. Henry Ford himself had described the individualistic qualities of his 'standard' product:

> No two things in nature are alike. We build our cars absolutely inter-changeable. All parts are as nearly alike as chemical analysis, the finest machinery and the finest workmanship can make them. No fitting of any kind is required, and it would seem that two Fords standing side by side, looking exactly alike and made so exactly alike that any part could be taken out of one and put in the other, would be alike. But they are not. They will have different road habits. We have men who have driven hundreds, and in some cases thousands, of Fords and they say that no two ever act precisely the same.[14]

Nevertheless, GM determined that something visible and tangible was needed to amplify their sales curve, a strategy that earned them 40 per cent of the North American market for new cars by 1935. Earl, Sloan and Fisher, whose division eventually built the bodies for all GM car brands, were dedicated to converting the car body into a mannequin, which they would dress in an annually changing procession of ornaments, paint colours and upholstery fabrics. These visual elements would be arranged in different combinations each

STYLE

WHEN it comes to style in motor cars—and today style
is all-important—all the world looks to Body by Fisher.
For Fisher is the authority, the leader, tried and proven;
the chief source and center of beauty in motor car design.

Cadillac · La Salle · Buick · Oakland · Oldsmobile · Pontiac · Chevrolet

year to freshen an old body and conceal the increasingly glacial
pace of their cars' mechanical evolution.[15] Soon that analogy
between car styling and fashionable dress was featured centrally in
GM advertising. McClelland Barclay's widely published illustration
Style for the Fisher Body Division of GM in 1928 conveyed an
explicit link between the latest clothing fashions and the newest car
styling, without even illustrating a car.

McClelland Barclay's elegant advertisement for the Fisher Body Division of GM made
the link between fashion and auto design explicit. His 'Fisher Body Girl' became a popular
pin-up.

Automotive DNA

Brand recognition, carried over from the bicycle trade, began with the ornamental nameplates attached to the earliest cars but was soon communicated by design features that were easily recognized from a distance. The radiator was the most prominent feature of the early motor car, identifying the chassis that would typically be supplied to coachbuilders, and therefore came in for special attention. For example, Wilhelm Maybach of Daimler Motors in Stuttgart designed the Mercedes model of 1902, designated Simplex to denote its ease of operation, with a clean and distinctively shaped brass radiator sporting the car's name in script set at a rakish angle. When Emil Jellinek, Mercedes' French agent, entered the first Simplex in the Nice-La Turbie hill-climb, he set new records, establishing the car's thoroughbred reputation. Immediately that radiator shape became widely recognized by car enthusiasts. It has evolved gradually over the past century, remaining recognizable even in the present-day S-Class. Similar significance is attached to the 10-hp Type A Rolls-Royce of 1904, the first model to wear the classical aedicule-shaped radiator that is still in use by the company as its key identity feature along with the Spirit of Ecstasy mascot.

The front of the automobile then remained its main identifiable viewpoint, the distinctiveness of its radiator or grille, the position, size and shape of its headlights and the proportions of its windscreen all suggesting the character of a face, human or animal. Just as the features of a human face tell us about the personality of an individual, the features of the car's face convey similar information about the brand or model. While this is a commonly understood phenomenon that plays a part in forming the bond between people and cars, it has rarely been examined systematically. One team of scholars representing the fields of psychology, anthropology and marketing carried out research at the University of Vienna using geometric modelling and statistical measurements to determine how ordinary people attribute personality traits to the shapes in automobile faces. Broadly, the study aimed to enhance understanding of how human perceptual strategies lead us to the phenomenon of animism, ascribing life to inanimate objects. By analysing reactions to various proportions and surface shapes in a selection of recently produced cars, researchers distinguished among cars that appeared sociable, happy, modest and female in contrast with those that respondents saw as angry, aggressive, arrogant and male. They concluded that, 'The better our subjects liked a car, the closer it matched the shape characteristics corresponding to high values of power. Thus, people seem to like mature, dominant, masculine, arrogant, angry-looking cars.' Car styling in the early twenty-first century suggests that

The Rolls-Royce 10hp of 1905 was the first car to be badged 'Rolls-Royce' and to be identified by the triangular-topped, 'temple-front' radiator the marque's main identification feature ever since.

manufacturers agree, responding with increasingly testosterone-laden designs emphasizing stealth, muscularity and power.[16]

When GM launched its first all-new post-war models, in 1948 and 1949, divisional design teams ornamented them with carnivorous-looking frontal features, dubbed 'dollar grins', but they also made their first coordinated effort to establish through ornament the distinctive appearance for each brand from *any* angle. The famous story told in memoirs by Alfred Sloan, Bill Mitchell, Harley Earl and others records how in 1938 Earl, an aviation buff, took two protégés, Mitchell and Hershey, to view a prototype of Lockheed's new P38 Lightning fighter aircraft. Its appearance impressed them all deeply. Designed by Hal Hibbard and Clarence 'Kelly' Johnson of the Lockheed aircraft design team, the Lightning featured a dramatic single-seat, twin-propeller layout with its engine fairings sweeping back separately in two long, graceful booms linked by a distinctive twin-tail assembly; the pilot sat centrally in a teardrop-shaped nacelle

General Motors' styling supremo Harley Earl identified the Lockheed P38 Lightning, designed by Hall Hibbard and Clarence 'Kelly' Johnson, as the inspiration for the styling of all post-war GM cars, but particularly for the Cadillacs of 1948–59. The P38 prototype is seen here entering a wind tunnel.

under a bubble of clear Plexiglas. This was an unusual aeronautical layout in that it was perfectly adaptable to the form of a car body. Frank Hershey, who was appointed head stylist for the Cadillac division after the war, eventually translated that composition into his design for the Cadillac of 1948, conferring the aeroplane's elegance and image of dynamic power on GM's top luxury brand.

That car featured the first embryonic tail fins on the trailing edge of the two voluptuous rear wings (fenders), clearly identifying the brand from the rear view. Yet it was not just the fins that resonated with potential buyers. The entire shape of the body aped the long integrated forms of the Lightning's fuselage and tail booms with a variety of sleekly sculpted lines beginning at the headlights and continuing along the side panels to the rear bumper. Hershey

The Lightning's unusual planform, with twin tail booms, central pilot nacelle, bubble canopy and propeller nose cones, transferred artfully to the pontoon body shapes of GM's post-war cars. Its twin tail fins sat easily on the rear fenders of the 1949–53 Cadillac and gave it a strong visual identity.

accented the blur of spinning wheels, which appeared as concentric circles of black, white and silver, with chrome speed lines running horizontally along the wings marking their wake. The bright, airy cabin was as much of a bubble as current glass technology would permit, with thin chrome edging emphasizing the overall horizontal sweep of the window openings. The car's marketing gained considerable attention owing to its overt appeal to the imaginative driver's heroic fantasy life, as dramatized in the 1947 film version of James Thurber's humorous story *The Secret Life of Walter Mitty* (1939).

The publicist-turned-car-maker Edward 'Ned' Jordan had done with words what Detroit stylists would later do with chrome (and what they do today with sculpted body panels), writing one of the most influential and controversial passages of copy in advertising history. The 'Somewhere West of Laramie' advertisement for his Jordan Playboy roadster, first published in the *Saturday Evening Post* in 1923, described a free-spirited flapper racing her car alongside a horse-riding cowboy through an abstract, magical landscape, just for the seductive enjoyment of the chase:

> Somewhere west of Laramie there's a bronco-busting, steer-roping girl who knows what I'm talking about. She can tell what a sassy pony, that's a cross between greased lightning and the place where it hits, can do with eleven hundred pounds of steel and action when he's going high, wide and handsome. The truth is – the Playboy was built for her.

Whereas early motoring commentators contrasted the 'clean' automobile with the horrors and filth of horse locomotion in cities, Jordan linked his car with the freedom and excitement offered by recreational horseback riding, demonstrating how the horse had changed since the advent of the car from a beast of burden to a symbol of freedom pursued through sport and leisure, possibly a premonition of how manually controlled ICE cars may be enjoyed in the future.

Although Jordan's hyperbole set a fanciful standard for American advertising in the 1920s, in European markets the appeal to motorists' brand loyalty worked somewhat differently. In France, for example, André Citroën's cars achieved a dedicated following of admirers and buyers attracted by their imaginative engineering and unique design. Yet Citroën, like Jordan, was also an aggressive and innovative promoter, and in the mid-1920s he secured the sole rights to advertise on the Eiffel Tower, which he set ablaze with the company name in giant illuminated letters. The Russian Futurist writer Ilya Ehrenburg, a critic of capitalist machine culture, described the famous tower's illumination, which was installed to coincide with the opening of the International Exposition of Decorative and Industrial Arts in the summer of 1925, and which remained in place for nine years: 'A foreigner arriving in the city at night . . . will see only one word: it blazes in giant letters on the Eiffel Tower. Monsieur André Citroën's calling card.'[17]

At the start of his car-making enterprise, Citroën was committed to providing the French consumer with cars that were both economical and stylish. His project combined Ford's concern for economy, employing a single model to achieve maximum savings in production, with Alfred Sloan or Walter Chrysler's concern for appearance. According to Ehrenburg,

> He was figuring how to combine American know-how with European poverty. He had to make low-priced cars. These cars had to consume very little fuel. These low-priced cars had to look very smart. The European was poor, but vainglorious, he was so proud of his thousand years of culture! He would put up with a feeble engine, but not ugly proportions.[18]

Future cars may take various forms, and among them will be personal vehicles that closely relate to the human form. Henri Peugeot's Seyan concept reveals this direction.

In 1934 Citroën launched the brilliantly engineered Traction Avant, gorgeously proportioned by André Lefèbvre and Flaminio Bertoni. It featured a low-slung unitary body with no separate frame, front-wheel independent suspension and, most radically, front-wheel drive. It quickly established a distinctive image of technical innovation and sophisticated styling that inspired a cultish following among 'Citroënistes', a devotion that persisted until the 1970s. Citroën's 2CV and DS models of 1948 and 1955 dominated the post-war French car market at opposite ends of the price scale, and were widely acclaimed by contemporary critics, including pundits of the art world, adding to an already unprecedented level of brand loyalty that we would now more typically associate with such niche manufacturers as Ferrari or Morgan.

Today's highly styled DS3 attracts a similar sort of enthusiasm and loyalty, despite conventional technology, because of carefully contrived features that remind us of Citroën's DNA. Brand identity relies to an extent on nostalgia. Popular affection for vehicles of the past is a widespread and important phenomenon in its own right, but it is also significant because it informs the way we admire and acquire new cars.

Fatal love

The commercial notion of brand loyalty may apply best to ordinary motorists, but a 'Citroëniste' enjoyed a more intense emotional bond with that make of car, and among some car enthusiasts the love of particular brands or types may reach a level of intensity that can be discussed in Freudian terms. That pioneer of psychoanalysis employed the word 'cathexis' to describe an irrational love or excessive investment of emotional or sexual energy in another person, an idea or an object such as an automobile.

No more amusing or vivid caricature has been written of that state of intoxication induced by the automobile than the story of Mr Toad in Kenneth Grahame's novel *The Wind in the Willows*, published in 1908. In the following passage, Mr Toad is about to 'borrow' a car from its distracted owner:

'There cannot be any harm', he said to himself, 'in my only just *looking at* it!' . . . Next moment, hardly knowing how it came about, he found he had hold of the handle and was turning it. As the familiar sound broke forth, the old passion seized on Toad and completely mastered him, body and soul. As if in a dream he found himself, somehow, seated in the driver's seat; as if in a dream, he pulled the lever and swung the car round the yard and out through the archway; and, as if in a dream, all sense of right and wrong, all fear of obvious consequences, seemed temporarily suspended.[19]

Toad's better judgement was clouded by an emotional kick akin to sex, stimulated by working the car's handles, pedals and levers. Many drivers feel that the slight change of pressure on the accelerator, adjustment of the steering wheel or flick of the gearshift is like manipulating the erogenous zones of a sexual partner, in this case a machine. Less charmingly eccentric than Toad, the Italian Futurist poet F. T. Marinetti described the experience of speeding through the night in his powerful 1908 Fiat: 'On we raced, hurling watchdogs against doorsteps, curling them under our burning tyres like collars under a flatiron. Death, domesticated, met me at every turn.'[20] His extravagant prose expressed the intensity of his relationship with the car and with what it represented for the modern world.

The drug of speed, its implicit sexual allure, the competitive thrill of overtaking and neck-snapping acceleration could all be *felt*, but speed also demanded *measurement*. In 1888 the Croatian inventor

Before the introduction of a driver's code of conduct, elite motorists were widely perceived as uniquely arrogant speed demons. Later, that sense of entitlement to behave extravagantly on the road trickled down to all drivers. *Puck* magazine, 1902.

Josip Belušić developed the speedometer, which was granted an Austro-Hungarian patent as a 'velocimeter'. The speedometer today remains the largest and most significant instrument on nearly every car's dashboard. Measuring speed was a double-edged sword, for although it could excite the driver to see the evidence of his prowess and his car's power, the speedometer also helped to enforce speed limits. One of the most draconian was the British Red Flag Law of 1865, which set the maximum speed for any self-propelled vehicle at 10 mph (16 km/h) but was subsequently reduced to 4 mph (6.5 km/h) in the country and 2 mph (3 km/h) in towns. This law resulted in the first British conviction for speeding in an automobile, with a fine of one shilling, in 1896. Similar laws restricted the speed of cars in various parts of Europe and in certain North American states and provinces until about 1900.

Thereafter speed limits rose gradually, with laws reflecting local conditions and the quality of roads. Today expressway speed limits vary from country to country, ranging from 90 km/h (56 mph) in Iceland to unlimited speeds on some stretches of German autobahns. And, of course, cars also vary in their top speed and acceleration. The world's fastest road car at the time of writing is Volkswagen's Bugatti Veyron Super Sport, which is capable of 431 km/h (268 mph) from an 8-litre, sixteen-cylinder engine. By contrast, the French-made Smart car, with its three-cylinder, 999-cc engine, is electronically limited to 145 km/h (90 mph). Consequently, drivers of both can exceed the speed limit on most of the world's roads.

The tragic potential of speed seems only to add to the car's allure, as demonstrated by the violent death of the actor James Dean in 1956, en route to a race in his Porsche Type 550 Spyder, a street-legal racing car, which he had named 'Little Bastard'. Famous for his role as a drag-racing hot-rodder in Elia Kazan's *Rebel without a Cause* (1955), Dean attempted to live out that erotic fantasy of speed-crazed American teenagers, a spirit borne of recklessness and peacock display that was celebrated and promoted in the media. Yet his crushed body and the crumpled remains of his Porsche became symbols of the hubris connected with the dreams of post-war American youthful rebellion.

Celebrity deaths in cars have always exerted a special fascination for observers of both pro- and anti-car persuasions. Such events have a louche glamour and a visibility that mark them as fair game for any and all to 'cluck and tut' about. Among the earliest and most scandalized of Hollywood death crashes was that involving the great German-born film director F. W. Murnau in 1931, while travelling the California coast road near Santa Barbara in a rented Rolls-Royce.[21] Sensational rumours, reported later by the underground film-maker and Hollywood gossip Kenneth Anger, suggested an orgy in the car at the time of the crash, although the true circumstances were apparently unremarkable. Twenty-five years later the Abstract Expressionist painter Jackson Pollock famously wrapped his speeding Oldsmobile convertible around a tree while inebriated, killing himself and a female passenger, and injuring his mistress.

Assassinations began taking place in cars early in the twentieth century. Among the most significant – the killing in June 1914 of Archduke Franz Ferdinand of Austria, heir to the Habsburg throne, and his wife, Sophie, while they were parading through Sarajevo in a stately Gräf & Stift Double Phaeton of 1911 – triggered the First World War. Since then the world has witnessed the murder of John F. Kennedy in the presidential Lincoln Continental while processing through Dallas in 1963. Other royals to die in cars included Princess Grace of Monaco, in her ageing Rover, and Diana, Princess of Wales, who was killed in a Paris underpass along with her lover, Dodi Fayed, and their allegedly drunken chauffeur while fleeing in a black Mercedes from paparazzi photographers on motorbikes. On a balmy evening in Nice in 1927, the progressive American dancer Isadora Duncan was strangled and hurled on to the road by her own flowing scarf, which caught in a rear wheel of the open sports car in which she was riding as a passenger.[22] Such famous individuals killed in cars join a long roster of top racing drivers, headed by the Formula One champion Ayrton Senna, who crashed his Williams FW16 at the San Marino Grand Prix of 1994 in Imola, Italy. If the bond with our cars is strong in life, it becomes eternal in death.

Many of these glamorous figures, both in their extraordinary lives and in the circumstances of their violent deaths, project an eroticism that was employed creatively by the British author J. G. Ballard as the central theme of his novel *Crash* (1973; made into a film in 1996 by David Cronenberg). It is the story of a young car-crash survivor who develops a condition known as 'symphorophilia', a sexual fetish aroused by participation in or the witnessing of automobile accidents or other types of violence perpetrated in cars. The fetish is aroused not only by the damage to the victims' bodies, but by the bodies of the cars in which they crash. In Ballard's narrative, the sheet metal and upholstery, the glass and chrome, all emit sexual vibrations. More recently, in an installation in 2014, the British artist Sarah Lucas presented crashed or vandalized cars themselves as 'victims' of brutal attack, surrounded by crushed glass and fragments of plastic and steel. Lucas transforms these powerful, charismatic objects into erotically fetishized totems of our modern love affair with speed and violence.

Breaking up is hard to do

Arthur Drexler, curator of the New York Museum of Modern Art's Department of Architecture and Design, wrote in the catalogue for the exhibition *8 Automobiles* (1951):

Automobiles are hollow rolling sculpture . . . They have interior spaces corresponding to an outer form, like buildings, but the designer's aesthetic purpose is to enclose the functioning parts of an automobile, as well as its passengers, in a package suggesting directed movement along the ground.[23]

Drexler was referring particularly to the Italian cars designed by Pininfarina, Ghia and other Italian *carrozziere*, who built many of the most elegant and refined automobile bodies on the greatest high-performance chassis available. That exhibition, the first on cars to be held in a museum of art, was curated by the architect Philip Johnson and presented a Mercedes SS of 1931, an MGTC of 1948 (see p. 142), a Talbot Lago of 1937, a 1938 Bentley, a 1946 Cisitalia (see p. 153), a Lincoln Continental from 1941, a Cord of 1937 and, perhaps surprisingly, a Willys Jeep of 1941, all of which were presented as sculpted forms with little attention paid to their interior spaces.

Taking the analogy with architecture and interior design further, the writer and critic Stephen Bayley focused his attention on that 'hollowness': 'Static controlled environment is called architecture. Mobile controlled environment is called a car . . . Inside a car you get a perfect little exercise in interior design.'[24] Like the interiors of our buildings, the car interior has become increasingly well serviced and atmospherically controlled over the past century, with more ergonomically adjustable seats, more efficient climate control and a better sound system than our haphazardly arranged living rooms, offices and bedrooms. In practical terms today's Honda or Audi is among the most carefully designed environments most people will experience daily. And many of us spend more time sitting inside that car than we do in our favourite chair at home. It is designed to be physically safe, and aesthetically safe, too.

Considering the huge emphasis in car design on 'user experience', it may seem surprising that colour has drained almost completely out of the interiors of mainstream cars in most of Asia, North America and Europe since the later twentieth century, yet this phenomenon reflects a general chromophobia in contemporary taste. From the smallest and cheapest up to the premium segment, car interiors are most commonly finished in grey: grey leather and grey plastic inside a shell of black or silver-grey. Like the minimalist architectural interiors that have been popular since the 1990s, cars are now shorn of colour in favour of the safest neutral, grey.

More fundamental comparisons between vehicle interiors and architectural space may be on the horizon, however. Current projects suggest the increasing use in both architectural and automotive interiors of more ecologically sustainable natural materials, such as bamboo in the Toyota MEWE concept of 2013. Materials now hidden within the bodies of Formula One racing cars, such as honeycomb composites of carbon fibre and aluminium, are expressed visibly as aesthetic elements in recent design concepts.[25] Thermochromic materials, which change colour in response to variations in temperature, could relieve the drabness of car interiors, while the car's traditionally lustrous paintwork may well give way to less glossy, self-finished surfaces with attractive ageing qualities, saving the massive cost of creating perfect finishes, but also allowing traces of the car's use, and thus of the user, to show in marks, scuffs and other minor signs of wear without spoiling its appearance – as with a well-worn Louis Vuitton suitcase.

Possibly the greatest changes signalled by the most important emerging technology in the first quarter of this century, autonomous driving, are new interior configurations, some of them adaptable to both personal control of the car and fully automatic running. Others appearing in the latest concepts reveal the potential in driverless

cars for flexible interior layouts, abandoning the forward-facing convention of most cars from the past and present, and reviving such types as the face-to-face arrangement of some early horse-less carriages and electric broughams. Such convivial arrangements must alter significantly the role of the driver, who could become more of a host than a captain, having the freedom to engage fully with other passengers or simply enjoy a stress-free journey alone.

Today's car interiors still provide us with that special opportunity to be alone and yet out in the world, moving about at will, delivering us, at least in theory, from door to door on almost any journey, no matter how long or short. That particular combination of privacy within the car and visual connection with the public realm is unique and, in the opinion of millions of motorists, irreplaceable. The emotional sacrifice, however, is a sense of engagement in community, treating it instead as a spectacle. It appears that greatly increased connectivity is about to become the main provider of that

The panoptic function of the car interior is revealed dramatically in Scottish photographer Colin Millum's *Stakeout*, 2011, the private sleuth in his Lincoln evoking the atmosphere of classic film noir.

link with the world outside the car, maintaining more effectively the motorist's attention to his or her personal life and work. Without the need to drive, such a technological and experiential shift promises drivers a more relaxed experience of road travel, unless manual driving is desired for pleasure or sport.

The car's interior, especially its roof and windows, provide various opportunities for serious personal or professional surveillance of activities outside. Detectives, police, insurance investigators, kerb-crawlers and jealous lovers are types often cited for using their cars to watch, to stalk and to record the activities of others. In cars they can watch unobtrusively and wait in relative comfort, and with today's mobile phones and laptops they can report on what they observe immediately, involving others from afar in their vigil. Ultimately, while observing the world from within the carapace of the car, drivers can become true voyeurs, especially if accommodated behind black-tinted window glass, surveying the public space and interrogating the world in a particularly automotive way. And the shape of the windscreen, the position of pillars and the proportion of metal to glass all configure the observer's view from within the car.

In the American Midwest, where burgeoning towns began spreading out into automobile suburbs in the early 1920s, the inhabitants were learning their terrain intimately from behind the steering wheels of their cars. The estate agent at the centre of Sinclair Lewis's novel *Babbitt* (1922) made it his business to know every building, neighbourhood, individual street and block in terms of their desirability, or its opposite, in the property market:

> He admired each district along his familiar route to the office: The bungalows and shrubs and winding irregular drives of Floral Heights. The one-storey shops in Smith Street, a glare of plate glass and new yellow brick; groceries and laundries and chemist shops to supply the more

immediate needs of East Side housewives . . . The market gardens in Dutch Hollow . . . The old 'mansions' along Ninth Street, like aged dandies in filthy linen . . . Then the business centre, the thickening darting traffic, the crammed trams unloading, the high doorways of marble and polished granite.[26]

George Babbitt was seeing and studying the streets of his entire town in a comprehensive way that would have been scarcely possible before the advent of the car. In the Internet age, Google cars prowl the planet, recording on camera every street, shop and house front for the public to use for a myriad of purposes, from finding a friend's new home before a visit to searching for the perfect holiday resort on the other side of the world. The intimacy of such an automotive view of the street is familiar to many people who are accustomed to viewing the built environment through the windscreen of their own car, yet with Google the virtual nature of 'the drive' is entirely new.

The anthropologist Michael Bull observed that the car radio also fundamentally changed the experience of motoring. An anonymous interviewee told him: 'When I get in my car and turn on my radio, I'm at home. I haven't got a journey to make before I get home. I'm already home,' defining the car as a detachable room of the house.[27] Whereas before the advent of radio drivers and their passengers had ridden with only one another for company, radio added a new relation to life on the road. It could create a party atmosphere for groups riding together, or a seductive background for romantic couples. Whether spoken word or musical performance, 'in-car entertainment', produced by an increasingly global communications industry, supplemented motorists' visual links to the places through which they passed with an addictive aural diet of synthesized information or entertainment. Many drivers never switch off the radio, considering it an essential element of their motoring experience, preferring it to live conversation or to the hum of the engine. And with it they are never really alone.

Radios began to appear in cars almost as soon as the apparatus appeared in homes. Yet the crude technology and bulk of early, battery-powered valve receivers gave way within a decade to well-integrated dashboard equipment that became an accessory as desirable as a powerful engine or an effortless gearshift. Although many cars of the late 1920s were factory-wired for radio, which could be separately purchased from and fitted by a specialist supplier, the first radios sold as factory-installed options by auto manufacturers appeared in the USA on GM's Cadillacs and LaSalles in 1930. Soon car radio was widely available and considered by many motorists to be essential above all other equipment – even a heater – and its significance was expressed through styling.

At any given time in the history of motoring, there have been dominant features in the typical dashboard. At first they were the speedometer and the clock, as time and speed were the *raisons d'être* for the car. By the 1930s the radio came to the centre of the

Car radios were initially an after-sale option. They brought the party to the automobile, introduced the notion of permanent connectivity to the motorist and made long drives less boring for the lone driver.

dash, a prominent position comparable to that which it occupied in the living rooms of most homes. In the car it was given an equally big presentation, confirming the car as a mobile concert hall and featuring illuminated selector windows and streamlined chrome speaker grilles, stylistically coordinated with other instruments and decorations. Its controls were accessible to all front-seat passengers, inviting them to serve as the radio operator or disc jockey while the driver attended to the road.

Today, the VDU screen holds centre stage as the key to the management of a computer-controlled interface between driver and machine, controlling the car's mechanical settings and communications functions. Tesla's upgradeable 17-inch digital touchscreen features information panels designed by Brendan Boblett with skeuomorphic (realistic) representations of traditional controls, instruments and live images, combined with icons employing a minimalist, Bauhaus-inspired 'flat design' language. Alternatively, visual information can be presented in a car's windscreen, as in the helmet visors of military pilots, enhancing a Walter Mitty-esque, game-like sense of adventure for the driver.

The French philosopher Gaston Bachelard compared man-made spaces to the primeval protection of the mollusc's shell, that place of ultimate safety for an organism in motion or at rest. This basic human urge for self-preservation has been expressed in the design of modern cars in a variety of ways: size and weight; the technology of seat belts, airbags, crumple zones and roll bars; and the appearance of solidity. The huge popularity of SUVs is justified by many motorists on the grounds that such cars offer maximum protection from all external threats, including collisions, carjacking and psychological intimidation.

Such feelings of invulnerability can lead to inappropriate behaviour that invites a variety of negative responses, from road rage to

ridicule. And despite statistical evidence that drivers and passengers are more likely to die in SUVs and pick-up trucks than in conventional cars (largely because of their tendency to roll over), their drivers often feel they *need* the level of apparent protection these vehicles signify through their sheer size, heavy stance and aggressive styling. The communications theorist Marshall McLuhan shared Bachelard's view, calling the car 'the carapace, the protective and aggressive shell, of urban and suburban man'.[28]

Some commentators envision an imminent retreat from mass addiction to the automotive carapace. The founder of the Welsh think tank Transport for Quality of Life, Dr Lynn Sloman, gathered evidence through extensive interviews that many drivers are ready

Today's dashboard is akin to the glass cockpits of commercial and military aircraft. Information is called up by voice commands to appear on large visual display units as and when required. Tesla Model S, 2014.

to come out of their shells and give up the car.[29] Proposed alternatives to driving include the usual options (walking, cycling, public transport and home working), which are sensible but seem to require some degree of sacrifice in the face of 'normal' standards of ease and convenience. She cites the Dutch *woonerfen* (residential streets) of Utrecht and other towns, where pedestrians and cyclists have priority over motorists, to demonstrate a planning concept that reduces the dominance of the car and requires the driver to give up some of that 'lordliness' that accompanies the car's traditional status as king of the road, in exchange for a more civilized city life.

This sensible argument advocates the 'strategic coordination' of transport and small environmental adjustments over major infrastructure projects, such as tramways and bypasses, and, most importantly, attacks the notion that any restriction on driving is 'an affront to civil liberties'.[30] It counters the belief, frequently espoused by politicians, in the negative economic effect of reduced car use. Instead, Sloman argues for the 'de-coupling' of automotive dominance and economic growth, concluding that 'it is possible to reduce traffic levels without damaging the economy of a town. We can even say that it is essential to reduce traffic levels in order to let a town thrive.'[31] This view defines the car as a social rather than a technical problem: 'Many people who think of themselves as environmentalists still have a blind spot about cars.'[32] And that blind spot is largely conditioned by love of their personal cars.

The transport analysts Daniel Sperling and Deborah Gordon propose a thorough revision of the way humans travel, and set out an image of the future that involves a fundamental global switch to low-carbon fuels for transport, and the abandonment of the 'gas-guzzler monoculture' and the psychological reliance on big vehicles that is nearly universal in the USA and endemic in most developed nations. Their information (as of early 2008) was authoritative and their logic convincing, until they present their vision of the future, cleverly dubbed Futurama III after the GM 'Futurama I' and 'Futurama II' exhibits at the New York World's Fairs in 1939 and 1964. In contrast with those earlier car-centred forecasts, Futurama III depicts a transportation world of 2050 with sustainability as its primary characteristic: 'efficient, affordable and civilized'.[33]

This vibrant new world, with a stable climate and no oil wars, would be characterized by varied mobility options for urban and suburban dwellers alike, with transport beyond the immediate neighbourhood – including car-sharing, ride-sharing and door-to-door multiple-occupancy minibus services – ordered electronically and arranged automatically and instantaneously. Transport options would also include the familiar mantra of walking, biking and busing, plus access to new types of machine (available in some places today) such as zero-emission neighbourhood electric vehicles or mobility scooters.

Such a proposal would be unassailable by any rational person, but not by a dedicated motorist. Its weakness is in the notion that those who have tasted the drug of personal motoring will ever again be willing to share automotive space with strangers, or to make any arrangements prior to travelling. Here I suggest considering the clothing metaphor. The premise of driving a Zipcar or similar car-club vehicle, regardless of how sensible an idea it may be, is akin to the notion of sharing our shoes, coat or gloves. Drivers use their car's storage compartments like the pockets of their jacket, which contain their loose change, their pens, their medicine and their tissues. The upholstery is as much theirs as the fabric of their trousers. The windows are as clean or as smudged as the lenses of their spectacles. The door handles bear only their fingerprints, as do the buttons of their coats.

Beyond this haptic connection is the sense that one's image is constructed by the style of a car as much as by the cut and cloth of one's suit, making us deeply resistant to sharing a car with anyone except perhaps a close family member, just as siblings might share a jumper. The car body offers further clues to this bond. Black-tinted windows serve a function similar to that of sunglasses, providing a view out while obscuring the wearer's gaze. A car can be 'thrown on' like a raincoat over pyjamas, if at any time of the day or night you want to pop down to the drive-through bottle-shop in Sydney, the drive-through drugstore in Cincinnati, or the drive-through McDonald's in Gujarat. The private car conceals, protects, isolates and represents its driver as clothes do the wearer. We don't easily share our clothes with strangers, and it could take a seismic shift in human expectations, or in the vehicles on offer, to encourage some individuals to share cars. In a TED talk, the former BMW design supremo Chris Bangle goes further, declaring that cars are even more personal than clothing. They are our avatars.[34]

In the long view, our attachment to the private car is probably here to stay, at least until the development of an alternative that provides the personal benefits of today's automobile without its undeniable social, political and ecological disadvantages. Such a change could be realized in part by devising new means of relating to vehicles, conducted more through software than through hardware and emphasizing convenience, connections and contentment over the swaggering seclusion of today's culture of private cars. Such designers as Adam Setter of the Royal College of Art in London focus on increasing the shape-shifting capability of the car, and particularly of its interior, as a way forwards. Setter says that in coming years, 'companies will need to reinvent their products to appeal to a new generation of intelligent, environmentally aware and technology-hungry customers, and therefore digital personalization will be of huge importance.'[35] This logic could apply especially to vehicles designed for sharing, endowing the generic car, a blank canvas, with the capability of becoming visibly and physically 'yours' just for the time you need or want it.

3 | Image

Mythical object

One of the most often-quoted paragraphs written about the car, describing it as *the* central emblem of twentieth-century culture, was published in an essay on the nature of contemporary myth by the French semiologist Roland Barthes in 1955:

> I think that cars today are almost the exact equivalent of the great Gothic cathedrals: I mean the supreme creation of an era, conceived with passion by unknown artists, and consumed in image if not in usage by a whole population which appropriates them as a purely magical object.[1]

To compare a common mass-produced product with the architectural glory of the Middle Ages was a daring idea in the mid-1950s, but it is one that today seems sensible, recognizing that deep human attachment to automobility and the tremendous industry and artistry that have gone into developing the car.

In 'The New Citroën' Barthes described the car as the product of 'unknown artists', those workers who built cars and jobbing craftsmen who delineated tail-light assemblies or sculpted in clay the ornaments decorating mass-produced cars, and who are now lost to posterity like the carvers of the gargoyles on York Cathedral or the artists who created the stained-glass windows of Chartres.

A relationship grew up between the car and new movements in the arts and philosophy from the early years of the twentieth century. The mythology of the car had entered the visual arts by 1900, when Fiat began commissioning paintings of its products, linking them with images from classical mythology to emphasize their quality and endurance. Illustrations by artists, including the classically named Plinio Codognato, Jack Le Breton, Enrico Sacchetti and Mario Sironi, combined mythological figures with images of Fiat cars to associate the rationality, heroism and power of the latest automotive technology with Graeco-Roman symbols. Even the company's circular logo,

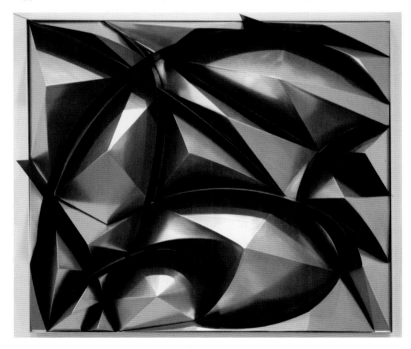

Giacomo Balla's *Sculptural Construction of Noise and Speed* (1914, reconstruction 1968) demonstrated the Italian Futurist's abstraction of those invisible 'lines of force' generated by the speeding automobile.

with the name inscribed in a laurel wreath, reinforced that symbolic connection with classical excellence, athleticism and nobility.

A succession of early twentieth-century art movements further linked the latest aesthetic ideas with automotive trends. Before the First World War, the Italian Futurist Giacomo Balla depicted the speeding car as a new reality in keeping with the French philosopher Henri Bergson's theory of the *élan vital* (creative vital force) that animates modern life. Similarly, Balla's mentor, Filippo Tommaso Marinetti, declared that a racing car 'is more beautiful than the *Victory of Samothrace*', that most dynamic example of Hellenistic sculpture.[2] With those words, Marinetti confirmed Italian Futurism as the earliest aesthetic movement to celebrate the car as a central subject of its art, and, in its dynamism, the most representative object of a new technological era.

Classicism has often been evoked in car design and automobile advertising to communicate a sense of high quality and endurance. FIAT used the laurel wreath, symbol of victory in ancient Greece and Rome, in the design of its logos dating from 1925 to 1931 and revived it in 1999–2006.

Even the aeroplane, seen against empty sky, could not convey the impression of speed as clearly as could a car roaring over the road. Balla struggled towards a pictorial language that expressed the car's speed, using the fragmented forms of Cubism in dynamic compositions of wheels and streamlined wings (fenders). In his *Sculptural Construction of Noise and Speed* (1914), he employed those overlapping shapes, repeated as in a kaleidoscope, dissolving the image of the machine to communicate abstractly the nature of velocity, the highest ideal of Futurism.

Whereas anthropomorphism, endowing cars with human qualities, had been commonly associated with the automobile from its birth, artists including the Dadaist Francis Picabia employed its opposite – mechanomorphism – to bestow human subjects with the characteristics of machines. Among a series of 'object portraits' of 1915, Picabia represented himself through the image of a car horn superimposed on a cutaway view of an engine's combustion chamber, alluding to his explosive pronouncements on the nature of art (the chamber), his self-promotion (the horn) and his sexual promiscuity (both the phallic horn and the combustion chamber). Picabia was a wealthy car enthusiast who amassed a large collection of sport and luxury vehicles by various makers, including Hispano-Suiza, Mercer and Rolls-Royce, over nearly fifty years. He wrote: 'The machine has become more than a mere adjunct of life. It is really a part of human life . . . perhaps the very soul.'[3]

The Surrealist painter Salvador Dalí portrayed cars through veils of ambiguity, paranoia and the grotesque. In one picture, in which a vine-covered Edwardian touring car blends into the ancient, rocky landscape of northern Catalonia, the antiquity of the landscape is contrasted with the precision of the machine, recalling the freakish surfaces of such architectural follies as Grotta Madama at the Boboli Gardens in Rome. Dalí never drove, but he acquired a series of

Cadillacs for his wife, Gala, beginning with a convertible of 1941, similar to one he portrayed draped in diaphanous cloth and sprouting branches, the car's glossy paintwork peeling away to reveal crumbling brickwork underneath. Dalí gave us images of cars drawn from his dreams, but they were very different from what became known as 'dream cars'.

Like ships before them, cars were mythologized as 'roving eyes'.[4] As early as 1905 the British academic painter, scenic designer and illustrator Hubert von Herkomer recognized the particular sequence of images available to the aesthete when driving in a closed car: 'The pleasure [of motoring] . . . is seeing Nature as I could in no other way see it; my car having "tops", I get nature framed – and one picture after another delights my artistic eye.'[5] Many other artists

Ant Farm's *Cadillac Ranch* has been dubbed an American Stonehenge, which projects the hubris of US Cold War power and of the consumer society. Chip Lord, Hudson Marquez, Douglas Michels, Texas, 1974.

subsequently explored the potential of the framed view provided by the windscreen.

The architecture of the car becomes most effective as a means of framing experiences when in motion.[6] The architect and film-maker Chip Lord combined that immediacy of kinetic observation with a historical perspective on the car in his video feature *Motorist* (1989). He recorded a vintage 1962 Thunderbird crossing the southern USA as its driver narrates the 27-year history of the car. Interwoven with his story are images and advertisements detailing the post-war history of the Ford Motor Company, its heroic factories and troubled labour relations. Lord treats the car's interior as both a confessional and a panopticon, while also making a visual inventory of its futuristic design.

In 1974 Lord and the experimental art collective Ant Farm built *Cadillac Ranch* in Texas. Sometimes classified within the genre of Land Art, *Cadillac Ranch* is among the most significant projects to

The 1955 Buick was described by *Industrial Design* critic Deborah Allen as 'having no more weight than the designer chooses to give it' and 'floating on currents of air'. Its design inspires suspension of disbelief.

address the theme of the car and to map its role as the ultimate symbol of consumer culture, 'a monument to the rise and fall of the tail fin'.[7] Installed alongside the former US Route 66, this 'American Stonehenge' comprised a line of ten Cadillacs, their noses buried in the earth at an angle of 60 degrees, their tails in the air, arranged chronologically from the first fins on a model from 1949 to their last appearance on a de Ville of 1964. Both *Cadillac Ranch* and *Motorist* exposed the hubris of the post-Second World War American Dream through the mythology of the car.[8]

Meanwhile, in mid-1950s London, the Independent Group, founders of British Pop Art (including the painter Richard Hamilton, the sculptor Eduardo Paolozzi, the historian Reyner Banham, the critic Lawrence Alloway and others), applied a mix of irony and appreciation to the imagery of American consumerism centring on automobility and on the appearance of the American car. Hamilton's painting *Hers Is a Lush Situation* (1958) draws its title from a review of the American cars of 1955 by the automotive critic and founder of *Industrial Design* magazine, Deborah Allen, a neglected pioneer of design analysis, who described the new Buick:

> It is logical, but only by its own standards . . . it is perpetually floating on currents which are built in to the design. This attempt to achieve buoyancy with masses of metal is bound to have the same awkward effect as the solid wooden cloud of a Baroque baldacchino. Unless you want to wince a purist wince at every Buick or baldacchino the best recourse is to accept the Romantic notion that materials have no more weight than the designer chooses to give them.
>
> The Buick's designers put the greatest weight over the wheels, where the engine is, which is natural enough. The heavy bumper helps to pull the weight forward; the dip in the body and the chrome spear express how the thrust of the front wheels is dissipated in turbulence toward the

rear. Just behind the strong shoulder of the car, a sturdy post lifts up the roof, which trails off like a banner in the air. The driver sits in the dead calm at the centre of all this motion; hers is a lush situation.[9]

Hamilton's painting combines the curvaceous forms of post-war organic design with abstractions of the human body to represent that 'lush situation'. This was the heyday of glamour models draped over the bodies of new cars at auto shows, and so in Hamilton's painting the texture of flesh melds with muscular bulges and pulchritudinous swellings of wings and bumpers, black rubber nipples and the orifices of exhaust ports. The sensuality of the painting directly reflected the erotic and fantastic character of the car Allen interpreted so elegantly.

The relationship of sex and speed was then still a largely unquestioned aspect of macho car culture, and the literature of the period unashamedly hymned the sensation of speed linked with masculine potency. In *On the Road* (1957), Jack Kerouac described that feeling: '[We] all realized we were leaving confusion and nonsense behind and performing our one and noble function of the time, move.' During their road trip the driver, Dean, and his girlfriend make out in the front seat as he 'hunched his muscular neck, T-shirted in the winter night, and blasted the car along . . . [he] beat drums on the dashboard till a great sag developed in it; I did too. The poor Hudson.'[10] The arrivals of Kerouac's voyagers at their various destinations always reflected a sense of ennui: the real fun was over, the thrill of movement displaced by the dreariness of stasis.

Crafted cars

At the same time as Kerouac was empathizing with that Hudson's stigmata, the first generation of car customizers were also imprinting personality on the body of the car in a new kind of automotive art in which individuals modified standard second-hand cars to create a unique image, often a self-portrait of the artist in automotive form. Grass-roots customizing found its first home in the car culture of California, but eventually spread to all parts of the motoring world, including the emerging car cultures of India, where several national chains of shops provide customization services, and China, where the China International Custom Car Expo is held annually in Beijing.

The origins of customizing can be found in traditional coachcraft, born in the age of the horse. That craft industry quickly converted to building car bodies, demonstrating special skills through hand-rubbed paintwork, pinstriping that highlighted the forms of the body, polished brass metalwork and luxuriously tufted and buttoned upholstery. Among the leading carriage builders turning to car bodies were London's H. J. Mulliner, Chapron in France, Brewster of New York, Schutter & van Bakel in Amsterdam, and Erdmann & Rossi of Berlin, all of which tailored their designs to the desires of individual customers.[11]

Coachcraft's key worker was the body draughtsman, ancestor of the stylist. The draughtsman's job was to conceive and communicate the complex shapes of the car body to pattern and die makers. Draughtsmen developed their skill on the job and in such institutions as the Carriage and Automobile Body Drafting School in New York. Like ambitious young North American architects who attended the École des Beaux Arts in Paris, some aspiring American automotive draughtsmen, such as the early designer and teacher Andrew F. Johnson, studied at the college of Louis Dupont in Paris, then the centre of high-quality carriage and automobile body design and construction. Or they could read the journal *Guide du Carrossier*, founded by Thomas Brice in 1858 and later carried on by his nephew Dupont.

Importantly, the guide detailed the translation of horse carriage types – *phaéton*, *coupé de ville*, *spider* – to cars.[12]

Some older coachbuilders in Europe and America flourished during the period of full mass production after the First World War, surviving as design consultants to manufacturers or building one-offs for private customers. Paul Wilson observed that the director of these small firms 'was almost always the chief designer . . . and often supervised the actual construction of the body'.[13] Such intimacy distinguished their classic products from mass-produced cars. Eventually, Rolls-Royce bought both H. J. Mulliner and Park Ward to build special coachwork for individual clients and all-steel bodies to standard patterns in small batches, while the largest independent American body maker, Fisher, was brought into GM as a senior division, enhancing the significance of image in the design of production cars.

The golden years of the classic coachbuilt car were the 1930s, on both sides of the Atlantic. This Hispano Suiza of 1934, designed by Swiss engineer Marc Birkigt, with coupé bodywork by Van Vooren, shows the classic line at its peak of refinement.

While Ford, Citroën and other manufacturers were building great car factories designed for mass production, the remaining coach-builders were making automobile bodies according to the traditions of handcraftsmanship, some in the same buildings they had used previously to build horse-drawn vehicles. Such workshops changed little in the first 40 years of the automobile age as they continued to employ traditional skills and materials to build bodies for the chassis of premier makers Daimler, Pierce Arrow, Renault and others. A view of Hooper's workshop in London around 1920 shows smock-clad carpenters toiling at workbenches in the atmosphere of a typical Victorian furniture workshop, each incomplete car body supported by saw horses, waiting for the next tradesman to complete his part in its fabrication – timber framework, metal skin, paintwork, upholstery.

Some coachbuilders and mail-order houses, such as Sears in the USA, marketed ranges of standard accessories, including upholstery slip covers, luggage racks, spotlights and decorative motometers, enabling motorists of modest means to personalize mass-produced cars and create an image for themselves. Similarly, the Ford Motor Company sold accessories to 'improve' the Model T. Henry Ford believed that owners should upgrade and extend the life of his cars, and so he bought the Lehman manufacturing company to supply Ford owners with special bodies that could be bolted easily to the sturdy Ford chassis when the original shell became dilapidated. Lehman's Lamcoline range included sporting, touring and racing bodies designed specifically to fit the Model T.[14] Alternatively, at the top of the luxury market, the French glass maker René Lalique of Nancy sold illuminated crystal Art Deco radiator mascots to personalize even the most distinguished car body further.

The new styling departments of big car companies demonstrated how the glamour of coachbuilt cars could be transferred to low-priced, high-volume cars. However, the sheer number of such cars

being made denied them the individuality of elite, custom-built vehicles. And so, in 1940s Los Angeles, small professional workshops, including the Coachcraft Shop, Valley Custom and Barris Brothers, began modifying Detroit cars for private customers. In such workshops carpenters were replaced by metalworkers, using welding torches rather than chisels, wearing goggles and respiration masks instead of smocks; yet the cars were stationary, raised on jacks, with various workers coming to perform their part of the construction process. The cars would be carried on dollies to the paint shop and trucked to the upholsterer's for trimming, as in days of old.

Radiator mascots offered makers of high-quality commercial sculpture in metal or glass the opportunity to adorn the most conspicuous position on the classic car body. This Lalique figure, titled *Chryssis*, is seen on a Rolls-Royce of 1956.

By the early 1950s customizing had become a practice with significant consequences for the styling directions of major manufacturers, who aped in their production models features developed by professional customizers, as they continue to do in the twenty-first century. Yet it was the private customizer who created some of the most unique automotive sculpture in motoring history. In 1997 the designer Victor Papanek noted: 'Young people in the United States spend four thousand million dollars each year to "customize" their cars, that is to make them look different . . . trying to tell car manufacturers and their captive designers that they are fed up with the dreary sameness of cars.'[15]

The automotive craft workshop is as different from a mass-production factory as the custom-built car is from the mass-produced model. Boyd Coddington's California Hot Rod Shop is seen here c. 1996 with the scratch-built Roadstar under construction and a scale rendering of the modified 1948 Cadillac Sedanette, CadZZilla, in the background.

Individual customizers would typically enlist various professionals, including a metalworker, upholsterer, pinstriper and performance specialist, to transform a stock car into a unique custom design. Their personal involvement in the conception and construction of such special machine sculptures confirmed them as a new breed of creative craftspeople practising a new folk art of the mass-production era, an art that separated the final product fundamentally from its factory origins. Daniel Miller noted that 'it is the car enthusiasts who . . . cultivate their cars to the degree that one feels the transformation of the car body is a vicarious expression of their sense of bodies generally.'[16] Miller's observation is echoed in the neo-gothic fashion for piercing and tattooing that has become ubiquitous among the young since the 1980s, and in the French artist Orlan's transformations of her own body through plastic surgery.

In the 1960s the journalist Tom Wolfe reported on an exhibition of Ford concept cars, observing that although their Detroit styling seemed flamboyant to some observers, to him it appeared austere – 'pure Mondrian, very Apollonian' – in contrast with grass roots customizing, which he labelled 'Dionysian'.[17] That Dionysian style evolved from relatively conservative efforts by individuals after the First World War to improve and personalize the appearance, performance and interior comforts of certain high-volume automobiles, such as standard Fords and Mercurys of 1939–40. Customs are classified as 'mild' or 'wild', depending on the extent of modifications. But in their early years they were mainly simplified versions of the production model, de-chromed, with running boards removed, their bodies lowered by 'chopping' and 'channelling' to exaggerate their sleekness. The point here is that Wolfe's interpretation of the two major approaches to car styling, in terms of a great dichotomy in classical Greek philosophy, elevates the status of the automobile image to the ranks of high art.

California customs were painted in unusual colours to convey the symbolism attached to each car by its owner or creator. After 1945, pictorial decoration was frequently added to express the driver's personal passions. Hand-painted flame motifs, mythological creatures and religious iconography were typically framed in lacy pinstriping executed by such artists as Kenny Howard (also known as Von Dutch). Popular ornaments were eventually sold globally as printed transfers that carried both cultural and branded messages.

Inside were tuck-and-roll upholstery, fur rugs and elaborate displays of instrumentation and controls. The addition of stock or handmade chromium trimming, 'continental' wheel kits and wing skirts contributed to the uniqueness of each car. Such extravagant ornamentation was not without its critics. The architect John Brenneman wrote in 1957:

> It seems to me that customizers do not try to improve the look of their cars, but instead try to make them more conspicuous . . . speaking as a professor of architectural design, the most highly customized business in existence, [I] am led to wonder what motivates this frenzy of dedicated activity.[18]

Wolfe offered some suggestions after an interview with the best-known professional customizer and authority on amateur customs, George Barris. A Barris car is like 'one of those Picasso or Miró rugs. You don't walk on the damn things. You hang them on the wall . . . In effect, they're sculpture.'[19]

Barris opened his first Kustom City workshop in Los Angeles in 1945 to repair and modify standard cars, and went on to design and build handmade cars, often for celebrity clients. As contributing editor to *Motor Trend* magazine, he encouraged a generation of home customizers to allow their imagination free expression through sheet metal, plastic and paint. Wolfe compared Barris's work to Eero Saarinen's flamboyant, organic TWA Airlines Terminal in New York, describing it as modern Baroque. He added: 'What we have here is no longer a car but a design object, *an object*, as they say.'[20] Like a Cellini salt cellar, these cars were works of decorative art for which use is secondary to image.

The custom car medium spawned a subgenre known as Art Cars, in which the car body is used as a canvas or an armature. By 1988 this movement had become sufficiently organized to merit the foundation of the Art Car Museum in Houston, Texas. Its collection includes automobiles amid other works by artists not normally shown in conventional fine-art settings. In his *Art Car Manifesto*, the museum's co-founder, James Harithas, wrote:

> Art cars are subversive and have in common the transformation of the vehicle from a factory-made commodity into a personal statement . . . the art car represents the degree to which minorities, subcultures and modern artists [create] vehicles which are metaphors of political and economic dissent.[21]

Cars conceived as singularly expressive objects by professionals such as Barris or by accomplished amateurs had originally become widely known via shows and magazines.[22] The publisher Robert Petersen, founder of the Petersen Automotive Museum in Los Angeles, began staging custom-car shows in 1948. Customizers learned of new designs and techniques in his magazines, *Hot Rod*, *Car Craft*, *Rod & Custom* and *Motor Trend*. By the late 1950s Barris cars were being reproduced by the AMT Corporation as 1/25-scale plastic model kits. Ed Roth, another leading California customizer, produced designs for similar kits made by Revell. In this way, the customized *object* became available to the under-sixteens as a purely imaginative

possession and as a product of their own craft skill, executed in miniature.

Wolfe recalled the colour studies of Goethe in describing Barris's original 'Kandy Kolors' as signifiers of emotion. The mythological status of custom cars was also signalled by their names: 'Orchid Flame', 'Lost in the Fifties', 'Heartbreak'. Inevitably, Barris, Roth and another customizer, Boyd Coddington, worked as consultant designers of 'concept' cars for the world's major manufacturers, just as the elite coachbuilders of earlier years had done before them.[23] They also worked for Hollywood, producing such iconic film cars as the Barris-built Batmobile, a reworking of Ford's Lincoln Futura show car of 1955.

Customizing proved one of the most fertile outlets for individual design creativity in the standardized material world during the

This 1953 Chevrolet ice cream van was customized to commemorate the eviction of local residents from Chavez Ravine in Los Angeles to build a new stadium for the Dodgers baseball team. Commissioned by the musician Ry Cooder and painted by the artist Victor Valdez, this car became a mobile canvas for political expression.

automotive era. Critically, styling has become an arena for the ongoing debate between rational, classical design (Apollonian) and romantic expressionism (Dionysian). The former represents 'good form', functionalism and refined taste; in the latter, symbolic and subjective values outweigh other considerations. The two approaches demonstrate the distinction between the illusions of individuality implanted in the design production cars and the more genuine individuality of handcrafted custom cars.

From beauty to branding

Historians of the car generally concur that until Harley Earl, 'the notion of style simply did not arise.'[24] Until about 1930, mechanical and production engineers, who made the major design decisions, were typically portrayed as rough mechanics, more at home with files and lathes than with pens and watercolours, and with an innate hostility to art. For purchasers of high-class chassis, coach-building firms supplied the art. With the near total separation of the chassis, engine and running gear from the body, those two stereotyped worlds of car design could remain peacefully apart.

Early publicity and journalism support this interpretation, concentrating on power, reliability and technical features. Yet by 1902 the standardized Oldsmobile runabout exhibited a graceful silhouette adorned with Art Nouveau ornament. Its sophisticated advertisements demonstrated the company's recognition that handsome appearance was an important sales advantage. Similarly, the Packard Model 'Thirty' of 1908, sold with stock factory bodies, was advertised as 'modish, comfortable, and elegant . . . a superlative creation of the body-builder's art'.[25] Illustrations used to advertise such cars in the early twentieth century frequently employed the elegance of Art Nouveau and the simplicity of post-Impressionism drawn from Japanese prints to communicate the car's sophistication and innovation.

With the establishment of the Art and Color Section at GM in 1927, derisively called 'the beauty parlour', there arose between engineers and stylists a conflict that was won decisively by the latter in the 1930s, distancing the car body as much as possible from the technology it cloaked. Harley Earl dramatized the 'problem' he had with hard-headed engineering and production staff in a story that has been retold many times. Earl's design for the Buick of 1929 involved a slight swelling of the belt line running under the windows and continuing forwards to meet the matching profile of the radiator. Without consulting Earl, production engineers raised the height of the Buick's body, distorting the bulge. Earl dubbed the result the 'pregnant' Buick, insisting that the interference of engineers had ruined the car's appearance, causing a sales 'disaster'. However, Buick retained sixth place in American car sales during that year of real economic catastrophe, and only from 1932, in the depths of the Great Depression, did sales of the Buick fall drastically for four consecutive years, revealing this styling 'disaster' to be a corporate myth.[26]

Among those early 'hard-headed' engineers, many were sensitive to the appearance of their cars, and some were genuine artists. Italian-born Ettore Bugatti was from a creative family, and studied art in Milan before turning to mechanics. Beginning with his first automobile, in 1898, Bugatti's cars were remarkable for both high performance and elegance. Their engines were conceived like pieces of mechanical sculpture, with an attention to form and finish echoed in the graceful proportions of their bodywork. From his tiny Peugeot Type 19 Bébé (1913) to the six enormous Type 41 Bugatti Royales he and his son Jean built between 1929 and 1933, this engineer's attention to the precise execution of elegant mechanics *and* of elegant bodies was a consummate expression of artful engineering.

'Style', like most words used in aesthetic judgement, is often employed carelessly, yet it properly describes a distinctive form in any medium that represents an artist's individual attitude (Jackson Pollock's expression of psychological states) or a particular moment (Art Nouveau). It can also refer to the finesse with which something is done, exhibiting unique taste. Bugatti certainly had it, and he operated as an *auteur* of automotive design.

Yet even Henry Ford ensured that the appearance of his cars was as refined as possible within the capabilities of his production process. The Model T was much loved for its characteristic shape, and later became a favourite of customizers. The designer Strother McMinn wrote of the 'new' model of 1923: 'Even its bare necessities possessed a sense of grace and logic that endeared it to its loyal customers.'[27] But if the Ford car is granted a modicum of beauty,

This 1938 Bugatti Type 59/50B III Grand Prix engine demonstrates a concern for form and finish compatible with the meticulous design of the cars' exteriors and interiors, spartan as those racing bodies are.

it is absolutely the result of the way its appearance expressed its fitness for purpose.

The functionalist car, exemplified by the Model T, had an unpretentious beauty that constituted a 'style' in the strictest meaning of that word – as it might be applied to the elegant concrete airship hangars (1916–23) by the French engineer Eugène Freyssinet – and the qualities of that style drew the admiration of the first generation of modernist architects and designers.[28] The Ford's egalitarianism appealed to the socialistic ideals of the post-First World War generation of artists in Europe, and also to some liberal intellectuals in North America, who saw the idea it represented as beautiful.

The engineer Alec Issigonis, chief designer of the Morris Minor of 1949 and the Austin Mini of 1959, was a significant post-war automotive functionalist. Although the Morris Minor was influenced by pre-war streamlining, the form of the Mini was determined by the radical and demanding brief given to Issigonis by the president of the British Motor Corporation (BMC), Leonard Lord: to create an entirely new type of very small, all-purpose car. Like the Model T Ford, the Mini developed a huge, classless following. These were cars that came to be known as 'people's cars', owing to their appeal to a very wide clientele at all levels of society and income.

Functionalist architects acknowledged the stylistic influence of motorized transport vehicles on their architecture, as can be seen in Le Corbusier's book *Towards a New Architecture* (1923). Le Corbusier illustrated cars, aircraft and ocean liners as 'products of engineering . . . designed to achieve economy of materials and simplicity in their purpose[;] architecture should do likewise'.[29] His appreciation of cars may even have led him towards a particular style of building, one of simplicity and lightness, and featuring machine-made elements, such as metal-framed windows – imagery that arose from his taste for those motor cars that *appeared* most functional.

Automotive style resulted from the trinity of mass production, mass consumption and advertising, and it subscribed to a system of rules established first in the fashion industry. Writing in 1923, Henry Ford scorned the use of styling as part of planned obsolescence almost at the same moment as Alfred Sloan was penning its mandate as GM policy. Ford wrote:

> The automobile trade was following the old bicycle trade, in which every manufacturer thought it necessary to bring out a new model each year and to make it so unlike all previous models that those who had bought the former models would want to get rid of the old and buy the new. That was supposed to be good business. It is the same idea that women submit to in their clothing and hats. That is not service – it seeks only to provide something new, not something better.[30]

As well as underestimating the critical faculties of women, Ford's dismissal of the influential fashion system lacked foresight, as within four years his Model T would be designated the greatest casualty of a new approach to car design modelled closely on the fashion system. That new approach would come to be called Sloanism, after the GM president, emphasizing the obsolescence of Fordism itself and giving title to the new reality of the consumer society. Yet the influence of fashion in automotive design was interpreted in various ways at the time. A brochure of the National Motor Vehicle Company, promoting its models of 1915, declared:

> An automobile is one of the most personal of possessions, as personal, almost, as haberdashery or millinery. If the car is to last a number of years, there must be elements of classicism in its design – beauty which will endure and stay good in spite of saneless style changes, made for sales impetus or some other ulterior motive.[31]

While acknowledging the relation between cars and clothing, this underestimates the importance of the fashion cycle, demanding constant updating.

In his lecture 'Of Cars, Clothes and Carpets: Design Metaphors in Architectural Thought' (1989), the British architectural historian Adrian Forty recalled the German historian Sigfried Giedion's admiration for modern sports clothing in the early 1920s, and for the unadorned cars of that period, which he saw as positive influences on the modernist dwelling because of their simplicity and apparent fitness for purpose.[32] Forty reasoned that the automotive model for new architecture ended when the fashion system infected car design, particularly in Detroit. He maintained that the car's

> history as a type object ended in 1926 when Ford started introducing new models. It is from around then that car design (though not car production) went into eclipse as an architectural analogy; by the 1940s ritual attacks on Detroit car styling provided a regular catharsis for European modernists.[33]

Although Forty points out the ascendancy of expressionistically styled Detroit cars and their fashionable relatives around the world (such as Vauxhall, Opel, Holden), the idea of a functionalist car remained important, or even dominant, both in mass production and in the construction of special vehicles, such as those designed for military purposes and for speed, both discussed later in this book.

When Ford was 'forced' to discontinue the Model T because of fashionable GM competition, the legend of 'history's most expensive art lesson' was born. Superficial comparison of various touring models of 1926 confirms that a Chevrolet was more dashing, more powerful and better-equipped, yet it cost significantly more than a comparable Ford.[34] It can be argued that the real advantage of any low-priced car over a Ford in 1926 was its nameplate. By then, the Ford was seen as a proletarian car, and many aspirational buyers would therefore prefer any make that was *not* a Ford. In 1925 my own grandfather, rising from immigrant roots, bought a new Durant Star touring car, as similar to the Model T as a Chevrolet, partly because it did not carry the Ford's stigma of austerity. In a somewhat desperate effort to lose that reputation, Ford's Model T advertising in 1925 appealed shamelessly to middle-class, multi-car families as a 'second or third car' in a 'stable' of grander makes: essentially, a runabout for the butler or nanny.

Nevertheless, with the rise of corporate styling the functionalist car was condemned to a lesser role in American motoring life. In Europe, however, it had a promising future, and remained the dominant type of car in that emerging mass market, even appearing in upper price bands.

Functionalism versus expressionism

Functionalism is a design theory according to which an object's form is derived substantially from a defined purpose or need, and communicates practicality, durability, efficiency and economy congruent with its purpose. Such a product's longevity also contributes to its 'economy' value. In post-war Europe, economy and longevity remained admired features of functionalist design long after North American car styling had committed itself fully to expressionism and disposability.

In Britain, the MG T series of two-passenger sport roadsters enjoyed such longevity. Engineered originally by Hubert Charles, the designer of all MG cars from 1930 to 1938, they were built from 1936 until 1955. Their slow evolution retained the original classic proportions, rectilinear body, vertical chromed radiator grille, fold-down windscreen, sweeping wings, cut-down doors and spare wheel mounted behind an independent fuel tank. MGs appeared to be composed of the bare necessities, yet each element was so carefully refined over time that it inevitably became stylized. The Museum of Modern Art's press announcement for its exhibition *8 Automobiles* of 1951 declared: 'The MG gives the illusion of being the unenhanced piece of machinery which the Jeep actually is, but unlike the Jeep, its stylistic understatement is the result of careful attention to appearance itself.'[35] All survivors of this series are revered classics today.

Perhaps the most beautiful British car of the 1960s was based on a sophisticated blending of form with function and modernism with tradition. After the war the founder of Jaguar, William Lyons, oversaw the development of a string of highly competitive racing cars, introduced the first of his modern sports cars, the XK120, and

The MGTC of 1948 retained and refined the forms of pre-war T-series roadsters. Curators of the *8 Automobiles* exhibition at the Museum of Modern Art in New York in 1951 presented this as functionalism influencing automotive aesthetics.

launched a range of luxury cars noted for their speed, performance and elegant lines. Jaguar's superb engineering, by William Heynes, was proven on the track by the Type C and Type D racing cars with bodies by the in-house designer, Malcolm Sayer, who domesticated their curvaceous lines for the company's greatest production car, the E-Type roadster and coupé of 1961.

Perfectly attuned to its time, but with a classic elegance that kept its appearance eternally fresh, the E-Type's sleek exterior form spoke of the wind tunnel and of the muscular bodies of jungle cats, science and nature, the latter reflecting the organicism popular in architecture and design at the time. Its cockpit recalled the finest aircraft of pre-war aviation, with an array of round, black-rimmed instruments, rows of toggle switches set in a brushed aluminium dashboard and lightweight, leather-upholstered bucket seats. In 1996 the E-Type became one of only six cars in the permanent collection of the Museum of Modern Art in New York, which was composed exclusively of functionalist designs. Ultimately, both the Jaguar E-Type and the MG T series came to stand for fundamental British aesthetic values shared by the London Routemaster double-decker bus and Giles Gilbert Scott's red K2 telephone cabin.

The most ubiquitous car of its era was developed by the Austrian engineer Erwin Komenda, who became head of the car-body-construction department at the newly formed Porsche design consultancy in 1931.[36] Before the Second World War, Porsche did not make cars under its own name, but developed projects for other manufacturers and for the German government. For one of those projects, Ferdinand Porsche himself designed early prototypes for a 'Strength through Joy' car ('Kraft durch Freude', also known as the KdF-Wagen or VW Type 1), based very closely on Hans Ledwinka's design for the Tatra 97 of 1936. More than 21 million of the rear-engine, rear-wheel-drive, four-cylinder, air-cooled, two-door VW sedans were eventually manufactured in fourteen countries between 1938 and 2003.

Although Komenda's original design of 1937, like the later Morris Minor, reflected the streamlining that was popular internationally at the time, the practical Germanic use of aerodynamics is distinct from its stylistic applications elsewhere during the so-called Streamlined Era. Influenced by the ideas of the aeronautical engineer Paul Jaray, Komenda used wind-tunnel testing in his reworking of Porsche's prototypes for the Volkswagen to refine what became the twentieth century's most familiar car body. Its appearance remained virtually unchanged for 65 years, and although it had been conceived as cutting-edge, it came to seem reassuringly traditional in the post-war environment of constantly updated jet-age automotive imagery. Simultaneously, it achieved a mythic status as the most powerful symbol of German post-war recovery, and as that country's olive branch to the peoples of its former enemy nations.

With his colleague, the aerodynamics expert Josef Mickl, Komenda also designed the sensational aluminium bodies of Ferdinand and Ferry Porsche's Auto Union Grand Prix-winning cars of 1935–9. After the war he worked with Ferry Porsche, Ferdinand's son, to shape the Porsche 356, and later developed the model 911, which has remained in production, subject to continuous refinement, since its launch in 1963. Despite their alternative reputation as impractical luxuries for professional men in mid-life crisis, modern 911s are the direct descendants of the practical people's car of the 1930s, and among the clearest exponents of functionalism in automotive design.

An innovative and diverse series of functionalist designs also emerged from the company founded by the former arms manufacturer André Citroën. In the early 1930s Citroën recruited two individuals to lead his design team, which produced three of the century's most mythologized cars. The Italian sculptor and car-body designer Flaminio Bertoni worked with aeronautical engineer and racing driver André Lefèbvre to create the elegant Traction Avant (1934), the utilitarian 2CV of 1948 and the magical DS19, launched to wide acclaim at the Paris Motor Show in 1955. Each of these cars, in its own way, demonstrated French technical innovation and purposeful aesthetics.

Long, low and sleek, the Traction Avant was produced in several body types (light or stretched sedans, coupé, roadster and hatchback) between 1934 and 1957. Like the Ford Model T, it was available only in black (except by special order), a feature that became part of the car's mystique. In addition to its revolutionary monocoque construction (see p. 60), its pioneering technology included front-wheel drive, independent torsion-bar suspension, rack-and-pinion steering, hydraulic brakes and radial ply tyres. The Traction Avant's extreme lowness was the product of its monocoque structure and front-wheel drive, which also permitted the cabin to have a flat floor. The car's fluid lines were the result of an impeccable set of proportions, with a very low belt line supporting an upright roof structure with large windows creating a bright, airy cabin, blending Lefèbvre's sophisticated engineering with Bertoni's harmonious forms.

Following the death of André Citroën in 1935, his firm was bought by the Michelin Tyre Company, which installed Pierre-Jules Boulanger as the director of engineering and design and later as company president. Boulanger was a brilliantly innovative manager of talented designers and engineers. For his project to design a minimal car (*toute petite voiture*), capable of carrying four people at 65 km/h (40 mph) or two farmers with a sack of potatoes and a basket of eggs over a rutted field without breaking the eggs, Lefèbvre and Bertoni again collaborated to create one of the most significant functionalist cars of all time, the Deux Chevaux (2CV).

Prototyping began in 1935, and by the time of its post-war launch the designers had refined the original concept, with corrugated-metal body panels providing structural stability, a two-cylinder air-cooled motor, front-wheel drive, resilient suspension, a rolling fabric top and tubular metal seats with slung canvas upholstery. Buyers instantly warmed to its low price, fuel economy, robustness and flexibility. It was fun to drive and could go almost anywhere.

The car's visual appeal resulted from the designers' strict adherence to a rigorously spartan brief. The 2CV's unique profile, accented by flaring, teardrop wings, gave the body its air of motion, while its aura of utility was signified particularly by the corrugated metal of the bonnet, which evoked tin-roofed farm buildings and 1920s airliners, but became as typical of French ingenuity as the Eiffel

Externally the Citroën DS balanced immense ingenuity with supremely confident aesthetics to become one of the most sophisticated production cars of the 20th century.

Tower. L.J.K. Setright described the 2CV as 'the most intelligent application of minimalism ever to succeed as a car' and as 'a car of studied utility, remorseless economy, and irrefutable logic'.[37]

In the early 1950s Citroën planned a replacement for the ageing Traction Avant, to be designed by Bertoni and Lefèbvre as nothing less than the most advanced production car in the world. It combined front-wheel drive with innovative hydro-pneumatic suspension and a uniquely long wheelbase, to achieve a cushioned ride while maintaining the excellent handling characteristics that helped it to European rally victories. For ease and safety, Lefèbvre provided hydraulic power steering, disc brakes and an automatic clutch. Plastic was used extensively, particularly inside the car, where a smoothly moulded dashboard and novel single-spoke steering wheel evoked a sense of travelling into the future.

The world of tomorrow was glimpsed in the interior of the Citroën DS of 1955. Its clean, organic forms, bright, modern surfaces, and use of new plastics distinguished it markedly from its contemporaries. It broke with tradition in every imaginable way.

To sheath this technical marvel in an appropriate shell, Bertoni employed his sculptor's technique of clay modelling to develop a shape of proportional originality and organic vitality, a characteristically French manifestation of organicism with an emphasis on lightness and transparency. The hydraulic suspension and wide, soft seats of the DS (pronounced Day-S, *déesse* in English 'goddess') induced a sensation of floating over the road rather than riding on it, while the slippery overall form and flat, smooth underbody contributed to the lowest drag coefficient of its time (0.38). The continuity of its surfaces was made more intriguing by the frameless junctions of side windows and body panels, and the miraculous neoprene gaskets holding in place its compound curved rear glazing between the silvered C-pillars, with their innovative roof-mounted indicator lights. That highly technical roof structure hovered lightly over the gracefully organic lower body and composed a spectacular, panoptic view from the interior. Roland Barthes analysed it famously:

> It is possible that the Déesse marks a change in the mythology of cars . . . despite some concessions to neomania (such as the empty steering wheel), it is now more homely . . . the dashboard looks more like the working surface of a modern kitchen than the control room of a factory: the thin panes of matt fluted metal, the small levers topped by a white ball, the very simple dials, the very discreetness of the nickel-work, all this signifies a kind of control exercised over motion, which is henceforth conceived as comfort rather than performance. One is obviously turning from an alchemy of speed to a relish in driving.[38]

Unsurprisingly, nearly all the cars described above were among the 26 nominees for the international Car of the Century award of the Global Automotive Elections Foundation, decided by a jury of journalists, supported by a public vote and announced at the Frankfurt Motor Show in 1999. The final results of the competition were as follows:

1. Ford Model T
2. Austin/Morris Mini
3. Citroën DS
4. Volkswagen Type 1
5. Porsche 911

All five belong to the functionalist end of the automotive design spectrum. At the opposite end of that spectrum lies the expressionist car, which flourished in post-war North America, where automobiles functioned most aggressively as expressions of taste, affluence and personality, displayed on the suburban driveway and in the street. They belonged to a style of art and design conveying an uneasy confidence and hawkish dynamism, touting American power during the Cold War, just as the Baroque sculptures in seventeenth-century Rome reasserted and dramatized the power of the Catholic Church during the Protestant Reformation.[39] These were the most ubiquitous of expressionist automobiles in motoring history. One of the most extravagant, yet typical, was a late design of the Harley Earl era. The Cadillac of 1958 employed ferocious anthropomorphic imagery particularly in its tail-light assembly, representing the image of a Mohawk warrior in full battle cry, similar to American Indian portraits by such popular nineteenth-century sculptors as Charles Henry Humphriss and, more recently, Jon Hair's *Cry of the Mohawk* (2004). Yet the language of that portrait is merged, and double-coded, with images of exhaust ports and fins drawn from fighter aircraft and rockets.

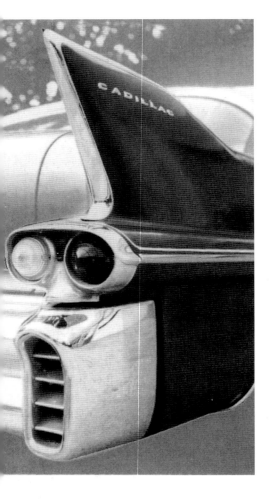

Whereas functionalist designs tend towards plain surfaces, carefully balanced proportions and an absence of ornament, the expressionist car conspicuously features highly sculpted surfaces suggesting turbulence, aggressively dynamic profiles, exaggerated proportions and lashings of trimming. Multi-hued colour combinations dramatize their combative shapes and set off their characteristically gaudy detailing. When Deborah Allen compared the Buick to the wooden clouds of a Baroque baldacchino, she was describing similar formal and stylistic methods of engaging the emotions of the viewer and of inviting his or her suspension of disbelief regarding the true substance of the object.

During the 1920s and '30s in Europe, small coachbuilding companies also treated the custom car body as an extravagant sculptural object. Figoni & Falaschi, Pourtout and Saoutchik, best known for their Delahaye, Delage and Talbot cars respectively, took the modern science of streamlining to its expressive peak, exploiting length and lowness in fluid designs often highlighted dramatically with chromium trimming. Despite their appearance of modernity, they were finished to the highest standards of traditional carriage building. Metal shells

'How like a Mohawk warrior', said the painter Benjamin West on first seeing the *Apollo Belvedere*. This 1958 Cadillac tail assembly could evoke the same comment. The Mohawk warrior in full battle cry has always been a familiar image in North American decorative arts.

were constructed over wooden frames; exotic paint colours were applied in dozens of hand-rubbed coats; interiors exploited the upholsterer's and cabinetmaker's most extravagant skill and materials to achieve a sumptuous look through time-honoured craft methods, comparable with the work of contemporaneous furniture makers and decorative artists Dunand, Ruhlmann and Lalique. Those *carrossiers* also operated in a similar way to the most imaginative and poetic couturiers, such as Schiaparelli and Vionnet, and served many of the same clients in the 1930s and '40s.

After the Second World War the mantle of European coach craft shifted to Italy, where the *carrozzerie* Pininfarina, Touring, Bertone and others promoted the new 'Linea Italiana', developing the fully integrated pontoon body to a state of high refinement. This simplified form combined the functionalism of racing cars with the organic sensuality of architecture and furniture, such as that designed by Carlo Mollino or Eero Saarinen. The latter trait showed in the soft ovoid or rectangular front air intakes of Pininfarina's Cisitalia 202 Berlinetta (1947) and the Ferrari Typo 166 Barchetta roadster (1949) – small, lightweight cars that provided the template for later sports cars including the Lotus Elan of 1962–73 and the Mazda MX5 Miata of 1989.[40]

Carrossieries Figoni & Falaschi created this 1937 Delahaye 135 Torpedo Cabriolet based on a design by Geo Ham. It demonstrates their characteristically sleek streamlining emphasized by elaborate two-tone paintwork.

Yet Italian design was also famed for the extravagance and aggressiveness of its later high-performance cars. Beginning in the 1960s, Marcello Gandini of Carrozzeria Bertone introduced wedge-shaped bodies with knife-edge definition, emulating rear- and mid-engine racing cars of the time. Gandini's Alfa Romeo Carabo concept of 1968, in particular, featured an unfeasibly low roof line over deeply raked windows, necessitating scissor doors for entry and exit. Its sharply creased surfaces and hard, rectilinear air intakes, lights and spoiler all suggested a race track, but perhaps one on another planet.

Italian supercars continued to epitomize passion in automobile design into the twenty-first century. Such cars as Horacio Pagani's Zonda (1999–2013) and Huayra (2012–) models, conceived by his Modena Design studio, are built of lightweight carbon fibre and powered by ferocious 670-hp Mercedes-Benz V12 engines capable of 349 km/h (217 mph). Their interiors feature a distinctive blend of racing-car austerity and svelte materials in luscious colours, with finely tailored details appealing to the most sybaritic tastes

In the 21st century Italian sports cars remain the beating heart of expressionist car design. Examples such as the Pagani Zonda tell a story of intense emotional involvement in driving through their extravagant forms and their representation of immense power.

of billionaire oligarchs. Yet it is their visual bravura, dynamic proportions and intricately curvaceous exterior forms that confirm such Italian design as the beating heart and throbbing pulse of twenty-first-century automotive expressionism.

Hyperbole versus understatement

In the early years of motoring, advertising stressed little more than the capability of the car to go. The first automobile advertisement, depicting the Benz Motorwagen in which Bertha Benz made the first long-distance motor trip, said little about the car, but it was 'live advertising', a reminder of her newsworthy expedition, which had been reported in the press. Bertha Benz's road trip was an entrepreneurial coup drawing attention to the capability of the motor car and specifically to that of her husband's car, an event so important historically that it is celebrated by a biennial antique car rally, the

In the years following the Second World War, Italian designers such as Pininfarina perfected the pontoon body form, as shown in the Cisitalia 202 coupé of 1947.

Bertha Benz Challenge, on an official industrial heritage route designated in 2008 by the State of Baden-Württemberg.

Believing that a good car should speak for itself, Karl Benz had scant respect for advertising, then referred to as a 'business recommendation', invoking the more respectable 'word-of-mouth' endorsement. However, his advertisement established car publicity as a trust-building exercise, appropriate in the first decades of motoring, when many ads were aimed at potential distributors rather than at the end-user.[41]

Growing competition among hundreds of car manufacturers in Europe and North America soon required more sophisticated tactics. The lure was 'lifestyle'. Advertisements for vehicles, from the humble Oldsmobile runabout to Benz's luxurious Mercedes, portrayed their cars in settings that suggested affluence and leisure. The fashionable German poster artist Ludwig Hohlwein portrayed the elegant Mercedes 37/90-hp touring car of 1911 at an early air show, with a Farman biplane passing over a well-dressed party standing in the large open car for a good view of the spectacle. The image was presented in Hohlwein's linear manner, which typified the German *Plakatstil* (poster style) popular into the 1930s.

The car maker Ned Jordan built 'assembled cars' of little mechanical distinction but elegantly designed, and by 1920 he had promoted body styling and lifestyle advertising to corporate priorities, primarily to attract women buyers. He argued that people who dress fashionably want to drive a fashionable car. Colour and fine interior finishes were their main attractions. Starting in 1916, Jordan used his own compelling copywriting, illustrated by various artists, to portray the lifestyle of the modern woman and to present the car as a purely mythical object.

Jordan expressed the dynamic spirit of the Jazz Age in his milestone advertisement for the Playboy model (1923), 'Somewhere

West of Laramie', which had a significant impact on American advertising through its fantastic prose and avoidance of factual information. Fred Cole's dynamic artwork showed the speeding car, flapper at the wheel, racing alongside a cowboy on horseback, supporting Jordan's mesmeric text to spin a romantic fantasy about driving *that* car. Sinclair Lewis satirized Jordan's style in his novel *Babbitt* (1922):

> Speed – glorious Speed – it's more than just a moment's exhilaration – it's Life for you and me! This great new truth the makers of the Zeeco Car have considered as much as price and style. It's fleet as the antelope, smooth as the glide of a swallow, yet powerful as the charge of a bull-elephant. Class breathes in every line.[42]

The earliest advertisements for production cars were informational recommendations, aimed as much at potential distributors as at private buyers. Benz New Patent Motorwagen advertisement, 1888. But by the outbreak of war in 1914, automotive advertising had become hugely sophisticated and aspirational. Ludwig Hohlwein's alluring *Plakatstil* portrayal of the 1911 Mercedes at an air show is among the finest.

As in the fashion world, status is an important element in the image of cars. And in North America, high status equals large size. The advertising critic Vance Packard noted in 1957 that the most influential factors in selling a car were appearance and size; economy was a poor second; and reliability succumbed to third place. Safety did not figure. Ads for Pontiac emphasized that it was a 'Big Car with Big Power'. Mercury was touted as 'The Big M', and 'Lincoln was running magazine spreads showing its car stretched the width of two pages: "Never before a Lincoln so long . . . *and so longed for.*"'[43]

Among the most glamorous and highly stylized advertising illustrations ever produced were those by Art Fitzpatrick and Van

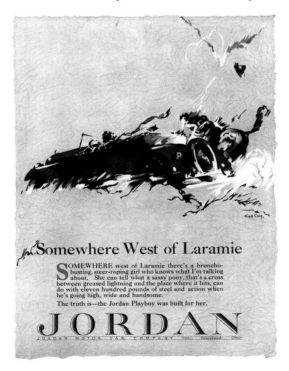

One of the most influential copywriters for the automobile in its early years was Ned Jordan. His purple prose had an enormous impact on the practice of advertising that has remained until today. Avoidance of facts and appeal to fantasy are the significant characteristics of his approach, as in this example from 1923.

Kaufman for the Pontiac Division of GM in the 1960s. In their vividly coloured paintings, the pair located the cars in exotic, aspirational settings – Paris, Nice, Acapulco or Hawaii, for example – surrounded by beautiful, elegantly dressed people. Kaufman provided the backdrops and figures, and at the centre of the composition was Fitzpatrick's luminous rendering of the 'wide track' car, its length and width significantly exaggerated, and viewed from the front to show off the body's broad stance and Pontiac's signature grillework. The vibrant colours of GM's Magic Mirror lacquers were enhanced and endowed with unfathomable depth by Fitzpatrick's brilliant highlighting technique, and by his deemphasizing of window frames, panel junctions and other distracting details. The result was one of the longest running and most commercially successful automotive ad campaigns in history.

In contrast to such artful manipulation of the public's susceptibility to glamour came a clever alternative. William Bernbach, of the

Stretching the car body was a feature of the highly successful series of ads for Pontiac illustrated by Art Fitzpatrick and Van Kaufman, 1959–71. Their lustrous cars were always located in elegant settings, but their outstanding feature was the exaggerated width of the cars, which signified stability and track-readiness.

Doyle Dane Bernbach (DDB) agency, declared that Volkswagen was 'an honest car' deserving honest advertising – but with a dash of humour that acknowledged the reader's intelligence. In 1959 DDB initiated a campaign created by the art director Helmut Krone and copywriter Julian Koenig, showing a tiny black-and-white photo of a VW Beetle photographed against a blank background, with the tag line 'Think Small'. A simple statement of facts established the minimalist virtues of the car while lampooning the extravagance of American automobiles. The layout was pure Bauhaus, using the Futura typeface designed in 1927 by Paul Renner. The text accompanying the original 'Think Small' advertisement confessed:

> Our little car isn't so much of a novelty any more. A couple of dozen college kids don't try to squeeze inside it. The guy at the gas station doesn't ask where the gas goes. Nobody even stares at our shape. In fact, some people who drive our little flivver don't even think 32 miles to the gallon is going any great guns . . . That's because once you get used to some of our economies, you don't even think about them any more. Except when you squeeze into a small parking spot. Or renew your small insurance. Or pay a small repair bill. Or trade in your old VW for a new one. Think it over.

This sort of copy not only established the VW as an antidote to conspicuous consumption, but also elevated its buyer above the manipulation of the ad men Vance Packard called the 'hidden persuaders'. 'Think Small' ads instantly made conventional car advertising look passé.

Subtlety worked well for cars at both ends of the price scale. David Ogilvy's advertisements for Rolls-Royce in the late 1950s employed classic British understatement to answer the question 'What makes Rolls-Royce the best car in the world?' in thirteen statements of simple facts that were notable and quotable.[44] A British transplant to the USA, Ogilvy wrote critically of the American style of aspirational car advertising: 'I have never admired the *belles lettres* school of advertising, which reached its pompous peak in . . . Ned Jordan's "Somewhere West of Laramie" . . . I have always thought them absurd; they did not give the reader a single *fact*.'[45]

Both Bernbach and Ogilvy, however, recognized that the semblance of rationality combined with dry humour ('At 60 miles an hour the loudest noise in this new Rolls-Royce comes from the electric clock') could trigger an emotional as well as reasoned response. This was fifteen years after the Second World War, when controversy continued over whether Jewish Americans should buy German cars. Using gentle irony in the VW advertisements, Bernbach, himself Jewish, captured both the reader's head and their heart.

Another evergreen advertising gambit for mass-produced cars was the myth of choice. From 1932 art director Jack Tarleton of the J. Stirling Getchell agency touted Plymouth and DeSoto in a series of homely campaigns featuring unglamorized photos of cars used by ordinary people. Human-interest copy included personal endorsements emphasizing the reliability and economy of the cars. Carefully scripted slice-of-life narratives were presented in a homely scrapbook format characterized by multiple images, slogans and blocks of text in various typefaces, and featuring the price outlined in a circle or square. Plymouth's virtue was value. The tag line 'I Priced "All Three" and Plymouth Won!' confirmed the Depression-era consumer as the judge.

By the 1950s American car manufacturers offered shoppers a wide selection of factory options, creating a role, real and mythological, for consumers in the design process. A print campaign run in *Motor Trend* and *Field & Stream* magazines by Campbell Ewald for Chevrolet in 1959 and 1960 presented stories of fictional buyers under the rubric 'I "built" my Chevy as a . . .'. The advertisements described how each character fashioned a unique automobile from a basic car and a list of optional equipment, producing a 'workhorse', 'robot' or 'sports car for five'. They promised: 'You can virtually design your own car, tailored precisely to your needs', whether sedan, convertible, automatic, manual, V8, Six, stripped or loaded, although the basic offering was always a big, sculptural showboat. Nevertheless, the idea of a 'build-it-yourself' motor car suggested the reclamation of personal identity in an alienating, mass-produced world. The Campbell Ewald series featured cars 'built by' a New York fashion model, a sporty architect with a young family, and a suburban housewife who collects antiques.

Among the most fundamental marketing gambits is the appeal to gender. While the car body itself featured gendered forms – the power bulge over the engine of a 'muscle car', or the cuteness of a Nissan Figaro – such imagery transferred readily to marketing. Bertha Benz brought a woman's perspective to the technical improvement of the car, but also launched its reputation as a family vehicle, driven by Mother. Since then, cars 'for women' were characterized in advertising as small second cars, as massive carriers of domestic consumer goods and children, or as convertibles to display youthfulness and glamour. The twentieth century's mythical object par excellence carried in its DNA an affirmation of gender stereotypes.[46]

More recently, the symbolic anthropomorphism of the car body was demonstrated in the design for a textile-skinned BMW concept roadster named GINA (2008), announced by BMW's chief designer Chris Bangle on YouTube for maximum public exposure. Its skin recalls earlier fabric-bodied cars, such as the folding Czech Velorex three-wheeler of 1943 and the luxurious Weymann bodies, fitted in the 1920s to many first-class European and American chassis, framed in ash and covered in ultra-lightweight Dupont Zapon synthetic leather or similar textiles, a technique derived from the aeronautical industry. Bangle and his team developed the tubular-framed, Lycra-skinned GINA to demonstrate the biomorphic, shape-shifting possibilities of new materials; the car's headlights blink open like lidded eyes, while the bonnet opens in the manner of human labia to reveal the engine through a slit in the fabric. Such provocative and multivalent imagery links this car with the surreal images of automobiles by Dalí and with the sexually ambiguous Pop Art references to automotive forms in the paintings of Richard Hamilton.

And so, throughout its history the car has been a central image in art movements including Futurism and Pop Art, and has reflected such design theories as functionalism, such cultural and political movements as feminism, and economic ideologies, especially consumerism. It has stood for these ideas through its form and through its representation in the visual arts, in literature and in the popular verse and jingles of advertising. Its form is seen by some in the industry as a work of art and by others outside the field as a canvas for self-expression. Yet however its appearance is conceived, represented or manipulated, and regardless of what it represents in terms of philosophy or ideology, it remains one of the primary icons of the modern world.

4 Road

The line

A recorded voice announces: 'May I take the pleasure of introducing Mr J. Widdecombe Billows, the inventor of the Billows Feeding Machine, a practical device which automatically feeds your men while at work. Don't stop for lunch: be ahead of your competitor.' Testing the Billows Feeding Machine on an unsuspecting assembly-line worker, played by Charles Chaplin in *Modern Times* (1936), goes comically wrong as the machine force-feeds him nuts and bolts along with his soup, pummels him around the head with its automatic mouth-wiper and ultimately pushes a cream pie in his face, triggering a complete nervous breakdown.

In 1929 Ilya Ehrenburg described the car assembly-line worker as one 'who doesn't know what an automobile is. He doesn't know what an engine is. He takes a bolt and tightens a nut. The wrench is waiting in the raised hand of the next worker.'[1] Ehrenburg then put a face to the anonymous worker and described the effect of his repetitive labour: 'Jean Lebaque worked in Suresne. He made joints. . . . He was paid four francs per hundred joints. He forgot about living.' Like Chaplin's character in *Modern Times*, 'he went berserk.'[2]

Not everyone working on an early production line took it so hard, however. A British psychologist employed incognito in a war-production factory in 1943 commented that her initial impression was 'definitely pleasant, rather like knitting in a fairly plain pattern . . . It is hard for anyone who has not tried it to realize the curious, almost exhilarating sense of the slipping away of all responsibilities that comes over people after a few days in this sort of work.'[3] Henry Ford commented in this vein: 'I have been told by parlour experts that repetitive labour is soul- as well as body-destroying, but that has not been the result of our investigations.'[4]

Ford believed that workers with imagination and ambition would progress into positions of responsibility, leaving only those who wanted undemanding jobs on the line: 'Repetitive labour . . . is a terrifying prospect to a certain kind of mind . . . but to other minds, perhaps I might say the majority of minds, repetitive operations hold no terrors. In fact, to some types of mind thought is absolutely appalling.'[5] Ford also wrote proudly about employing non-English-speaking immigrant workers, about hiring the 'handicapped', about employing women and black workers, about the safety aspects of machinery and about wages (he initiated a $5 day for his top-class workers in 1914). But when he characterizes the assembly-line worker, his image is as singular as the car they were building.

The working conditions of the Rouge plant in Detroit were the subject of a series of murals commissioned by Henry's son, Edsel Ford, and executed by the left-wing Mexican muralist Diego Rivera in 1932–3. These large, dense compositions, which line the inner courtyard of the Detroit Institute of Arts, represent the simultaneous ugliness and beauty of mass production, showing the entire process of manufacturing a car, from mining iron ore to the finished product. Rivera concentrated equally on the intense, repetitive actions of the human workers and on the monumental forms of the factory equipment. Recognizing the functional beauty in machine forms, he wrote: 'The dynamic productive sculptures which are the mechanical masterpieces of the factory are active works of art, the result of the genius of the industrial country.'[6]

Ultimately, Ford's complacency regarding workers was shattered by labour unrest in America and England that eventually led to the decline of car making in Detroit and Coventry. David Gartman described the persistence of Fordist 'workplace repression' into the 1970s: 'Major corporations like the automakers tightened managerial surveillance and control of workers on the shop floor, hiring more supervisors to enforce intensified labor.'[7] For car makers, the solution was the robot. Just as the car had replaced the horse, so the robot would replace the assembly-line worker.

The earliest practical industrial robot, Unimate, was developed by the American inventor George Charles Devol in 1954 and led to the formation of the original robot-manufacturing company, Unimation. In 1961 GM installed its first Unimates for die-casting and spot-welding, and they showed such promise that the company began 30 years of heavy investment in robotics. Their poor initial application, however, led to manufacturing chaos, such as a notorious incident in 1988 at a GM plant in Michigan, when uncoordinated robots smashed windows and painted one another.

Despite their shaky start, by the year 2000 some 50 per cent of all manufacturing robots were involved in some aspect of car production. They welded more precisely than human workers, performed at a steadier pace, were never absent and didn't strike. Humans were increasingly responsible for detailed assembly, quality control and the maintenance of the robots themselves. In 1979 Fiat dramatized the mechanized assembly of its new model, the Strada, in an advertising film directed by Hugh Hudson to communicate the perfection of robotic production, without a single human worker in view. The film conveyed the drama and elegance of the production process as a mechanistic ballet, accompanied by the best-known aria from

Mozart's opera *The Marriage of Figaro*, remixed with factory-type sounds by the Greek composer Vangelis. The film concluded with a brace of completed cars in jelly-bean colours racing in formation around the rooftop test track of Fiat's Lingotto factory in Turin, under the title 'The Strada, Hand Built by Robots'. In 2012 Hyundai advertised that its company produced the robots that make its cars, ensuring the highest quality. And so the relationship between product and production became less fragmented and more consistent as the object increasingly belonged to the same race and culture as its makers. They were all machines.

Whether cars are mass-produced by robots or hand-built, like British Morgans, they are always seen to be 'born'. Ehrenburg wrote ironically of the process, while in 1983 the novelist Stephen King described the delivery into the world of his homicidal 1957 Plymouth Fury, Christine, as a supernatural event. No other machine carries such deeply personal, anthropomorphic, empathetic and erotic

A robotic ballet is the characteristic feature of the modern automobile factory. Here German-built Kuka robots perform spot welding on a car assembly line.

qualities in its mechanical genesis. The sight of any new car, glossy, virginal, promising adventure and freedom, remains an uplifting sight, regardless of one's knowledge of the danger, damage and futility of that machine. The human bond formed with such an object will not easily be severed.

The design of cars and the design of assembly lines are two halves of a single process, as the factors affecting each affect the other, and they evolved together, initially to produce a better car at a faster pace, to lower the price and increase sales. Those were the goals of mass production that Citroën, Fiat, Ford and Morris all pursued, first to make money and secondly to make cars. In motoring history, the assembly line became one of the early notorious black spots largely for its impact on those workers who stood at its side repeating basic tasks to the point of mental and physical burnout. They were the immediate participants in the black magic of car production described in prose by Ehrenburg, parodied on film by Chaplin and memorialized in paint by Rivera. That highway of steel, glass and rubber flowing past them carried the parts of what would become a retreat from their mind-numbing work, their own car. The assembly line is the first of all 'magic motorways', the one from which mass-market cars have always sprung. And without it no other road would have purpose in the modern world.

The moving assembly line for car production was devised over a period of years, most significantly by Ford and his associates at his Highland Park factory in Michigan, where until 1915 it still served only a small part of the manufacturing process and constituted just one step towards a mature mass-production process. The building in which it was housed was designed by the most prolific and innovative factory architects of the twentieth century, Albert Kahn and his brothers, the engineer Julius, who devised the 'Kahn System' of reinforced-concrete construction, and Moritz, the firm's strategist and manager. The Kahns had built Detroit's first concrete-framed, fireproof factory, Building Number 10, for the luxury car maker Packard in 1903 (see p. 8).

Ford recognized the potential in reinforced-concrete construction for the linear process of making high-volume, low-priced cars, and commissioned Kahn to build him a plant like Packard's for his recently introduced Model T. The plant opened in 1910, when Ford and his chief production engineer, Charles Sorensen, were just beginning their experiments to cut production time by increasing the division of labour and by bringing the work to the worker. The bright, open spaces of the structure, with its long metal roof trusses, large windows and saw-tooth roof lighting, allowed Ford to experiment with the route or height of the line and to make other changes without structural impediments. The electrification of the line in 1914–15 cut the production time for a single car from more than twelve hours to just 93 minutes.[8]

Kahn's offices eventually designed more than 1,000 buildings of various sorts for the Ford family. They included a Cotswold-style manor house for Edsel and the luxurious neo-Georgian Dearborn Inn, one of the earliest airport hotels. Since the Kahns were Jewish sons of a rabbi, Henry Ford's continued patronage demonstrates the complexity of his notorious anti-Semitism, which was intertwined with his loathing of banks and bankers.

Kahn's greatest commission for Ford was his gigantic River Rouge factory in Dearborn, Michigan, known as 'The Rouge'. Many of its buildings were planned by Kahn, and construction began in 1917; by the time it was 'completed' in 1928, the Rouge was the world's largest manufacturing complex, with an area 1.6 × 2.4 km (1 × 1½ miles) and consisting of 93 buildings with nearly 1.5 million sq. km (16 million sq. ft) of floor space. Sited on the Detroit River, the complex had its own docks, an electrical power plant and production facilities for steel and glass, as well as its own parts-manufacturing and assembly plant. At its peak in the 1930s, the River Rouge factory employed more than 100,000 workers. It accomplished Ford's aim of creating a 'vertically integrated' company, owning all its suppliers and manufacturing processes, meaning that in the single facility raw materials from Ford-owned sources were transformed into finished cars. In this way the production road extended virtually from his Brazilian rubber plantation, Fordlandia, to showroom floors.[9]

As the assembly line evolved, other architects and engineers found ways of expressing its fluidity within an envelope of concrete, metal and glass. Fiat's giant Lingotto factory in Turin, designed by the engineer Giacomo Mattè Trucco and built between 1916 and 1923, presented the production process even more literally as a road, demonstrating the manufacturing principle of vertical integration through its stadium-shaped spiral floor plan. Raw materials entered at street level and rose along a continuous ascending ramp, emerging as finished cars on to a rooftop test track for final proving.[10] The Lingotto factory's majestic expression of the car-making system was eventually outmoded by the arrival of automation in the 1970s, and the building was transformed by the architect Renzo Piano into a cultural centre, shopping precinct and hotel; but the test track was preserved as a historic exemplar of Italian car manufacturing and of architecture animated by the car.

The Anglo-Iraqi architect Zaha Hadid composed a similarly spectacular construction road in the plant she designed for BMW in Leipzig in 2001. In a dramatic statement of deconstructivist architectural theory, Hadid introduced an assembly line interwoven with the managerial and clerical activities of the factory. As cars under construction passed through the building on their assembly highway, they could be seen by employees engaged in a full range of company activities, reminding them of the object of their enterprise. In this way the line became a tool in the creation of a self-conscious corporate community by partly blurring the traditional segregation of employees in 'blue-' and 'white-collar' status groups. It also emphasized the image of the car as the key element of a monumental, kinetic, sculptural environment.

The typical car today comes into being on assembly lines, as it has since the days of Ford and Citroën, although the process is now executed mainly by robots with human assistance. Following the conversion of raw materials into the component parts of the car, robots assemble the heaviest pieces, such as chassis and suspension, with their long, articulated arms. Workers help in fitting panels and by ensuring quality, as demonstrated when the shell is subjected to 'body in white' inspection under brilliant light to identify defects,

BMW's Leipzig factory, designed by architect Zaha Hadid in 2001, integrates the assembly line and the cars it carries with all other activities of the plant. Significantly, they process past white-collar workers who might otherwise become oblivious to the product.

which are repaired on the spot by skilled workers before the car is spray-painted by robots. Overhead conveyors carry the body through the painting process before it is baked in a high-temperature oven to cure the finish. Workers then outfit the cabin with wiring, lighting, seats, linings, instruments and windows. In the assembly of unibody vehicles, robots and workers fit the remaining mechanical parts – engines, transmissions and wheels – on to the body shell. For body-on-frame vehicles, robots assemble the chassis on a separate line. Then the chassis and body assembly lines merge to mate the two main elements of the car, before workers bolt them together and the car is complete.

Street, road, highway, motorway

Once through the factory gate and the dealer's showroom, where it typically passes to its first owner, the car's world is mainly a ribbon of black asphalt – even for SUVs with off-road capability. That world of roads was conceived and constructed mainly for cars, and is shaped by their capabilities and the desires of their users.

The global road network in 2013, including paved and unpaved routes, was more than 64 million km (40.5 million miles). The largest national road network was that of the USA (6.6 million km/4.1 million miles), followed by India (4.7 million km/2.9 million miles), China (4.4 million km/2.8 million miles), Brazil (1.8 million km/1.1 million miles) and Japan (1.2 million km/0.75 million miles). The development of that huge US road network began shortly before the advent of the car, and its inception can be credited mainly to the Good Roads Movement, begun by an organization of bicycle enthusiasts. In 1880 the League of American Wheelmen (still going today as the League of American Bicyclists) was founded to lobby state and federal governments to build and improve roads, particularly outside cities, where few paved roads existed. They held conventions, supported road-friendly candidates to public office, enlisted the support of farmers and published *Good Roads* magazine to spread their gospel.

In Britain a 'golden age' for cyclists existed for a time, as portrayed in H. G. Wells's comic novel *Wheels of Chance* (1896). Wells later wrote in his autobiography: 'The bicycle was the swiftest thing upon the roads in those days, there were no automobiles and the cyclist had the lordliness, a sense of masterful adventure, that has gone from him altogether now.'[11] The rise of the car not only overthrew the cyclist and the horse as kings of the road, but also caused far more physical damage to existing roads than before. This was because of the motor car's weight and speed and its pneumatic tyres, made by Dunlop, Michelin and Goodyear, which sucked up the soft, unstable road surfaces of the early twentieth century.

In 1893, the year when the Duryea brothers built their first horseless carriage and the US Post Office introduced Rural Free Delivery, the American Department of Agriculture initiated a survey of existing highways, which sparked a nationwide acceptance that economic growth and prosperity would depend on improving communication by road. With the rapid spread of car ownership, motorists assumed leadership of the Good Roads Movement, promoting the construction of an east–west, coast-to-coast paved road, the Lincoln Highway. Dedicated in 1913 and running 5,454 km (3,389 miles) through thirteen states to join Times Square in New York City with Lincoln Park in San Francisco, the new road was a significant achievement, a symbol of national unity and a validation of the car as the primary national transport vehicle.

The French were proud of their roads, which had been developed since the time of Napoleon I (1769–1821), and France was well ahead of the rest of Europe and North America in its network of surfaced highways when it became the leading motoring nation in the late 1890s. In 1905 the French novelist and enthusiastic motorist Octave Mirbeau, travelling through northern Europe, gave a good review of Dutch roads, which he described as 'smooth, springy and dust-free, surfaced with well-laid bricks'. But he warned that 'you have to drive slowly across the polders, along the dykes . . . there is no rule of the road for cars except those you make up for your own safety as you go.'[12] Mirbeau reserved his scorn for the Belgian roads: 'It is really maddening to have driven from the frontier over those ghastly stones – wave upon wave of them – through the grimy mining country of the Borinage.'[13]

By the end of the 1920s most main roads in the advanced motoring countries of Europe had been surfaced with asphalt or tarmacadam (commonly interchangeable terms), eliminating the worst dust and rutting. However, in what was by then the largest car culture, the USA, the sheer scale of the problem with the roads meant that in rural areas many main routes were still poor throughout the 1920s. F. Scott Fitzgerald wrote of the horrible state of some main roads in the rural South in his story *The Cruise of the Rolling Junk* (1924), in which his Marmon touring car 'plunged through impassable streams and surmounted monstrous crags' between punctures and breakdowns.[14] He described the transition from rough country road to city street as he and his wife, Zelda, entered Richmond, Virginia: 'At about nine o'clock the road became hard and smooth beneath us and trembling lights glimmered into our consciousness until the city . . . developed on all sides of us.'[15]

Similarly variable conditions can be found in the surging economies of the twenty-first century, such as China, where urban roads have been built to a high standard and the quality of new expressways exceeds those of established networks elsewhere. Yet roads in the vast rural areas make the craze for four-wheel-drive

SUVs seem almost sensible, as two-lane paved roads might rapidly and unexpectedly degenerate into rough tracks or rutted fields. In *Country Driving* (2010), the writer and journalist Peter Hessler, echoing Fitzgerald, recounted his adventures motoring in rural China, guided by a set of Sinomaps, which were quickly rendered out of date by the rapid construction of roads in developed areas, but proved even more fickle in the countryside, where 'two or three times a day I'd find myself Sinomapped: Sinomapped into dead ends, Sinomapped into washouts, Sinomapped on to grass tracks that led nowhere.'[16] Hessler frequently drove a hired Chinese-built Jeep Cherokee, with robust springs and plenty of ground clearance, features reminiscent of the earliest automobiles.

Cars evolved in response to the reality of the roads, which is why most early ones were set on high wheels, with their chassis and running gear kept well away from the uneven ground over which they

Road's end. A motorist in New York c. 1910 finds that the lane disappears into undergrowth, an experience reported by country drivers in rapidly motorizing China today.

drove. Throughout its production run, the Model T Ford retained a high stance to provide ample clearance over rutted roads, which had largely disappeared by 1927, when the model was discontinued. The desire of car makers to advance the design of their vehicles, and the increasing economic and political power of the largest manufacturers, forced the improvement of streets and highways (despite varying definitions, I use 'highways' to mean main ex-urban public roads), and eventually the creation of motorway networks.

Major milestones in the modern development of roads included the first divided highways exclusively for motor traffic, the Berlin

An automobile approaches an overpass on the newly opened German Autobahn in the late 1930s. Continuous high speed with no stops was a reality on very few of the world's roads before the 1950s.

AVUS (*Automobil-Verkehrs- und Übungsstrasse*, Automobile Traffic and Training Road), planned in 1909 but not opened until 1921 because of the First World War; and the Long Island Motor Parkway, conceived and financed by the motor racer William K. Vanderbilt II and opened in 1908. Designed for racing as well as private motoring, these were graded and banked, divided highways with guard rails, tarmac-surfaced reinforced-concrete construction and limited access, meaning that there were no crossroads, only unidirectional on and off ramps. Germany, Italy and the USA led in the construction of the first superhighways during the Depression of the 1930s, when governments saw their construction as a remedy for high unemployment.

The days when pedestrians, horse-drawn vehicles, trolleys, bicycles and cars shared the road equally were short-lived. Traffic density and the increasing speed of cars made the road space too dangerous for such a mix, and it soon became clear which form of transport would dominate. Trolleys were eventually eliminated in most cities, partly owing to the danger of mounting and dismounting in the middle of the street with cars whizzing past. Cyclists were forced into the gutters until the advent of designated cycle lanes from about 2000. Pedestrian controls soon arrived, and specially assigned crossing places and jaywalking rules were put in place in North America and elsewhere after about 1910, when motoring lobbyists promoted the notion that the street should be a pedestrian-free zone. That idea damaged city and town life everywhere for decades, until anti-car groups, such as Reclaim the Streets (begun in London in 1991), began agitating through direct action for a change in attitude. Meanwhile, road-pricing schemes, enacted in some cities in the early twenty-first century, approached the reduction in urban car use primarily through legislation, rather than through direct action.

Showing off

At the beginning of the motoring age, with few legal restrictions in effect, the car could be parked in front of nearly any destination, from the village pharmacy to a Ritz hotel, making an impression on those witnessing its arrival or departure. Initially, the great height of cars made a graceful entrance or exit from the vehicle challenging, but as cars became lower, and with the elimination of running boards in the 1940s, the proper form of entering or leaving a car took on an importance comparable with using the correct fork at dinner or performing the latest dance step. Ladies entered by first sitting down and then swivelling their feet up on to the floor of the car. Men stepped in with one foot first, then sat down, and finally lifted the other foot into the car. Sporty types made a display of jumping in over the sides of such low-slung sports cars as the MGT series, with their rakishly cut-down doors. A gentleman always

Will Crawford's cartoon of 1913 for *Puck* magazine, 'Don't Blame the Motorist', shows the street shared by pedestrians, cyclists, children playing, push-cart vendors, trolley men and dogs, accompanied by a familiar plea, stay out of the way, to those less fortunate than the driver of the enormous brass-era touring car.

opened the (passenger) door for a lady. She might then courteously reach over to unlock his door.

This element of performance extended from the kerbside to the open road, where the driver's posture at the wheel became a conveyor of style and a signifier of prowess and confidence. Observable stereotypes include German businessmen at the wheel of their Mercedes, cruising at 160 km/h (100 mph) on the autobahn, who often adopt an upright posture with arms fully extended, a pose suggestive of command over the powerful machine. The proverbial 'Little Old Lady from Pasadena' behind the wheel of her Dodge characteristically positions herself close up to the wheel, hunched forwards, demonstrating her careful attention to the road and her tight grip on the controls. A hot-rodder portrayed by Paul Le Mat in the nostalgic cruise movie *American Graffiti* (1973) slouched nonchalantly over the steering wheel of his Deuce coupe, right hand draped over the wheel, left elbow dangling out of the window, that studied repose signifying his erotic coolness and latent aggression before the inevitable drag race.

Passengers, too, performed for spectators through their self-presentation in the car. The diva seated in the back of a chauffeured limousine was free to emote and gesture, to express dramatic ennui or to display her finery and a disdainful profile to pedestrians or to those watching from lesser vehicles. In 1950 Gloria Swanson, the star of Billy Wilder's film noir classic *Sunset Boulevard*, displayed herself to such grand effect in the rear seat of her character's anachronistic Isotta Fraschini Tipo 8A Transformable by Castagna (1929).

Cars have always presented a spectacle for the roadside observer. The glamour of the new, the dilapidation of the old or the appearance of something unique hold a fascination as magnetic as that of sculptures displayed in an art gallery or a first glimpse of the new season's fashions. With the re-emergence of electric vehicles, the sight of a Renault Twizy parking at a roadside charging station draws crowds, out of curiosity, admiration or derision. The journalist Erin Baker reported on her experience driving one in London: 'The Twizy electric quadricycle must be doing wonders for the French brand . . . I had small boys pointing, mothers laughing, men staring.'[17]

Such responses may rest on aesthetic judgement, at least in part. The size and baroque ornamentation of American cars as they rolled conspicuously through the streets of war-torn European and Asian cities in the late 1940s appeared as symbols either of Western prosperity and 'the good life' or of arrogance, self-indulgence and occupation.[18] On the other hand, the appearance in 1955 of the Citroën DS attracted the admiration of many observers, as Roland Barthes wrote: 'The DS – the "Goddess" – has all the features (or at least the public is unanimous in attributing them to it at first sight) of one of those objects from another universe which have supplied fuel for . . . science-fiction.'[19] According to one of the car's first British owners,

> driving through London's streets . . . was an eerie experience, it was like sitting in a glass house, continuously stared at, fingers pointed . . . As for the constant activities of the DS suspension, many other drivers of lesser machines, as well as pedestrians, gaped open-mouthed in wonder and astonishment, necks craning to get a closer look.[20]

A more ritualized type of car spotting is the cruise, a regularly occurring event with or without municipal approval, which originated during the 1940s in the small towns of southern California, in the suburbs of Detroit and eventually around the world. These were events staged to show off peacock cars such as hot rods, low riders, muscle cars or custom cars. And although the drivers were the stars of these events, their cars were used like carnival costumes, paraded slowly, sometimes bumper to bumper, along a popular commercial strip or highway where the car parks of diners offered drivers places to congregate and socialize.

The cruise is predicated on the act of looking and of being seen, a free-form activity portrayed in *American Graffiti* and in the Swedish film *Raggare! (Blackjackets!)* of 1959. Wherever it occurs, cruising is a type of driving with no fixed destination, a kind of automotive line dancing that involves several of the key modes of personal interaction associated with the community dance – eye contact, pursuit, leading and following, sitting out for refreshment and conversation. Raggare (from the Swedish *ragga*, 'to pick up') is a working-class subculture inspired by the American hot rod, 'greaser' lifestyle. Its origins can be traced across Scandinavia, Germany and Austria, where young working-class men and women took up cruising in the late 1950s, using big American V8 Pontiacs and Chryslers or the finned Mercedes and Opel models of the 1950s and '60s to pursue their hard-drinking, sexually promiscuous leisure time.[21]

Raggare has remained a popular subculture into the twenty-first century, giving rise to several regular gatherings, among which the annual Power Big Meet is the best known. As a result, Sweden has become home to thousands of 1950s American cars, whether original, restored or customized. They continue to be imported in significant numbers at the time of writing, making Power Big Meet one of the world's largest vintage American car gatherings, attracting tens of thousands of spectators and as many as 12,000 participating cars. But despite its international profile and attendance, the ethos of the event remains essentially blue-collar, with participants there to show off their cars and to party.

In such cruise events worldwide, drivers of cars outside the normal cycle of mass production, consumption and disposal – classic products of Italian *carrozziere*, backyard hot rods, well-loved jalopies or restored antiques – naturally use the road differently from the drivers of ordinary modern cars. For them, the road is a uniquely recreational space, an automotive catwalk, a parade ground, psychologically apart from the serious transport infrastructure, even when the two are physically mingled. That alternative road is a distinctive space for display, competition or seduction. The impression made by the car and its occupants on other motorists and pedestrians is the essence of the experience.

Parking problems

Although the natural habitat of the car may be the road, most automobiles spend the majority of their time parked. And while

A group of happy raggare demonstrate the spirit of the annual Power Big Meet aboard a 1957 De Soto in Västerås, Sweden, 2007.

roads occupy an increasingly significant percentage of the earth's crust, accommodating the parked car on and off road presents equally significant challenges for engineers, architects, town planners, port authorities, drainage experts and many other professional groups. Such vast acreage of tarmac has big implications for the environment, particularly since the recognition of global warming. The car while running may be a leading cause of climate change, but the parked car must also be included in the equation.

At the start of the twentieth century, the problem of accommodating cars in cities led to the conception of the first 'automated' parking structures. As Paris was the leading automotive city at the time, it was there that the earliest innovations appeared. The great French pioneer of concrete construction, Auguste Perret, designed one of the earliest multi-storey parking garages, the Garage Ponthieu, in 1905–6 (it was destroyed in 1960). This radically modern building employed the earliest mechanisms for moving cars about its interior – the automobile lift, rolling bridges joining cantilevered parking galleries, and the mechanical turntable – which together enabled parking attendants to negotiate the interior space efficiently, accommodating the maximum number of cars within the smallest possible building footprint.

Garage Ponthieu was not only a structural, technical and conceptual marvel, but also employed a new vocabulary of forms to give the parking structure a specific architectural identity, both inside and out. Its visible concrete framework made a nascent link between the early aesthetic of the car and an emerging functionalism in building design. On the facade, the concrete structure held large panels of glass set in thin metal channels. Dominating the composition, an imposing 'rose petal' window, decorated with a radiating geometrical pattern, ascended through two floors above the garage entrance. Behind this enormous showcase the majestic cars of the

Edwardian period moved across the bridges that linked the parking decks. The form of the interior was that of an arcade, flooded with light from the glass roof and the glazed street frontage.[22]

The subsequent history of the parking garage involves many twists and turns related to suburbanization and increased pressure on the use of land in city centres. It included the development of above- and below-ground parking structures and attempts to beautify such utilitarian buildings, some incorporating various service facilities, refuelling and charging stations, car washes, toilets and crèches for shoppers with children. During the Cold War underground garages were also proposed as potential bomb shelters. Whatever the new building type offered in terms of convenience and amenity, parking garages developed a stubborn reputation as grim and potentially hostile places, making them excellent settings for crime dramas and horror films. They drained life out of urban neighbourhoods and contributed to localized traffic congestion. Very few became lovable places, despite the ingenuity of their architecture or the mechanical glamour of their occupants.[23]

Among the most significant of innovations in the design of multi-storey garages was the development of ramped structures. According to the architect and historian Shannon Sanders McDonald, a controversy raged over the relative merits of the 'automated' mechanical garage, such as Garage Ponthieu, and the ramped garage. In 1921 *Architectural Forum* magazine hymned the ramp as 'the older solution, even older than a stair', and saw its direct relationship to the expression 'of the desire for freedom that driving your own car provided . . . [that] individual experience for the driver'.[24] The ramp enabled motorists to continue their journey directly from the road into the parking bay and thereby to maintain continuous control of their car, rather than relinquishing it to a valet. This reflected changes in attitude that also heralded the passing of the chauffeur.

An early model for the multi-storey garage with circulation ramps was Boston's Fenway Garage, completed in 1914. This innovative building was designed in two sections, one wing half a storey above the other, the two connected by gently sloping ramps to allow continuous movement through the structure. Congestion was thus minimized when hundreds of cars arrived simultaneously to park for baseball games at the adjacent Fenway Park Stadium, which opened in 1912 as the home of the Boston Red Sox baseball team.

A similar ramping system was patented by the engineer Fernand d'Humy in 1918, arranged in two sections with split-level floors, and it was this plan that became the most common pattern for parking garages thereafter. The split-level garage achieved a mature Expressionist aesthetic in the hands of the American architect Paul Rudolph in his design for the Temple Street Garage in New Haven, Connecticut (1963). That influential building followed the d'Humy plan, but was executed in exposed reinforced concrete, revealing the rich impression of the timber forms into which the concrete had been poured. The weighty structure, with columns that flared grandly into the floors above, created strong patterns of light and shade in the open parking decks, generating a profound sense of permanence and drama in a building type generally considered expendable and prosaic.[25]

In 1924 the American architect Frank Lloyd Wright proposed a radically integrated use of the ramp in his design for the Gordon Strong Automobile Objective and Planetarium, which was intended for the summit of Sugarloaf Mountain near Frederick, Maryland. This unbuilt project was conceived as a tourist destination for visitors from nearby Washington, DC, and Baltimore. Wright's design included a domed planetarium and other facilities for visitors, but the main element of the scheme was the drive up a spiral ramp that followed the contours of the mountain and wrapped around the

building to enable motorists sitting comfortably in their cars to appreciate the 360-degree view of the surrounding landscape in a sweeping, uninterrupted climb. They would then park on downward-spiralling ramps, a configuration that would merge the ramp and the parking bays, maximizing capacity and achieving a continuous flow of movement.

Although the client abandoned the project, Wright carried on experimenting with the continuous spiral. His investigations culminated in his Guggenheim Museum in New York, which proved over time to be a better space for the exhibition of vehicles than of paintings, and in a later garage design for the Point Park Civic Center in Pittsburgh, which demonstrated his determination to integrate the car and the road with the function and experience of the building as a whole.[26]

The controversy over automated versus ramped parking structures continues today. Reformers argue that ramped structures waste land and ruin city centres for pedestrians, whereas automated parking

Architect Paul Rudolph's Temple Street Parking Garage in New Haven, Connecticut, of 1959–63, represented a serious attempt to find an appropriate aesthetic for such unlovable structures.

constitutes a more efficient use of space (doubling the number of cars parked per square metre) and has the advantage of reducing pollution and the consumption of energy by requiring little mechanical ventilation or lighting. With the revival of electric cars and the development of autonomous city microcars and prototype folding cars in the early twenty-first century, concept designs for structures tailored to their specifications and charging methods have emerged, lending the parking garage a new green tint. Yet long before that concept had any meaning, there were commercial garages built specifically for electric vehicles.

Among the earliest were those built in the 1890s for taxis and delivery vans in London and New York, with other cities following by about 1900. Walter Bersey's electric London taxis, introduced in 1897, eventually comprised a fleet of more than 75 vehicles, serviced from a centrally located garage in which battery exchange could be carried out in just a few minutes. In 2012 Renault claimed the battery-exchange process as an original idea it called 'quick-drop' and described as 'a little like driving into an automatic car wash, only the machine will remove your car's battery and replace it with another' in three minutes. The scheme was tested in Israel and planned for implementation in Australia and Denmark.[27] But, as with other innovative automotive projects, finance has so far proved elusive.

Another sustainability initiative was pioneered by the landscape architect Theodore Osmundson, who established his reputation in 1958 by installing a planted roof over the garage of the Oakland Kaiser Center in San Francisco, one of the first roof gardens to make use of grasses to soak up excess rainwater and to absorb airborne pollutants. It established a model for subsequent green-roof projects that attempted to improve the ecological performance and the jaded image of both parking structures and the problematic cars they house.

The most significant breakthrough in the design of garages, however, has been the revival of interest in automated garages, latterly known as Automated Vehicle Storage and Retrieval Systems (AVSRS). By the year 2000 hundreds of AVSRS garages were taking cars robotically from their owners at the reception area, transporting them via computerized lifts and trolleys into storage spaces without human assistance, and returning them when required, achieving a better use of space by reducing the area needed for circulation, operational cost and toxic emissions (as cars would not run their engines while in the building). Since few people enter such buildings, the need for lighting and other atmospheric controls is also substantially reduced. In this way, AVSRS garages reduce the carbon footprint of car parking in cities where they have been built, from China to the Netherlands. With the advent of autonomous, self-parking cars, such buildings could adopt entirely new identities, with little or no human activity taking place within them. Driverless cars could also eliminate the need for much of the mechanical infrastructure of all previous garages, because the cars themselves will do the parking.

Perhaps the direct converse of the parking garage is the car showroom, where, instead of being tucked away, the car is displayed for the purposes of advertising and attracting buyers. But like the garage, the sales room is a temporary storage facility that shares similar problems of access, internal circulation and use of space. The typical location of such buildings – along major roads in cities or along suburban retail strips – is also significant in establishing their high visibility to passing traffic and in forming the imaginative link between the car as an object of high desirability, encased behind glass in a gallery-like setting, and its liberation on to the road, its site of action.

Of early car showrooms, one of the most artful in dramatically displaying the car was Citroën's Garage Marbeuf, built in Paris in

1928. The architects Albert Laprade and Léon-Emile Bazin designed the Art Deco structure with a monumental display window six storeys high, creating an epic showcase with the cars arrayed on six levels of balconies that zigzagged back from the window against three walls surrounding a spotlit atrium. Laprade understood the potential of electric lighting to dramatize the architectural interior, and used spotlights in combination with indirect lighting and other effects to focus attention on the cars during the day and to create a magical impression of them at night, highlighting the glamorous surfaces of the car bodies, their colours and

The automobile showroom is, at its best, a glamorous building type, practical and attention-grabbing as a branded advertisement. This Mercedes-Benz showroom in Munich is a jewel-box setting for elegant silver cars, 2013.

the sparkle of their nickel and chrome ornaments. The overall effect was that of a Surrealist stage set, or a monumental jewel box with its glittering contents exhibited on trays for the delight of those passing outside.[28]

Later development of the car showroom followed the general architectural trends of Modernism and, since the 1990s, the development of so-called super-sheds with simple open-plans and increasingly large walls of glass. Most were built along out-of-town retail strips accommodating lower, broader buildings with more outdoor space for storage and presentation of the vehicles. As these buildings were seen by motorists passing at speed, their attention-grabbing signage and techniques for displaying cars became increasingly extravagant. Audi's West London showroom in Brentford, completed in 2009, designed by the architectural firm Wilkinson Eyre, demonstrates the manufacturer's progressive, high-technology image and the sleek design of its cars. The architect gave the building a dynamic geometry with curved floor plans and a sweeping, angled glass facade that provides a spectacular view into the three floors of double-height showroom spaces, in which cars can be set out at fantastic angles and in unusual attitudes, like free-standing sculptures.

In addition to the ways in which modernist architecture presents the car from fresh perspectives, designers today are attempting to counteract the negative reputation of cars as major contributors to climate change by introducing conspicuously energy-saving elements into the design of their showrooms. For its new UK showrooms, Honda's architect Pick Everard employed several sustainability techniques including rainwater harvesting, ground-source heat pumps, solar power, underfloor heating and cooling, and waste-water recycling. By contrast, Honda's 'Green Center' showroom in Oakland, California, was staged to showcase the company's lower-emission hybrid and natural gas-powered cars in an environment that appeared consistent with the advanced technology of the vehicles on display. However, as the existing building incorporated none of the latest sustainable technology, its loft-style bare-brick walls, exposed timber structure and potted plants only suggested 'Greenwash!'

Drive-in

In addition to parking garages, one of the most ubiquitous and long-lived building types conceived specifically for the car is the drive-in restaurant. Restaurant owners were quick to realize that the dedicated motorist's favourite place to eat was *in* the car, which combined a weatherproof private dining space with the transient character of a picnic. Credited as the grandfather of drive-in restaurants, Kirby's Pig Stand opened in 1921 on the Dallas–Fort Worth Highway in Texas, where motorists pulled their cars up to the kerb for a 'carhop' literally to hop up on to the running board in order to take the order and serve the food.[29] As the chain expanded, new Pig Stands included a forecourt where diners would park after placing their orders at a kiosk in the shape of a giant pig or a pagoda. Carhops would then deliver food to the cars.

The great fast-food chains that spread around the world in the last quarter of the twentieth century were all descendants of Kirby's Pig Stand and its generation of drive-in eateries. McDonalds, Kentucky Fried Chicken, Dunkin' Donuts and many others later became global food retailers offering drive-in or drive-through facilities at which ordering, payment and delivery were conducted via a sequence of external windows in the main restaurant building. The entrepreneurs who created these brands appreciated that many customers preferred the privacy of eating in their cars to the communal experience of the restaurant interior. Diners wanted to listen to their own choice of music, enjoy the comfort of their favourite chair, and feel free to talk intimately and not worry about their children's table manners, in their personal car equipped with folding trays and cup-holders designed for 'dashboard dining'. The car became a true dining room on wheels.

The USA was the birthplace of commercial drive-in culture, but the broader notion of carrying out the routines of daily life without leaving one's car eventually spread worldwide. Feeding the car itself was among the first of those routines. In the early years of the internal combustion engine, motorists bought fuel from ironmongers, livery stables or pharmacies, as Bertha Benz did on her first long-distance drive in 1888. In the first years of the twentieth century some oil companies offered home delivery of fuel to motorists, whose chauffeurs then filled their cars' tanks from large cans. Around the same time the first purpose-built petrol stations were constructed in various countries. In 1905 the American inventor Sylvanus Bowser developed the outdoor fuel pump, the Bowser Self-measuring Gasoline Storage Pump, which introduced the form of dispensing fuel that has been used in most places ever since. The pumps were first installed typically at the kerb outside rudimentary garages. Yet around this invention grew the culture of the forecourt 'service' station, which would offer motorists not only a fuelling service, but also a check-up including oil and water levels and tyre pressure, plus the option of having the windscreen cleaned by a uniformed attendant while the driver remained at the wheel. Many stations also had mechanics in attendance and a car-washing bay. By 1913, in Pittsburgh, the Gulf Oil Company had built the earliest known architect-designed drive-in service station, using Bowser-type pumps.

After a flirtation with exotic or historical architectural styles in the 1920s, the mature American-style drive-in service station evolved

The forecourt of a filling station quickly became a social space with high utility value. Its rituals are an important part of everyday life across the world; talking about cars and tending cars have become natural adjuncts to driving cars and arise naturally in places with established car cultures.

by the mid-1930s, when the Texaco Company hired industrial designer Walter Dorwin Teague to standardize their nationwide chain of service stations. Teague's design of 1936 was drawn from the canon of architectural functionalism conceived by European architects a decade earlier. His white boxes, some sheathed in enamelled steel panels, were proportioned according to the golden section; their only ornament consisted of three parallel green lines running horizontally above windows and doors and extending around the projecting canopy that sheltered the fuel pumps. Those sweeping lines echoed the streamlined design of the cars of that period and signalled a setting appropriate to the spirit of modern drive-in living.[30] These havens of comfort and safety, refuges along the highway, were also located at the heart of neighbourhoods and villages. Typically seen as a friendly social hub, they could also be portrayed as dark or explosive, as in Dutch novelist Tim Krabb's *The Golden Egg* (1984) or Alfred Hitchcock's film *The Birds* (1963).

Texaco gas stations were conceived in the 1930s as a kit of parts, their designs based on Golden Section proportions by pioneer of industrial design Walter Dorwin Teague. They represent an architecture neatly attuned to the mass-produced product they served.

Another automotive accretion was the drive-in movie theatre, as the film and motor industries developed in parallel. Viewing films in the car shared the advantages of drive-in dining, and the cinema constituted a similar tributary of the road, conceived as a sculpted car park with its tarmac surface contoured in waves radiating from a large projection screen with ranked cars ramped, nose up, towards the picture for unobstructed views. An entrepreneur in New Jersey, Richard Hollingshead, patented the standard form of drive-in cinema in 1933. His original design employed loudspeakers strategically placed throughout the parking area, but in 1940 the electronics company RCA began manufacturing small individual speakers, with adjustable volume. These were located on stanchions next to each parking bay and would attach to the driver's window, greatly improving the quality of the sound.

Service stations themselves sometimes transcend the mundane to become magical architectural features of the urban and suburban streetscape. William Pereira and Gin Wong's elegant roof structure, intended for LAX airport in 1963, was used instead to shelter the forecourt of this Beverley Hills Unocal 76 station, where it became a much-admired landmark.

Such facilities defined the car as a physical element of the entertainment industry. Its specifications – length, height, ground clearance, turning circle – dictated the detailed design of the drive-in cinema, as it did that of the drive-in service window. It liberated families with small children from the need for babysitters; young dating couples enjoyed a privacy that was lacking in their family homes; and friends could talk and joke during the film without disturbing other viewers. Yet the drive-in film was a seasonal enterprise in some climates during its heyday from the late 1940s to the 1960s. It was killed finally by the development of home entertainment systems. However, the enjoyment of watching films in the car continues in the digital age with the development of miniature flat-screen displays mounted in the car's seat backs for the entertainment of rear-seat passengers. With the addition of head-phones, such devices offer a completely private cinematic experience for each passenger. Among rare survivors of the drive-in era, the

The parallel trajectory of commercial film and the car is the subject of Roger Welch's elegiac installation of twigs, bamboo, twine and cinema trailers, representing a 1959 Cadillac at a drive-in movie theatre. The work was shown at the Whitney Museum in 1982 and is now in the Guggenheim collection.

Mission Tiki Drive-in Cinema in Montclair, California, boasts four screens with digital projection from a panoptic booth atop the food concession and sound broadcast directly to the FM radios of viewers' cars.

Other drive-in facilities that became popular in various parts of the world include drive-in banking, employing a cashpoint or a clerk seated at a window in the exterior wall of a bank building, positioned at an appropriate height for a driver to access from the seat of an 'average' car. That standard deviation proved increasingly problematic as the dimensions of cars became significantly more variable in the late twentieth century; the difference in height between such popular cars as the Mercedes SLK roadster and the Toyota Land Cruiser was approximately 780 mm (30½ in.), placing drivers at significantly differing heights.

The relationship between the dimensions of the car and the dimensions of the structures that serve it become critical at the drive-in window. Kodak Fotomat, 1974.

In Australia, drive-in 'bottle shops' selling alcoholic drinks became an established feature of retailing. Drive-in pharmacies also proved popular in the USA, where more than 3,000 were in operation in the year 2000. Australia followed, and Britain's leading chemist, Boots, opened its first drive-through in a former McDonalds restaurant in 2008, aiming to fulfil prescriptions in two minutes while customers waited behind the wheel with the motor running. The initiative was intended to help mothers with children strapped into car seats, customers with mobility problems and commuters in a hurry.

Like the drive-in cinema, drive-in churches were established most commonly in places with sunny climates and dedicated motoring parishioners, but also in less gentle climates such as Portrush, Northern Ireland, where the drive-in church became a fixture of Sunday worship. As in Portrush, many drive-in churches made daytime use of a drive-in cinema, catering for people with small children, invalids and worshippers who wanted to attend a service on the way to the golf course or beach. In Florida, outdoor churches flourished because attending Mass in the car avoided the need for worshippers to dress formally, and 'parking spaces were often filled with cars carrying surfboards and golf clubs.'[31] Such facilities confirmed the car as a new type of contemplative space, a private alternative to the church hall. Some drive-through churches offer a quick prayer with a minister via a confessional window. Drive-in wedding chapels prosper in such locations as Las Vegas and Reno, Nevada, where a couple can be divorced or married, or both, without leaving their car.

The car itself was the subject of a proposed drive-in museum planned in 2009 by the Italian architect Francesco Gatti, whose Nanjing Automobile Museum project for China would enable visitors to view the collection from their own cars en route through the ramped building to park on the roof, and then to inspect exhibits more closely on foot as they descended along a spiral route, a system also reminiscent of Wright's Guggenheim Museum in New York.[32] Similarly, in an underground parking garage in Utrecht, the Drive-in Museum Woerden houses a collection of archaeological artefacts dating from Roman times, arranged to be viewed from the visitor's car while descending through the ramped structure, while above ground galleries contain further Roman exhibits, to be inspected on foot.

Similar to Germany's Bertha Benz Memorial Route, the Lincoln Highway Heritage Corridor opened in the USA in 2004 as a highway 'experience', paying homage to the first coast-to-coast road across North America and transforming a 322-km (200-mile) stretch of the highway into a linear open-air museum with interpretation stops along its length, drawing the motorists' attention to sites of architectural or historic interest, and interpreting the history of the road in a coordinated narrative. As the automotive infrastructure ages, such reverential treatment of historically significant highways may become increasingly common. The southwest stretch of US Route 66 awaits a comparable memorialization, given its rich and colourful role in automotive history and legend.

The car at home

If the production line is the birthplace of most cars and the public road is their natural habitat, then the private driveway and domestic garage are where they merge with the home. In the early days of motoring, the car occupied the stables of the rich, where their horses and carriages were traditionally kept when not in use and where the footman or chauffeur might live, in constant attendance, prepared to 'bring the car around' at any hour. However, the desire of motorists from all social classes to drive themselves, and the rise of suburban living, led to the design of houses that incorporated the garage.

That dedicated motorist, Frank Lloyd Wright, pioneered the inclusion of the car in the design of his later Prairie Style houses in the suburbs of Chicago. He designed the Frederick Robie House (1908–10) for a young engineer and manufacturer of sewing-machine parts, bicycles and motorcycles, who was branching into car design with his prototype Robie Cycle Car of 1906–7. This belonged to a class of light, inexpensive vehicles (also called 'voiturettes' or 'quadricycles') that were popular into the 1920s and anticipated later high-production small cars such as the Austin Seven and the Peugeot Bébé.[33] By 1914 Robie had incorporated the Robie Motor Car Company and refined his prototype vehicle into a sleek machine intended for production in Pennsylvania and England, although the venture foundered.[34] His house, the most important of Wright's domestic designs before the First World War, was built in Oak Park, a railway suburb of Chicago. Frederick Robie and his wife, one of the first women in Illinois to obtain a driver's licence, were both enthusiastic motorists, and so Wright included in

The Robie Cycle Car prototype was an elegant version of an auto type conceived to democratize motoring in its first decades. However, it resided with other grander cars in the triple garage of Frederick C. Robie's house, Oak Park, Illinois, designed in 1909 by that other early gearhead, Frank Lloyd Wright.

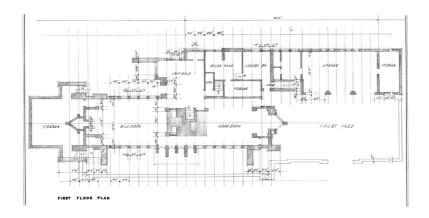

FIRST FLOOR PLAN

the ground-floor plan a three-car garage with a mechanic's pit. The Wright historian Daniel Carson Bruechert wrote:

> It is due directly to Robie's interest in mechanical endeavours that Wright elected to use an attached garage, rather than the typical stable-styled garage, to store Robie's cars. The Robie House brought the 'garage inside the house' for the first time, as the earliest documented use of an attached garage.[35]

At the same time Wright added a garage to his own home and studio near by. He included underground fuel tanks and a fuel pump for each of the three parking bays, as petrol stations were still rare in the suburbs of Chicago.

By the 1930s, when Wright conceived his Broadacre City proposal for an ideal suburban living and working environment based on the car as the primary means of mobility, he also reconsidered the car's domestic accommodation and began designing a more informal and economical space for it in the simply constructed, low-cost 'Usonian' homes he envisioned for the project. Bruechert noted:

The groundplan of the Robie House shows the 'front door' tucked away at the rear of the house while the walled and gated courtyard leading to the garages becomes the real main entrance.

'Wright proposes the eradication of the garage and is credited with creating the term "carport". A carport will do, with liberal overhead shelter and walls on two sides.'[36] Bruechert also pointed out that the carport itself evolved as Wright developed the Usonian house over more than twenty years. Its simplest form is seen in Wright's first house for Herbert and Katherine Jacobs, built in 1940 near Madison, Wisconsin. Here, the building's cantilevered roof simply projects over the end wall of the building far enough to shelter the car.

Another early Modernist architect who conspicuously incorporated the car, its specifications and its ritual activities into his house designs was Le Corbusier. This Swiss architect, famous for declaring that 'the house is a machine for living in', cited the car as a model for a new architecture in his theoretical writings of the 1920s. When in 1929 he designed a weekend house outside Paris for a wealthy client, Madame Savoye, the turning circle of his own Voisin C14 Lumineuse of 1928 provided the dimensions for the sweep of the driveway and for the radius curve of the ground-floor plan, which included a large reception hall, servants' rooms and a three-car garage, all sheltered by the overhanging square of the floor above. In the grand foyer next to the garage, he featured an elegant ceramic handbasin, raised on a pedestal like a piece of sculpture, acknowledging that driving was a dirty business at the time and asserting the perfect hygiene of the house where it met the car.

Whereas Wright and Le Corbusier promoted the car to the A-list of modern elements within the houses they designed, alongside central heating and fitted kitchens, a younger generation of architects and ordinary house-builders confirmed it aesthetically as *the* significant element of the post-war suburban house, especially in the USA, where the private car quickly became the only convenient means of reaching new, far-flung suburban communities. The

garage moved to the front, where porches had previously reigned, some becoming multi-purpose spaces used as home workshops or as practice studios for 'garage bands'. If sufficient land were available between the street and the garage door, a broad driveway would provide a place to park and display the resident's vehicles.

In the warm, dry climate of southern California during the 1950s, Craig Ellwood, John Lautner, Pierre Koenig and other modernist architects developed the notion of Wright's carport to dramatize the presence of the car and to present it as a piece of decorative art within the spare machine aesthetic of their rectilinear, open-plan, glass-walled houses. In their hands, the sculpted car body exhibited the essence of the relaxed, mobile California lifestyle. Transparent walls provided views of the car from both outside and inside the house, as

A 'Loewy Studebaker' displayed on the driveway at the front of a suburban American home, 1953.

in Koenig's Bailey House of 1958, lending it a fetishistic quality – that object of desire, never out of sight.

In suburban neighbourhoods from Melbourne to Munich, the grounds of homes were landscaped and paved to optimize the display of cars, signifying the status of the resident motorists. Increasingly prominent two- and three-car garages, equipped with electric remote-control doors, became the main entrance to the home despite the continued presence of a 'front door', which was relegated to a largely symbolic function.

In places where land was at a premium, ingenious solutions to residential parking became necessary. The urban transportation planner Scott Silsdorf described the regulations controlling private parking spaces in the Japanese city where he lived:

> One of the many steps required to register a vehicle in Japan is to prove that there is parking available for it off-street . . . To demonstrate the availability of parking, each residence has a certificate indicating the length, width and height of the off-street parking spot. (I can't really call these 'driveways' as we do in the US, because most of these spots are barely larger than the vehicle – and in fact, all Japanese cars' side-view mirrors either fold in automatically or manually to provide a few extra centimetres from an adjacent wall or column.) The local police station verifies the parking spot dimensions, receives a small fee, and issues you a sticker.[37]

Silsdorf recorded various ways of accommodating cars on very small plots of land in his neighbourhood of Yokosuka. These included tandem parking and the use of driveway lifts to stack two cars within a single parking bay. He also warned North Americans about the effect of uncontrolled parking on the cost of urban development and design, on car dependency and on urban sprawl.

His argument counters the unquestioned pre-eminence of the automobile in the world's leading car culture, a privileged position that it also gained in those other motoring nations with a relative abundance of land to population.[38]

The writer and academic Alison Lurie described the hegemony of the car in Los Angeles, which could stand for car-centred communities anywhere in the world. In *The Nowhere City* (1965), she described the cars of Los Angeles as

> a race apart, almost alive. The city was full of their hotels and beauty shops, their restaurants and nursing homes – immense, expensive structures where they could be parked or polished, fed or cured of their injuries . . . few people were visible. The automobiles outnumbered them ten to one. Paul imagined a tale in which it would be gradually revealed that these automobiles were the real inhabitants of the city, a secret master race which only kept human beings for its own greater convenience, or as pets.[39]

Suburb and newurb

Many suburbs pride themselves on the *absence* of such public pedestrian amenities as pavements and buses. Lawns stretch to the road with no intervening pedestrian zone. Homes are connected to the larger world only by ribbons of asphalt: winding avenues, boulevards, highways, parkways and motorways. All residents arrive by private car, as journeys are often too long to make taxis a realistic daily alternative. And only domestic workers come by bus.

With local variations, that 'ideal' scenario of suburban living spread to all motoring nations and throughout their class structures. Yet by the end of the twentieth century, when problems of car dependency began to disturb the public consciousness and seep into the minds of planners and environmentalists, the suburban model of living began to lose its lustre. Increasing traffic congestion and intensified regulation dimmed the pleasure of those drives required to carry out every aspect of daily life, although this remained delicately balanced with the secret pleasure of private automotive space.

Suburban sprawl has gradually extended to newly car-centred parts of the world. With the development of motoring in China after the turn of the millennium, the country's road network expanded rapidly, but few support facilities were provided on main routes and especially in the countryside. Refuelling stations, garage mechanics and comforts such as toilets for women are sparse, requiring Chinese drivers to plan their trips in detail before setting out. Their experience in the 2000s was comparable in many ways to that of French motorists 100 years earlier. And the development of suburban housing and decentralized shopping facilities around the country's burgeoning industrial cities mimics the growth of suburbs around Chicago at the turn of the twentieth century, when Wright built his Prairie Houses. The establishment of safety consciousness also remains haphazard in China, as it was in Europe and North America in the early years of the car. Drivers using new motorways have little experience of the road and, as a privileged elite, pay scant attention to those regulations that are in place. Yet motoring is a national priority, as it was in older car cultures in earlier times.

The construction of highways in the USA was a major element of Franklin D. Roosevelt's New Deal recovery programme during the Great Depression of the 1930s. Then, during the presidency of Dwight D. Eisenhower (1952–60), a lifelong motoring enthusiast, encouraging women to drive and to buy cars was seen as an important tool of economic growth, its two principal elements being the automatic car and the superhighway. The design of a national motorway network with wide traffic lanes, smooth surfacing, clear directional signage, elimination of traffic lights, one-way entry and exit ramps, and bright overhead lighting after dark was necessary to make driving easy and pleasant even for timid or lazy new motorists.

Governments who pioneered the construction of motorways also considered the military potential of a modern motorway network, although these roads have not notably been used for such purposes. It is commonly thought that the autobahn network built under the National Socialists in Germany was central to their strategy for European military domination, whereas the majority of troops and military goods moved during the Second World War were actually carried by rail or horse. But Adolf Hitler liked fast cars, and flashed all over his new highways in powerful, impressive Mercedes. To put the German people on somewhat smaller wheels, he commissioned the KdF Wagen (German for Strength through Joy Car), which became the Mark I Volkswagen, designed specifically for travel over the smooth surfaces of the autobahn at continuous high speeds. He thus created an outstanding example of a government introducing into an otherwise market-driven industry a non-market-driven car, which, as we have seen, eventually dominated that market.[40]

Motorways became a ubiquitous element of the built environment in many nations, and their impact is the subject of fierce debate. Yet there is little argument that they are one of the most prominent features of the modern physical world, and they provide the primary infrastructure for our mobile lives. While air-traffic patterns and shipping lanes are ephemeral, motorways are monumental, and from the perspective they offer us, we see and understand the world in a specifically automotive way. They take us about independently, and they relegated communal, scheduled forms of transportation during their period of ascendancy. But as their wider impact has come under increasing scrutiny, planners in various parts of the world have proposed alternative forms of settlement accessible by public transport.

New Urbanism, also known as the Urban Village Movement, is an approach to planning intended to reduce dependency on the car and to re-create a sense of community. In 2001 the charter of the North American Congress for New Urbanism declared as its policy principles: 'Neighbourhoods should be diverse in use and population; communities should be designed for the pedestrian and transit as well as the car.'[41]

Such revisionist proposals aimed to curb the ubiquity of the car in the spaces of everyday life. They reduced the prominence of the road and consigned the car to a less central position in the domestic and community landscape. In New Urban villages, the car is not displayed in front of homes, but is instead parked in a block behind the houses, which face streets that are friendlier to pedestrians and cyclists, where children can play, and where naturally occurring observation of the public realm from the private home can enhance security.

One of the best-known examples of New Urbanism is Seaside, Florida, because of its use as the morally ambiguous setting for the film *The Truman Show* (1998), directed by Peter Weir. Seaside was designed to echo the appearance of an old-fashioned Florida beach town, composed of timber-clad houses in a variety of vernacular and postmodernist styles, and planned by the founders of New Urbanism, Andrés Duany and Elizabeth Plater-Zyberk. Its primary aim was to generate a healthier community than that of the typical motorway suburb. Every building was uniquely designed, many by leading international architects associated with the postmodernist movement, including Robert A. M. Stern, Aldo Rossi and Léon Krier. Perhaps because of the elaborate architecture and generally wealthy population, Seaside projects an atmosphere of unreality that is typical of such relatively car-free master-planned communities.

In England in the 1980s, Krier planned Poundbury, a new suburb of Dorchester, supported by the Prince of Wales and his Duchy of Cornwall estate. With the appearance of a traditional high-density stone-built English village, the town aimed to be orientated towards pedestrians rather than cars, which are accommodated inconspicuously. Yet Poundbury's wealthy residents, like those at Seaside, continue to prefer cars for most journeys except those made very locally on foot. Similar New Urbanist communities have been built in the Netherlands, Sweden, Belize, South Africa and Canada, all promoting the virtues of traditional high-density towns connected to nearby cities by fast trains and relegating the car to a more recreational role.

The rules of New Urbanist planning vary, but all aim to reduce the car's importance in town life. Defining points of the urban village relating to the car were the dispersal of traffic through a dense network of narrow, pedestrian- and cycle-friendly streets, and the placement of parking spaces and garages at the rear of houses or flats, accessed from alleys. Such principles attempted to reinstate the road as a public space shared among all those moving about the town by every mode of travel. Most of all, they directly overturn the arrangement of the twentieth-century automobile suburb by eliminating the privilege of the car and undermining the pride in car ownership signified by its ubiquitous, prominent display.

On a recent visit to the Brandevoort district of Helmond in the southern Netherlands, I saw the results of a New Urbanist town with a master plan designed by Rob Krier, brother of Léon, and built in collaboration with the architects Paul van Beek and Christoph Kohl. The aim there was to create a dense town fabric with a traditional architectural character, connected to the city centres of

Eindhoven and Helmond by fast train lines. Yet despite its admirable aim and intelligent execution, and the inconspicuous accommodation of cars within the estate, the generally empty streets and squares lack the vitality and animation of a modern town, instead generating the atmosphere of a theme park.

<table>
<tr><td>**5**</td><td># Chaos</td></tr>
</table>

Speed demons

During the 1970s and '80s, international sports-car rallying adopted a particularly frenzied character that attracted a passionate following. In those years major car manufacturers competing in the Federation Internationale de l'Automobile (FIA) World Rally Championships were allowed to enter cars unlimited in weight and horsepower. Those cars in a new rally class, designated Group B, boasted as much as 500 hp and were built on ultra-lightweight tubular frames sheathed in Kevlar bodywork typically styled to bear a family resemblance to the manufacturers' 'hot hatchbacks', and to promote them. Although rally cars were traditionally standard automobiles, stripped down and hopped up, most of these cars were constructed without many major components from a genuine production car. And while power and speed increased dramatically, the protection of the driver was minimal, as safety consciousness had not yet penetrated the daredevil culture of motorsport.

The most successful Group B cars were the brutish Lancia Monte Carlo and Lancia Delta S4, the sure-footed Audi Quattros designed by Roland Gumpert, and the Jean Todt-designed Peugeot 205s, which revitalized the image of that brand and revived its sales in the 1980s. As the old adage goes, 'race on Sunday, sell on Monday.' Spectators

loved these cars and revelled in the unregulated atmosphere of the race and its absence of crowd control along the routes, which varied from winding stretches of asphalt to gravel tracks, often deep in mud, snow and ice. With no barriers, unrestrained and unruly spectators performed daredevil feats in the road to get the best view of passing cars and to feel involved. The result was mayhem, as in the Rally de Portugal of 1986, when the Portuguese champion Joaquim Santos, driving a 420-hp Ford Escort RS200, swerved to avoid fans in the road and careered into a crowd of spectators, killing three and injuring 32. Following the fiery deaths of two drivers later that season in the Tour de Corse rally, FIA officials finally took action and banned Group B racing in Europe.

This chapter discusses the ways in which cars designed for a variety of purposes have achieved historic reputations or notoriety in that twilight zone between order and chaos, on roads and in uncharted wilderness. Their exploits have produced thrills, brought about disorder and destruction, attempted to restore calm, or provided safety and comfort in extreme situations of weather, war or

The Lancia 037 was a so-called 'silhouette racer', resembling the Lancia Montecarlo/ Scorpion road car, although nearly all its mechanical parts and kevlar body panels were significantly different. Its purpose was to create a direct link in the public mind between track success and the manufacturer's production cars.

competition. The acceptance of carnage as part of motor sport was a racing tradition that dates back to the nineteenth century. The earliest great road races were French intercity competitions, beginning with the Paris–Bordeaux–Paris event of 1895. This began a series of similar races culminating with the Paris–Madrid event of 1903, notorious for its six fatalities: competitor Marcel Renault, four spectators and a race marshal. Despite, or perhaps because of, the danger, these and other early races were widely celebrated and memorialized, as in the series of tiled depictions decorating the Art Nouveau Michelin House, opened in 1911 as the tyre company's London headquarters. Those hand-painted ceramic panels, created by the Parisian tile maker Gilardoni, portray early racing cars taking part in those precursors to the French Grand Prix series, which began officially in 1906. Yet none show the unruly crowds of drunken spectators who contributed to the grisly crashes that occurred in those earliest races, just as they did in the Portugal rally

This hand-decorated Art Nouveau ceramic tiled plaque by Gilardoni on London's Michelin House of 1911 depicts Léon Serpollet leaving Nice in the Coupé Rothschild of 1903.

of 1986. The Paris–Madrid event of 1903 was dubbed the 'Race of Death', although the historian Malcolm Jeal argues that such versions of the 'massacre' reflect journalistic hysteria and lack empathy with victims. Nevertheless, that competition established violent death as an integral feature of car racing.[1]

Ninety years later, enthusiasts mourned Group B as a Golden Age of motorsport, but if its ban acknowledged safety as a problem in racing, Group B cars represented a significant investment by manufacturers, and were therefore entered in other competitions, including the Paris–Dakar Rally, one of the wildest off-road race events of all time owing to the harsh terrain through which it passed and the difficulty of navigating the western Sahara before the advent of global positioning systems (GPS). That exportation to Africa (1978–2007) of the race's madness, and the deaths that followed,

Marcel Renault is seen here competing in the notorious Paris-Madrid 'Race of Death' in 1903, shortly before his fatal accident.

eventually raised ethical questions typically overlooked in the macho, cut-throat ethos of car competitions.[2] Although the fascination for this fixture proved stronger than concern for the risks it presented, the extreme Dakar Rally became more problematic because of the effect it had on the poor communities through which it passed. When local spectators were killed, the Islamic fundamentalist group al-Qaeda rejected the rally as a form of 'neo-colonial' foreign 'invasion', which offered little to local communities. Yet the race moved on to South America after 2008, confirming the resilience of extreme motorsport.

Despite popular fascination with the danger of racing, and the generally slow pace of reform, racing cars were progressively made safer for drivers, while the security of spectators at track events has also improved. This was thanks in great part to the efforts of racing drivers, such as the three-time Formula One world champion Jackie Stewart, who doggedly pursued race organizers to tighten rules and establish design criteria that prioritized safety over spectacular risk. Under the regulations of the FIA's Circuits and Safety Department, innovations in Formula racing car design included reinforced survival cells, driver restraints, crumple zones, detachable steering wheels, rear and lateral headrests, fire-resistant fuel tanks and full-face helmets with elastic anchorages to avoid whiplash, among many other improvements. In 2012 the FIA launched a sustain-ability programme, a concept alien to traditional motorsport values and attitudes, and it initiated a Formula E class for electric racers, beginning international competition in 2014.

In addition to specific safety improvements, the great milestones in the evolution of the racing car were technological advances that improved performance in competition. These included the intro-duction of disc brakes in the mid-1950s and the shift from front to rear engines following Jack Brabham's victory in the Formula One

World Championship of 1959 driving the British Cooper T51. The appearance in 1962 of the Lotus T25, with an aluminium monocoque structure designed by the founder of Lotus, Colin Chapman, reconfirmed the virtues of lightness, strength and fine handling over brute power, as did the Edwardian Bugatti Type 10 in 1908. Lotus also initiated increasing reliance on electronic driver assistance with its active suspension system, first used in 1982. Chapman then pioneered the development of 'ground effect' aerodynamics, which helped to glue the car to the road by creating downforce (aerodynamic grip) and increasing stability when cornering. As performance improved, casualties fell. In 1994 Ayrton Senna and Roland Ratzenberger were the last two drivers to die behind the wheel of Formula One cars.

Throughout its history, motor racing was a world of contrasts: heroics and hubris, stunning success against tragic failure, pandemonium versus tight regulation. The racing car embodied both a

The winning Lotus 25s driven by Jim Clark and Graham Hill in the Dutch Grand Prix of 1963 demonstrated the virtues of lightness and fine handling over brute power.

mad craving for the sensation of speed and the most intelligent design for efficiency and safety at the leading edge of automotive technology. Yet the sport's aesthetic of danger and daring was lodged in the popular consciousness as early as 1909, when Filippo Tommaso Marinetti famously wrote:

> The world's magnificence has been enriched by a new beauty: the beauty of speed. A racing car whose hood is adorned with great pipes like serpents of explosive breath – a roaring car that seems to ride on [machine-gun fire] is more beautiful than the *Victory of Samothrace*.[3]

And that sense of beauty accompanies many drivers when they slide behind the wheel of ordinary road cars every day and set off to work or to run errands. The sensation of power underfoot, the urge to feel the G-force of acceleration and the response of the machine to every gear-change or slight turn encourages motorists

Looking like mini-Dymaxion cars, teardrop-shaped, recumbent electric racers start in the 2008 annual World Econo Move endurance competition in Ogata-Mura, Japan.

to treat driving as play, even in a short break from the drudgery of heavy traffic, in poor weather conditions or between closely spaced traffic lights.

Carapace

In contrast with the madness expressed in Marinetti's portrayal of the car, the perception of most motorists is that the automobile body encloses a secure space that is entirely under their control. The family car is a detachable room of the house, as solid as a building, with walls of steel and 'unbreakable' safety glass in the windows. Sophisticated electronic alarms provide deterrents against theft, while deadlocks keep out carjackers.

The toughness of even the smallest mass-produced cars gives their owners a sense of privilege and exemption from the threats facing pedestrians or passengers on public transport, even if that threat is simply the sharing of space with people of a different social status or ethnicity. The private car shields its occupants from contact with potentially unsavoury sights in the diverse neighbourhoods through which it passes, transforming those encounters instead into spectacles. Such an impression of the car recalls Bachelard's comparison of domestic shelter to the mollusc's shell.[4] Bachelard also noted that storms demonstrate the strength of any shelter, while its robustness enables its occupant to appreciate the aesthetic drama of the tempest in safety and comfort. That idea of an interior protected against what lies outside is a central attraction of the car.[5]

The role of the car in dramatic weather is exposed vividly in storm-chasing, the search for any extreme atmospheric activity motivated by thrill-seeking, meteorological research or reportage. The main tools of storm-chasing, which began mainly as a sport in the American Midwest during the 1950s, were initially a car and a camera. With the advent of digital technology, mobile phones, data recorders, GPS and IMAX cameras joined its armoury. From the early days of driving ordinary cars to positions where they could safely observe the behaviour of hurricanes and tornadoes, storm-chasers' growing ambitions required more specialized vehicles to penetrate the heart of violent weather events.

The most robust purpose-built storm-chasing cars are the Tornado Intercept Vehicles 1 and 2 (TIV 1 and TIV 2) developed by the film-maker Sean Casey. Based on a heavy-duty truck chassis armoured with a 3-mm (⅛-in.) steel shell and bullet-resistant windows of tempered glass layered with polycarbonate sheet, the six-wheel-drive TIV 2 was powered by a modified 6.7-litre Cummins turbo-diesel engine capable of propelling the 6,486-kg (14,300-lb) monster

Film-maker Sean Casey's two Tornado Intercept Vehicles were built to chase storms and to film inside tornadoes for his IMAX movies and *Storm Chasers* television series. The vehicles are constantly modified on the basis of experience in severe weather events.

at more than 160 km/h (100 mph). Armoured skirts could be lowered to the ground to protect and stabilize the vehicle, while four hydraulic spikes anchored it to the earth. This level of protection, which allowed storm-chasers to savour the full ferocity of the weather, realizes Bachelard's ideal shelter. But Casey frequently upgrades and modifies his vehicles in response to their performance in the harshest of weathers.

For ordinary motorists living in hot climates, car air conditioning has become an everyday defence against nature. Ever since air-conditioned cars became commonplace in the 1960s, a class of people once dubbed 'the no-sweat set' were able to live without ever feeling the heat outside. From Atlanta to Ahmedabad, the air-conditioned car linked multi-purpose building complexes with homes, to make a seamless internal environment, which was beneficial to the infirm or to newborn infants, but also had a debilitating effect on healthy people, intensifying their reliance on their cars as insulation from relatively normal temperatures.

Such privileged motorists also retreated inside large SUVs. In safe, salubrious neighbourhoods where the defensive function of those cars was almost entirely symbolic, they were disparagingly labelled Toorak Tractors (Melbourne), Chelsea Tractors (London) or Borstraktors ('stock exchange tractors'; Oslo). Their protective image, however, generated a styling fashion that has spread to all sizes of car since the 1990s, partly as a response to our heightened fear of terrorism and urban violence, exacerbated by the increasing economic divide between rich and poor.[6] Examples among smaller models include BMW's Mini Countryman crossover-SUV and Fiat's 500L mini-SUV.

Land Rover's chief designer, Gerry McGovern, amplified that aesthetic of stealth and defence for the Range Rover Evoque SUV of 2011. Its massive substructure, with wide shoulders emphasizing the

car's large wheels, contrasted with the slice of blacked-out windows reminiscent of eye slits in a medieval knight's helmet, providing the driver with equally limited visibility and requiring five exterior cameras to compensate for blind spots. McGovern's design team recognized the Evoque's role as a streetwise, urban mother's runabout, announcing: 'Don't mess with me!'

Mud Plugging, however, is a long established off-road motorsport in the UK, Australia and other countries worldwide. Like those other favourite off-road challenges, Dune Bashing and Rock Crawling, it is subject to the scrutiny of environmentalists and is now offered as a pay by the day driving experience at many motorsport parks, where environmental impact can be controlled.

The mythical life of the SUV is portrayed most clearly in images of would-be adventurers leaving the official matrix of modern roads

Mud Plugging.

to venture into an uncontrolled landscape, detached from the stabilizing influences of work and community. Yet such a sophisticated carapace against the unruliness of nature can blind SUV drivers to the damage they may cause to wilderness and wildlife. Statistics gathered in the millennium year, 2000, counted over 36 million SUVs registered in the USA alone, drawing criticism from environmental pressure groups Greenpeace, Tread Lightly and the Sierra Club over their CO_2 emissions on- or off-road, and their off-road contribution to land erosion, wildlife stress, the loss of species and the degradation of habitat. Those groups promoted the development of trail ethics and encouraged more consistent enforcement against illegal off-road activities, which they compared with the illegal dumping of toxic waste.[7] Yet the emotional security such big, defensive cars offer as family casts a powerful spell and ensures a large and fiercely loyal consumer group.

From Land Rover to CityCar may seem a big step for Man, but the appearance of the first car on the Moon in 1971 was a hugely impressive scientific and technical achievement dramatized by a North American love of motoring and particularly of off-road driving. The nifty Lunar Roving Vehicle (LRV), built for NASA's Apollo space programme in 1971 and 1972, was a 3-m-long (10-ft), 210-kg (460-lb) aluminium-framed quadricycle seating two astronauts conducting experiments in the wider environs of the Lunar Module not easily reached on foot. Built by Boeing and GM's Delco division, the four examples were powered by electric hub motors, one in each of the four steerable wheels, an arrangement that anticipated some of today's most innovative prototypes, such as the MIT CityCar. Like the City Car, the LRV, better known as the 'moon buggy', also folded in half to fit inside the Lunar Module.

Costing $38 million, four LRVs were built, and three went on subsequent Apollo missions to the moon, where they remain, their

two non-rechargeable 36-volt silver-zinc potassium hydroxide batteries dead. The astronaut Harrison Schmitt, who drove an LRV during the *Apollo 17* mission, said: 'Without it, the major scientific discoveries of Apollo 15, 16 and 17 would not have been possible; [neither would] our current understanding of lunar evolution.'[8] But the LRV was also presented to the public in films and photographs as a sports car, a joyride vehicle bouncing over the unfamiliar, dusty lunar surface carrying a pair of spacesuited gearhead astronauts having the time of their lives tossing it around at its top speed of 18.5 km/h (11½ mph). This was truly Top Gear.

Lunar Rovers enabled Apollo astronauts to expand the research area around their landing vehicle and to collect data and samples more quickly and efficiently than they could do on foot. It also provided them ultimate off-road automotive fun on the moon's surface.

Conflict

A somewhat more conventional understanding of off-road capability supported another compelling design imperative in the military build-up to the Second World War, when the US Army identified the need for a light, manoeuvrable, tough and versatile general-purpose reconnaissance car with four-wheel drive. The engineer Karl Probst quickly designed a prototype for the American Bantam Car Company, whose manufacturing capability proved too small to produce the vehicles in the required numbers. Willys-Overland and Ford therefore joined Bantam to perfect the design and manufacture the car. Although the origin of the name 'jeep' has been disputed throughout its history, the Willys-Overland company was finally granted the trademark brand name Jeep in 1950.

In the course of its war duties, the quarter-ton jeep proved its capabilities over the harshest terrain, from African desert to bulldozed tracks in the Pacific islands. Jeeps performed as troop carriers and as attack units armed with a .50 calibre gun. Equipped with radio, they could unobtrusively approach enemy lines as forward command posts; and fitted with flanged wheels, jeeps became light railway locomotives. The car had a macho reputation, but many women also served as jeep drivers for organizations including the Mechanized Transport Corps and the Women's Transport Service.

Later jeeps were built internationally under licence by manufacturers including Hotchkiss in France, Beijing Jeep Corporation of China and Toyota in Japan. Meanwhile, Willys and other American manufacturers continued producing military jeeps until the 1980s, when they were finally replaced by their larger offspring, the Humvee. By the end of the Second World War, the jeep had attained a heroic status and created a popular thirst for a no-nonsense, go-anywhere civilian vehicle that was fun to drive. Willys developed

two civilian versions, initially for agricultural use, the four-wheel-drive CJ-2A and a Utility Truck, both suitable for travel on unmade roads and over open country.

The most significant variant, however, was the Willys Utility Wagon announced in 1946. Ironically, it was styled by 'the prince of planned obsolescence', Brooks Stevens, who retained in its proportions, character and details a strong family resemblance to the wartime jeep.[9] This was the original mass-produced station wagon, designed as a family car, with an all-steel body (some painted to simulate wood) at a time when other station wagons were still built with genuine coachbuilt wooden bodies. From 1948 it came with four-wheel drive, making it the mother of all SUVs. Stevens also styled the Jeepster, an exotic sports phaeton with detachable side-curtains. The Jeepster anticipated later four-wheel-drive sports cars such as the Ford Bronco or Suzuki's Vitara.[10]

The mother of all SUVs was the Willys Jeep Utility Wagon, styled by Brooks Stevens and announced in 1946.

The purposeful design of the original Willys Jeep earned it unique adulation when viewed primarily as an aesthetic object or as an exemplar of functionalism by designers, critics and, significantly, the Museum of Modern Art in New York, where – as we have seen – the curator Arthur Drexler selected it for his first car exhibition, *8 Automobiles* (1951). Yet no matter how stylish its SUV descendants became over time, they all carried its military DNA.

Other special vehicles also crossed over between military and civilian roles. Marshal Chang Tso-lin was a luxury-loving governor general of Manchuria during the Warlord Era in China (1916–28). In that dangerous political climate he enjoyed the protection of an armoured Packard Twin-Six limousine, engineered in Detroit by Jesse Vincent. Chang's car was fitted with an armoured body by Brooks-Ostruck of New York and armed with a cowl-mounted machine gun, a rear-facing gun port and grab-handles for outriding guards. For the Russian tzar Nicholas II, Packard built a similar

Tzar Nicholas II's Auto-Sled was a Packard Twin Six modified with a specially designed Kegresse caterpillar mechanism replacing the rear wheels for traction over open country. Its front wheels were fitted with skis for winter running.

Twin-Six with touring body by Fisher, further modified by the French military engineer Adolphe Kégresse, who designed the original 'Kégresse track' for that car. This lightweight caterpillar mechanism replaced the rear wheels, enabling the vehicle to traverse the Russian countryside, where there were few paved roads; with skis attached to the front wheels for winter running, it was described as an 'auto-sled' and goes down in history as one of the earliest off-road luxury cars.

Although neither Chang's nor the tzar's specialized cars could protect them from being killed in the political upheaval of their time, such vehicles anticipated later cars constructed for VIPs requiring high-level security, whether travelling inconspicuously or in parades.

The bitter end for open-topped parade cars. John and Jacqueline Kennedy on their last ride together, the Lincoln approaching Dealey Plaza in Dallas on 22 November 1963.

The performance of such vehicles was thrown into stark relief in 1963, when President John F. Kennedy was assassinated while processing through Dallas, Texas, in his stretched Lincoln Continental. That car had been developed from a standard Lincoln 74A four-door convertible of 1961 by the specialist coachbuilder Hess & Eisenhardt of Cincinnati.

Known by the US Secret Service code name SS-100-X, Kennedy's Lincoln was lengthened and fitted with a variety of security features specified by the Secret Service, and highly styled to create the most glamorous parade car of the time. Although a transparent Plexiglas 'bubble top' was available mainly for weather protection, Kennedy liked open cars and the full public exposure they allowed. The rear seat could be raised by 25 cm (10 in.) to allow the President to be seen better by the public, and there was also a hand grip enabling him to stand. The lethal result was seen through the media by millions of spectators around the world. Following the assassination, that historic car was quickly returned by the Secret Service to Hess & Eisenhardt, stripped down to its chassis and rebuilt with heavy armour plating, a permanent, bulletproof roof and 2.5-cm-thick (1-in.) window glass; it was used until 1977 by a succession of presidents before retiring to the Henry Ford Museum. Later presidential cars – fundamentally different in design from such modified production convertibles – were closed cars designed to resist far more aggressive threats in the age of global terrorism.

Such was the bulletproof and blast-resistant Cadillac limousine (2005) ordered for the second inauguration of George W. Bush, built by the specialist security coachbuilder Centigon, the corporate descendent of Hess & Eisenhardt, on a lengthened GM four-wheel-drive truck platform. Designated 'Cadillac One', the car's special equipment included night vision and run-flat tyres that ensured the car would not be immobilized by gunfire. The floor-pan

Bunkers on wheels, US presidential limousines are now a species of car devoted to defence against any sort of attack, from a lone gunman to a full military chemical assault. Yet they are styled to resemble urbane, branded limousines. President Barack Obama works in the rear passenger compartment of 'The Beast', also known as 'Cadillac One'. Considering the car's enormous exterior, its cabin appears small due to the thickness of its body armour.

was armoured against bombs, the interior was hermetically sealed against chemical attack, and it carried a bank of the President's blood type. The vehicle's communications devices could transform it into a military command post in the event of a full-scale attack upon the commander-in-chief. At the time, a safer mobile carapace could not be constructed, and it became the model for the subsequent presidential fleet.

By using many of the Cadillac brand's familiar visual devices, and through a carefully controlled set of proportions, the designers of the car's body approximated the appearance of a conventional limousine with sleek, urbane lines; but the enormous scale of this behemoth told a different story, earning it the Secret Service nickname 'The Beast'. In this sense, the car was conceptually akin to the Group B rally cars of the 1980s, highly specialized vehicles thinly disguised, using branding cues, as variants of familiar production cars.

Military armoured cars began to be developed in the days of the horseless carriage. The French manufacturer Charron, Girardot

EN L'AN 2000

At the start of the automobile age, potential military uses of motorized vehicles were already eagerly anticipated, as seen in this cartoon looking ahead to the year 2000, but showing the hardware of 1900.

& Voigt (CGV) constructed its first armoured vehicle, the 40-hp *Automitrailleuse blindée* in 1902, designed for the Imperial Russian war ministry by the Georgian engineer Mikheil Nakashidze.[11] By 1904–5 Charron had begun limited production of an improved design that *Popular Mechanics* magazine described as 'an early step in the practical adaptation of the motor car to the purposes of warfare'.[12]

The magazine enthused over the features of the first twelve vehicles built for the Russian army: Hotchkiss gun projecting from a rotating roof turret; portable steel bridges enabling the car to cross trenches; bulletproof skin; wooden wheels covered with steel plates; early run-flat tyres; and an automatic engine starter operated from inside the car. It reported:

> Driver and gunner have a good outlook on the enemy through loopholes in the turret and front of the car . . . [which] is capable of making 30 miles [nearly 50 km] an hour . . . The facility with which it can be handled, backward, forward, up hills and across ditches, is astonishing.[13]

Armoured cars, soon used in the First World War, closely followed Nakashidze's design for CGV. Minerva in Belgium, Mors and Peugeot in France, and Lanchester, Austin and Rolls-Royce in England all built them, as did Fiat and Lancia in Italy. The Belgians used them effectively in their Auto-mounted Machine-Gun Corps (ACM), undertaking aircraft reconnaissance, intelligence-gathering and infantry attacks. Typically of the attitude to cars and motorists in Europe at the time, this was deemed an elite corps, billeted handsomely in Paris. The leading Paris couturier Jeanne Paquin designed their dress uniforms with caps, jackets and trousers of black cloth and battle uniforms immaculately tailored in black leather.

The Germans used similar cars made by Daimler, who had been experimenting with armoured fighting vehicles since 1904, when

Paul Daimler, eldest son of Gottlieb and an officer of the Joint German Imperial and Austro-Hungarian Army, designed and built a prototype four-wheel-drive car, fully armoured with 4-mm ($\frac{1}{8}$-in.) steel plates, powered by a four-cylinder 35/40-hp engine. Although this car was even more innovative than the CGV, it followed a similar pattern, demonstrating that the development of military vehicles was following parallel trajectories in the major automotive and military nations. Despite its advanced features, smoothly rounded surfaces, armoured radiator and hemispheric dome over the gun turret, Daimler's design never went into production, as traditionalists quipped that such noisy machines would frighten the cavalry horses. Yet this sophisticated experiment provided a pattern for later German armoured cars.[14]

The American development of the armoured motorized fighting unit was spearheaded by Colonel Royal Page Davidson. In 1915 he displayed a fully armoured car and seven specialized support vehicles at the Panama-Pacific Exposition in San Francisco. The formation of such a fleet was significant as a tactical model for a fully mechanized and technologically equipped automotive combat unit. Davidson placed the armoured car at the heart of a column of vehicles that included reconnaissance scout cars fitted with the latest observation instruments, a radio communications car, a field kitchen vehicle, an ambulance equipped with an X-ray machine and operating table, an anti-aircraft car and a supply vehicle.

The so-called Davidson-Cadillac armoured car followed the CGV pattern, but was also comparable with armoured vehicles built in England for the Royal Navy Air Service, which became active at the outbreak of war in 1914. Davidson's car had a complete carapace of 7-mm ($\frac{1}{4}$-in.) steel plating with radiator doors that were adjustable from inside. With its slow-revving eight-cylinder Cadillac engine, the car was faster and easier to restart after stalling than its

British equivalent, the Rolls-Royce, which nevertheless became a uniquely important war machine.

Light armoured vehicles (LAVs) continue to play a role in military action and peacekeeping. Those sent to Iraq and Afghanistan by British and allied armies since the 1990s transport personnel through extreme landscapes and unspeakable danger. Cars such as the latest North American-built Humvees and the Land Rover-Ricardo Snatch are so heavily armoured that when they go over an improvised explosive device (IED), reportedly, the car behind in the convoy has to radio the information to the crew ahead. The Canadian War Artist and poet Suzanne Steele described those armoured cars in which she rode during her stays in Afghanistan as a womb: 'in a number of my poems I refer to the Light Armoured Vehicle as "Mother LAV" because when one is squished inside it along with 7 or 8 men all of us wearing 30lbs of protective armour, one feels like an octuplet . . . protected and cosy.'[15] In her poem 'So Beautiful', Steele

In 1904–5 Charron Girardot & Voight constructed this armoured car designed for the Imperial Russian war ministry by the Georgian engineer Mikheil Nakashidze. It was described then as 'an early step in the practical adaptation of the motor car to the purposes of warfare'.

refers to such a ride, 'mother LAV humming', 'brothers sleeping upright in the belly of the LAV, shoulder-to-shoulder, knee-to-knee crammed'.[16]

Civilian commercial cars also achieved long-lasting heroic status during the First World War as troop transporters. In September 1914, when German forces had massed outside Paris and the Allied Sixth Army was desperate for reinforcements, the military governor of Paris ordered 10,000 infantrymen to the front, along the River Marne. Lacking sufficient dedicated transport vehicles, he conscripted 600 Paris taxis to ferry at least 6,000 soldiers into battle. The Renault Type AG1 FL (1905–10), designed by Louis Renault, was the first motorized taxi to be produced in France in large numbers. Great processions of those stately '*taxis de la Marne*' were hailed as a symbol of French national resolve and popular unity, bringing a semblance of order and security to the most hostile of situations by maintaining mobility when it was most needed.

Cars and cops

As Paris basked under beautiful spring skies in May 1968, revolution was brewing in French schools, universities and factories. On the night of 10 May protests became riots at 60 locations in the Latin Quarter, where students constructed barricades of pilfered building materials, cobbles torn from the roads, and cars, battered, overturned, many set alight. A reporter for *Le Monde* described the scene:

> Almost everywhere in this chaos . . . one can see the carcasses of burned cars, vehicles with their windscreens smashed to smithereens – with bodies crumpled when they were piled up in constructing the barricades. From this view the rue Pierre and Marie Curie and the rue Gay-Lussac offer a particularly sorry spectacle: spread across the street, sometimes

lying on their sides or overturned on their roofs, the carcasses are scattered about in their dozens.[17]

Before the end of the month, the pitched battles of the Latin Quarter had provoked a general strike by more than 10 million French workers, led by car workers at Renault. President Charles de Gaulle secretly left the country, and Prime Minister Georges Pompidou eventually resigned. In the world's first motoring nation, the car became a key symbol of civil disorder and social discontent.

'La barricade ferme la rue mais ouvre la voie' ('Barricades close the street but open the way'), declared the philosopher and Marxist theorist Guy Debord in his pamphlet 'Report on the Construction of Situations', the founding manifesto of the Situationist International (SI), published in June 1957. The SI was an international revolutionary group inspired by the European artistic avant-garde. In his book *The Society of the Spectacle* (1967), Debord portrayed capitalism and its commodity culture as the ruin of human experience communicated through manufactured 'spectacle', its key elements the private car and the media. The SI was seen as a stimulus for the riots of 1968, and cars were its ideologically pregnant material.

Images of overturned automobiles, the most easily accessible and readily identifiable components of the Parisian barricades, quickly became emblematic of the consumer society the students wanted to tear down. Just as the rioters had absorbed it into their armoury for civil disobedience, Debord targeted the car as a significant factor in those problems he saw afflicting modern urban culture. He wrote: 'It is not a matter of opposing the automobile as an evil in itself. It is its extreme concentration in the cities that has led to the negation of its function. Urbanism should certainly not ignore the automobile, but even less should it accept it as a central theme.'[18]

Designating the car as a *theme* rather than as a tool, Debord maintained, underscored its futility as a primary factor in urban planning: 'To want to redesign architecture to accord with the needs of the present massive and parasitical existence of private automobiles reflects the most unrealistic misapprehension of where the real problems lie.'[19] In the barricades, a new urban architecture was formed from the very material central to Debord's 'problems'. Deprived of its status and useful function, the appropriated car was transformed into a building block, along with cobbles and cafe chairs, in an instantaneous architecture of protest and confrontation.

The DS Citroëns, Renault 4s, Dauphines and Simcas forming the barricades were the same makes and models that the French police used at the time. Those police cars were supported by the ubiquitous Citroën Camionette H-series vans, with corrugated-metal bodies by Currus, which served as personnel transporters in the arrest of thousands of protesters. Designed in the late 1930s and produced between 1947 and 1981, the chunky rectilinear vans were police workhorses that incorporated the front-wheel drive and four-cylinder engine of Citroën's 11cv Traction Avant. Only the Paris police livery of dark blue and white and the flashing dome light distinguished its appearance from the standard corrugated-steel delivery van.

Like auto-ambulances, funeral cars and other small-volume professional automobiles, police cars never constituted a large enough market in any country to warrant the mass production of a purpose-designed vehicle. Whereas ambulances and hearses were custom-bodied, pre-Second World War police cars were typically standard production models painted in a police livery. Alterations usually included only a set of lights and a siren, bell or repeating horn, although some were sold with 'towing packages' including heavy-duty cooling systems and brakes. By 1950, however, the volume of fleet sales in the USA was sufficient that Ford introduced a specialized 'Police Package', offered with its fast flathead V8 model, which combined those standard options most often specified by police forces. They included heavy-duty shock absorbers, suspension, brakes, drive-train and cooling systems. Inside, they featured '24-hour duty' seats with reinforced frames, anti-sag springs, washable vinyl upholstery and heavy rubber floor mats. The package was designed to provide law-enforcement officers with the quickest, most reliable and most durable mass-produced car possible, creating a new breed of automobile, customized at the factory, with tailored performance and bearing.[20]

Other American manufacturers entered the field with more powerful engines for motorway pursuit, and new equipment, such as radar. Packages were designed for specific climates and topography, such as desert flatlands or snowy mountains. They were mainly full-size cars with spacious boots to accommodate a growing range of emergency equipment used in day-to-day police work, and the most successful was the Ford Crown Victoria Police Interceptor P71, which became so ubiquitous in North America that its image became generic for 'cop car'. Manufactured between 1992 and 2011, the 'Crown Vic' was a rear-wheel-drive V8 sedan with body-on-frame construction, which was appreciated by police for its toughness, robustness and stability in hard manoeuvres. It was so highly respected by law-enforcement officers that the last P71 to be built was bought by the Kansas State Highway Patrol for permanent display in the agency's museum 'as a tribute to the car's prolific past'.[21]

A European equivalent of the Crown Victoria was created by BMW with its 5-Series (announced in 1977), a car that needed little special equipment other than lights and sirens to be fit for police duty. Police forces throughout Europe used standard production models, as European cars were thought to be fast and robust enough to serve without modification in crime prevention and public-order duties. But, like Ford, BMW's factory eventually offered a police package.

Britain traditionally has a less aggressive approach to the maintaining of law and order, and when patrol cars were first introduced, in the 1960s, small Ford Anglias, with their snappy Z-line reverse-slant rear windows, and Austin Minis were typically benign-appearing choices. Despite being low-powered, they were relatively agile and represented a major step forwards in police efficiency, although they also contributed to a distancing of police constables or 'bobbies' from the local denizens they had previously served mainly on foot or by bicycle. The so-called panda cars, originally painted in large patches of black or light blue over white, provided the constable with a haven from wet weather, and, when equipped with a two-way radio, became part of a law-enforcement grid covering large areas of city or countryside, enabling the police to reach potentially far-flung crime scenes more quickly.

The Ford Crown Victoria in police livery. This popular civilian automobile was also the classic North American service car of the late 20th and early 21st centuries. Its other great role was as a taxi, where its robustness was also an advantage.

An important pioneer of police radio during the early 1920s was a senior constable in Victoria, Australia, Frederick W. Downie, who identified wireless communication as a particular advantage in the state because of the huge distances between police stations and the dispersed settlement patterns outside cities. Downie demonstrated the capability of radio to quicken responses significantly, although bulky valve sets and their batteries crowded even the large Lancia patrol cars of the time, which were crewed by three officers, including a dedicated radio operator.

Given the even greater scale of law enforcement in the USA – activity that grew dramatically after the introduction of Prohibition in 1919, and later with the construction of interstate highways – police radio became an urgent requirement. Detroit, the 'Motor City', was a pioneer in police broadcasting to squad cars, establishing station KOP-Detroit in 1922, licensed as a commercial entertainment station with music broadcasts interrupted by police announcements of burglaries and stolen cars. Years of experiments led to the establishment in 1929 of Michigan State Police station WRDS, a dedicated, state-operated, one-way police radio service. Since then the advent of two-way radio and of digital communications technology such as GPS systems, the Internet and mobile telephony operated from laptop computers and other specialized devices inside police cars has greatly extended the capabilities of officers operating in the field. But those early experiments in mobile police communications established the principle.

If the culture of the American police car is often stereotyped in popular literature, films and television, the reality of its interior was carefully designed for its effect on those taken into custody. The front seat became a landscape of digital equipment and electronic displays, typically littered with cups of takeaway coffee and boxes of doughnuts. In the back, the absence of interior door handles signals

incarceration, while heavy-duty vinyl upholstery in neutral colours approximates the decor of a prison cell. A low seating position was devised to suppress agitated or violent passengers, while steel mesh grilles isolate prisoners, and the squab of the driver's seat is armoured to prevent knife attack from behind. 'Run-lock' ignition allows officers to leave the engine running to power lights and other electrical equipment for extended periods at a crime scene, without risk of the car being stolen while unattended.

Although it has been a recognized tool of repression or injustice when misused by institutions or individuals, the police car is primarily an instrument of social order, whether a standard Toyota sedan, a tiny Smart car for urban patrolling (see p. 46) or the

Police cars are supplied with highly specialized communications apparatus, heavy-duty mechanical specifications and tough interior fittings as part of a typical factory-installed police package. The Australian Holden is typical.

320-km/h (200-mph) Lamborghini Gallardo donated by the super-car manufacturer to the Polizia di Stato in 2006 for use on Italy's autostrada. Yet it has also been a symbol of comic anarchy, as in the American cult film *The Blues Brothers* (1980), in which the protagonist, a petty criminal named Elwood Blues (Dan Aykroyd), describes in a nasal twang his latest second-hand car, a retired Dodge Monaco police interceptor still painted in the livery of the police department of Mount Prospect, Chicago:

> It's got a cop motor, a 440-cubic-inch plant, it's got cop tyres, cop suspension, cop shocks. It's a model made before catalytic converters so it'll run good on regular gas. What do you say, is it the new Bluesmobile, or what?

The 'new' Bluesmobile was used to create untold mayhem in the course of a madcap plot, which featured a series of extravagantly choreographed chase sequences in which 60 police cruisers were destroyed in their relentless pursuit of the magical Bluesmobile, literally flying from the posse. In this screwball narrative, the police car attained a status of outlaw heroism and reckless daring reminiscent of the Model T Fords used to similar comic effect in the early silent films of Mack Sennett's Keystone Cops. At the end, the exhausted Bluesmobile spontaneously falls to bits just as the flivvers did in Sennett's comedies.

Learning to share

Although it is common for vehicles of any police motor pool to change hands regularly among the officers of that force, such acceptance of car-sharing at work is greatly overshadowed by the attachment of private motorists to their personal cars. In this section

I will discuss various exceptions to private car use, and investigate their potential for the creation of a new car consciousness and possibly a more civilized transport culture.

An early outcome of the Situationist International collaboration between Guy Debord and the painter Asger Jorn was the *Guide Psychogéographique de Paris*. This collaged map identified relatively under-appreciated areas of the city that were deemed worthy of study achieved by wandering through them on foot, an SI practice known as the *dérive*, meaning drift. The map indicated how to reach each neighbourhood by taxi, bringing the individual *dérive* into a more ambitious, wider-ranging undertaking. As Debord's wife, the writer Michèle Bernstein, wrote in 1954,

> Only taxis allow a true freedom of movement. By travelling various distances in a set time, they contribute to automatic disorientation. Since taxis are interchangeable, no connection is made with the 'traveller' and they can be left anywhere and taken at random. A trip with no destination, diverted arbitrarily en route, is only possible with a taxi's essential random itinerary.[22]

Bernstein also reported on a proposal of 1954 to solve the increasingly chaotic parking problem in the centre of Paris by democratizing the taxicab. In Paris, as in most cities, the generally high cost of taxi fares restricted their use to the well-off (although OPEC states are currently notable exceptions):

> The prohibition of all private vehicles within the city limits and their replacement by a large fleet of moderately priced taxis . . . would have the invaluable advantage of allowing large sectors of the population to break free from the routes imposed by the Metrobus, and enjoy a hitherto rather expensive means of *dérive*. This proposal has our

unqualified support. We all know how important taxis are for the recreational activity we call '*dérive*', from which we expect to draw educationally conclusive results.[23]

Those results would be concerned with conditions of contemporary life in the city. In this way, the taxi would become a tool of the social sciences as well as an instrument in the poetic-artistic interpretation of urbanism.

The major technical innovation in the history of the taxi was the invention in 1891 by a German, Wilhelm Bruhn, of the taximeter, which measured the fare over distance and time. It was fitted to a Victoria-style motorized taxicab built by Gottlieb Daimler in 1897 and put into service in Stuttgart. Although everyone knows that travelling by car costs money, the illusion created by the private automobile is that driving is free. However, when the traveller is confronted by the rising numbers on a taximeter, the real cost becomes acutely apparent. Since early last century that ticking machine has exercised a mesmeric effect on many middle-class urbanites, such as an amorous New Yorker played in the film *Manhattan* (1979) by Woody Allen, who famously says to Diane Keaton as they glide through a starlit night in the back seat of a yellow cab: 'You look so beautiful I can hardly keep my eyes on the meter.'

Among the cars that have served as taxis during the past century, two purpose-designed vehicles stand out for their character and longevity. In the early 1930s the New York Taxi Cab Commission deemed that the city's taxis would be purpose-built vehicles, and for the rest of the twentieth century the city's taxi fleets were dominated by purpose-built Checker cabs, made by Checker Motors of Kalamazoo, Michigan, until the company ceased production in 1982.

The most distinctive, memorable and ubiquitous of all Checker models was the A8 Marathon, which was manufactured essentially unchanged from 1956 to 1982, becoming the most recognizable taxi in the USA during those years. This exceptionally conservative product of mid-1950s American automotive aesthetics was so purposeful and well-balanced a design, shorn of the theatrical elements of typical mid-century Detroit styling, that it never dated despite its long production run. While it was not considered a beauty, the A8 was a large, spacious and satisfyingly proportioned vehicle with a dignity that properly expressed its distinctive commercial purpose and social status within the metropolis. Midtown Manhattan seen from any high vantage point appears as a Mondrian-esque grey grid dotted with black limousines and yellow taxis, those ant-like yellow rectangles animating the picture.

In its stretched six- or eight-door form, the Checker Aerobus became the quintessential airport limousine when mass air travel was becoming a reality. By then, the earlier stretched Packards and Cadillacs that had transported the first generation of elite pre-war air travellers from city centre to outlying airfields had become uneconomic and seemed inappropriately luxurious for what was becoming a more routine shuttle ride. The larger and less ostentatious Aerobus properly filled the gap as a special vehicle serving larger groups of passengers taking ever larger planes, before the 'airport limo' became an upgraded city bus seating 60. With the relaxation of New York's regulations requiring taxicabs to be purpose-built vehicles, ageing Checker cabs were gradually replaced by long-wheelbase cars derived from such standard models as the Ford Crown Victoria and the Chevrolet Caprice, or by a variety of anonymous, mainly Japanese minivans.

Only one other taxi compares with the Checker for quality, longevity, uniqueness and character: the London black cab. In

1906 the London Public Carriage Office laid down 'Conditions of Fitness', which stipulated a tight 7.6-m (25-ft) turning circle for all London taxis, a capability then uncommon in ordinary production cars of a similar passenger capacity. The first Austin taxis, built in 1929, fulfilled the Conditions and were so much more efficient than previous taxis that they quickly dominated the field. From that time on, the London taxi underwent a gradual evolution but retained its basic characteristics for more than 80 years. The Coventry coachbuilder Carbodies, which from 1919 supplied standardized bodies to MG, Alvis, Rover and other manufacturers, also built the taxi bodies for Austin and eventually produced the whole car for British Leyland, Manganese Bronze and London Taxis International, each of which assumed the rights to the iconic car and continued to develop its classic design.

The British equivalent to the Checker A8 was the Austin FX4, launched in 1958 and produced without any significant change to its appearance until 1997, although many technical improvements were made over the years. Austin's engineer Albert Moore, designer Eric Bailey and Carbodies production engineers collaborated with the London dealership Mann & Overton, which commissioned the cars, to create a durable modern design of traditional character. The FX4 was spacious and easy to enter and exit, and provided a stately ride for its passengers and a comfortable cabin for its driver. It was succeeded by the sympathetically designed TX range. In 2012 ownership of London Taxis International was transferred to Geely of Shanghai, which declared its intention to develop the quintessentially British vehicles and manufacture them in China for a global market.

Throughout its history, the taxi has been a symbol of privilege, capable of generating animosity from those who objected to the established class order, as illustrated by the French Situationists. China, the world's most rapidly advancing mobile society in the

late twentieth century, demonstrated the tension caused by access to cars and specifically to taxis. In May 1985, during a football riot in Beijing,

> Gangs of angry young men roamed the streets outside the stadium after the game, detaining every passing taxi to shout and jeer at the drivers. One particularly vociferous rioter screamed: 'Fuck it, while I spend my hard-earned money to go to some lousy game, these guys are sitting in their cars pulling in a coupla hundred bucks a night. Get the bastards!' The mob soon set to spitting on windows, kicking doors and beating bonnets.[24]

The historian Geremie Barmé explained the problem:

The London taxi or 'black cab' represents a slowly evolving vehicle form based on specifications tailored to the British capital in the early 1900s. Yet its charming character, that of a large traditional limousine with a chauffeur, may form part of a more diverse range of hired personal transport options for Londoners in the future.

It was not surprising that taxis attracted such ire, for they provided the first privileged private spaces in reformist China, for drivers and passengers alike. Long before car-owning drivers appeared in the 1990s, taxi drivers were a class apart: they were mobile, free from the fetters of their original work units, and their wages were based on kilometres travelled rather than on the old, rigid socialist pay scale.[25]

The Chinese taxicabs of the 1980s were large, even by North American standards. Many were stretched Audi 100s and Dodge sedans built under licence in China as Audi-Chrysler-Red Flags, vehicles of exceptionally high status, seeming to offer counter-revolutionaries swinish luxury and immoral glamour. Their interiors represented a specifically Chinese aspirational taste:

> [their] passenger windows were often cloaked with green or brown gauze shades, while the back seats were covered in tan cloth with fussy antimacassars or woven-mat seat coverings – often still a feature – making the taxi a miniaturized version of the official audience hall or meeting room.[26]

Such decorations suggested the personal initiative of the driver, who also owned or rented the vehicle. In later years, the licensing authority required taxi companies to post public service announcements and portraits of Mao in their cars.

In the USA during the early years of the twentieth century, alongside the development of taxi fleets, the self-drive car-hire industry emerged. It put independent drivers at the wheel of a variety of standard passenger cars, primarily the ubiquitous Model T Ford, the operation of which was familiar to masses of prospective customers. Simplicity and familiarity were crucial to the success of a rental vehicle, and the Ford offered those qualities first. Yet there was also a need for larger cars, as demonstrated by advertisements from 1913 in the *Washington Herald* listing five separate companies offering seven-passenger self-drive touring cars for hire at $2 per hour.[27]

One of the first dedicated car-rental agencies was founded in 1918 by Chicagoan Walter Jacobs, using a small fleet of Fords. In 1923 John Hertz, who had formed a taxi company in Chicago that became known as Yellow Taxi, bought Jacobs's business, renaming it Hertz-Drive-Ur-Self-System, which went on to become the global industry leader. Another pioneer was Joe Saunders of Nebraska, who began his car-rental firm in 1916 also using Fords fitted with a mileage meter. By the mid-1920s he had agencies in 21 states and a turnover of more than $1 million a year. His fleet included the newly fashionable cars of Walter P. Chrysler, which were highly standardized in operation but also offered power, comfort and style, appealing to increasingly demanding Jazz Age consumers.

Customers were primarily commercial travellers who made long-distance journeys by train but then needed independent transportation to reach business or sales meetings in locations far from town centres and without frequent bus services. Since time was money, they needed freedom to move about the countryside according to their appointment diary rather than to the timetable of public transport. As a result, rental agencies grew quickly in the American Midwest, where business was booming in far-flung prairie locations. Early entrepreneurs collaborated with railway companies, who provided space for car-rental desks in station ticket offices and parking outside for their vehicles. Railway stations also offered a telegraph service that enabled train travellers to reserve a car at their point of departure, collect it at their destination and drop it off elsewhere, providing a convenient, coordinated system.

Car hire continued to grow with the rise of air travel. As early as 1932, Hertz had opened its first airport franchise, at Chicago's Midway Airport. After the Second World War, the Avis Airlines Rent-a-Car System captured the lead in the airport car-hire market, starting with a branch at Detroit Willow Run Airport and then opening agencies across North America and around the world. Airport locations were distinctive from the earlier franchises in railway stations, since those tended to be in city centres, while airports were out of town, served by the rapidly expanding freeway system. While business travel shifted from the train to the airliner, Avis also led the way for tourism, pioneering fly-drive holidays, reinforcing the relationship between the private car and the mass- transportation network.

The boom in car hire during the post-war period made major car manufacturers take an interest, and GM, Ford and Chrysler all acquired rental chains. The shift in global car manufacturing to Asian companies from the 1970s also affected the rental market. When Toyota became the world's largest car manufacturer, in 2008, it had been in the car-hire business as a Hertz partner for a decade. Its subsequent growth was partly attributable to the simplicity and familiarity of its car interiors, where every switch, dial or button was in the easiest place to find and its operation was essentially foolproof. The Japanese reputation for reliability also confirmed Toyota's cars as popular among renters.

Manufacturers involved in the rental market also recognized car-hire as a form of advertising, realizing that a one-day rental serves as a test drive. The Alfa Romeo rented on last month's holiday in Tuscany becomes the new choice at trade-in time. In addition to short-term car rentals, a potentially significant, if subtle, effect was wrought by the spread of car leasing on the culture of private ownership, long established as the standard mode of automobility.

Although to all intents and purposes the leased car 'belongs' to its user, it is more easily traded in and represents less of a personal investment than the privately owned car, which may be selected for substantially different reasons than a leased car. Factors include its physical sturdiness, the durability of its appearance and its potential trade-in value.

Environmentalists who promote more sustainable personal transportation, including car-sharing schemes, welcomed the advent of car clubs such as Zipcar (subsequently acquired by Avis), the world's largest organization for occasional hourly car rentals, operated with electronic booking and charging mechanisms. Such schemes are also aimed at customers who might want the temporary use of a different type of car from that which they own or lease. By 2012 car-sharing schemes, run by local civic authorities, car-rental companies, car manufacturers or cooperative organizations, for profit or not for profit, operated in more than 1,000 cities globally. These systems rely to some extent on the user's ability to organize their travel by booking a car in advance of departure, and on their willingness to use a car that is also used by many other people – essentially a taxi minus the chauffeur.

Cycle-sharing schemes, such as Vélib' in Paris, have shown up one of the most serious obstacles to a smooth-running urban car-sharing project, and that is distribution. Bicycles are often in the wrong places: one rank has none while another is full, leaving no place to park yours. Car-sharing ranks suffer similarly. The folding Hiriko car, the sole fully developed outcome of the MIT CityCar project of 2003, provides a good model for a shared city car, yet only the implementation of fully autonomous vehicles will enable such a system to work optimally. When cars can be summoned electronically to a specific location, and be moved about remotely from one location to another, independently of the driver, then car-sharing may finally become a more universally satisfactory system of personal transportation, even extending beyond city limits to destinations in distant suburbs, from which the car could return on its own to wherever it is needed. The economic advantage of a driverless taxi is clear, just as the effect of autonomous vehicle technology for all professional drivers will be challenging and controversial.

One of the earliest car-sharing schemes, Sefage, was launched in a housing cooperative in Switzerland in the late 1940s. In response to the growing pressure of urban traffic, parking problems and car-induced air pollution, more ambitious schemes began to appear in Europe in the 1970s, including the short-lived ProcoTip (Promotion Cooperative du Transport Individuel Publique) system in France and Amsterdam's Wit Car scheme, based on the Dutch White Bicycle Plan of the 1960s, whereby white-painted bicycles were left on the street for anyone to use, in an attempt to cut car traffic and pollution in the city centre. But car-sharing schemes did not gain

The Parisian Autolib car-sharing scheme may be the harbinger of a new personal transport system for this century. With the fundamental infrastructure in place, the need is now for better cars.

momentum until the advent of computer technology.[28] By the late 2010s the car-hire chains Hertz and Avis were running online car-sharing services to simplify the process of reserving a car.

Housing agencies and building developers also began to promote car-sharing as an incentive to environmentally aware residents and as a way of meeting 'green' planning targets. The British architect Bill Dunster designed such a sustainable development, the Beddington Zero Energy Development, known as BedZED, which was built in south London in 2002. BedZED's 82 homes and work units were near the local railway station, but the development also provided a selection of cars operated by Britain's leading independent car-sharing organization, City Car Club, as an alternative to

The jury is out while car-sharing is still in its infancy. Since 2008 Daimler AG's Car2go subsidiary has been providing car-sharing services in Europe and North America, using exclusively Smart Fortwo EVs and offering one-way, point-to-point rentals. Charged by the minute, hour or day, customers access the service on the street via a smartphone app.

private ownership. The cars themselves were mainly hybrid and electric cars that could be recharged in the development's dedicated charging bays. Such a coordinated approach to personal mobility was intended to offer a model for future housing developments both in urban centres and outside towns, giving residents a variety of convenient transport options that would leave the smallest possible carbon footprint.

The question remained, however, whether residents would subscribe to the fundamental notion of sharing that cherished vessel of uninhibited personal mobility and self-expression, the car, regardless of how much that act might contribute to a more orderly world. A change in vehicle architecture is one approach currently filling

Descendant of the 'taxi meter', Car2go's digital touchscreen is the user's simple interface with the car and the service.

the portfolios of young designers, to promote a change in public attitudes to the car, particularly for shared use in cities and for suburban driving.

In 2012 Lino Vital García-Verdugo, a PhD student at the Royal College of Art in London, proposed a series of alternatives to today's large, heavy motorway cruisers for city use. The concept recalls the minimalism of Edwardian cycle cars or post-Second World War European microcars, such as the BMW Isetta, which at their best offered motorists affordable thrills and practical basic transportation in contrast to the bigger, more expensive automobiles of the time. The highly adaptable minimal architecture of Vital's electric quadricycle, devised for short drives at low speed, reflects

a new design strategy, where apparent technical limitations are used to reinforce [the vehicle's] urban performance and user acceptance . . . transferring the individuality of the design from the container to the contained space.[29]

And it is precisely that shift from display to experience that could make such innovations in personal transport healthier and more enjoyable than most current options.

6 Afterlife

Longevity

FOR SALE, – Winton phaeton in first class condition, has 1900 equipment, 8½ horse power motor. Front wheels 32 in. in diameter, with 3 in. tires. Rear wheels 36 in. in diameter, with 4 in. tires. Hydraulic brake, besides the two regular brakes. Extras, – One new 4 in. tire. Two 3 in. tires. Full set of tools special. One new driving chain. Carriage lamp. One new extra wide touring top and cushion. Seats comfortably three persons. Can be put on and off in five minutes. This carriage is a bargain. A new one with the same equipments will cost $1,200.00. Price F.O.B. Plymouth, Pa., D.L. & W.W.R., $800.00. Reason for selling, am getting a two-seat Winton. FRANK L. McKEE, M.D.[1]

In its first issue, one of the earliest motor trade magazines, *The Horseless Age*, displayed Dr McKee's familiar-sounding advertisement for his nearly new Winton under the 'Special Notices' section. By 1913 the *San Francisco Call*, like most other city broadsheets, featured 'Automobiles and Supplies' among its classified advertisements. There, the city's Don Lee Cadillac agency featured a selection of traded-in 1910–12 cars, boasting: 'Each one has been overhauled and is in first-class running order.'[2] A two-year-old Buick, Winton or Peerless, which offered power, style and comfort, could be bought for the same price as a new Ford, and many thrifty but status-conscious buyers were choosing them. Eventually, hire-purchase schemes and, alarmingly, second mortgages enabled aspiring motorists not only to make their first purchase of a new car, but to buy second-hand ones. That system of down-cycling used cars soon spread with the export of cars to countries without their own car-manufacturing industries, a practice that continues today.

While conducting research in Ghana, before the local auto industry had grown beyond the limited assembly of foreign-made cars, the anthropologists Birgit Meyer and Jojada Verrips became aware of the fundamental importance of the car in Ghanaian life by observing the activities of one of their neighbours, a long-distance taxi driver. He owned a Peugeot 504 Break (station wagon), which was an unroadworthy shell when the pair first encountered it and its owner. Like thousands of other cars, and particularly 504s, the car had been imported at great expense from the Netherlands by a Dutch aid worker in 1991. At that time, the 504 would have been so old as to have dropped out of the European used-car market. But for Africa it was just entering its prime.

Peugeot's 504 was designed as a comfortable family car for the French domestic and international markets. More than 3 million were built in France from 1968 to 1983, yet they continued to be assembled under licence in several Latin American and African countries including Kenya, Egypt and Nigeria, where tens of thousands more were built from knock-down kits until 2006. Spacious, robust and mechanically simple, the 504 became so ubiquitous as a bush taxi that it earned the title 'King of the African Road'. The most prized model for bush taxis is the 504 Break, because of the extra space it provides. The particular example encountered by the anthropologists confirmed the model's reputation for having nine lives, as it was repaired and rebuilt numerous times after being gutted by fire, suffering major mechanical failure and being involved in several serious accidents.

The two researchers watched daily as the driver and a few other young men worked tirelessly to restore, after a near-fatal accident, the worn-out hulk that was the owner's means of livelihood. By observing the work, tracing the car's history in Ghana and following the driver's relationship with the 504 for more than three years, Verrips and Meyer compiled a picture of the car's use, maintenance, accidents, repairs, rising or falling exchange value, breakdowns and revivals. Such a history was starkly different from that of similar cars used by a typical sequence of owners in wealthier consumer cultures, where it would pass through the new- and used-car markets much as it had left the factory and then be scrapped when the cost of further repair exceeded the market value. In Ghana, however, such cars were not only rebuilt and repaired many times, but

Taxi drivers repairing and maintaining Peugeot 504s in Nigeria, 2006.

also 'adjusted' and 'tropicalized' to function with the country's bad roads, punishing climate, lack of spare parts and approach to maintenance, which involves as much faith, magic and ritual as it does technical know-how and innovation.[3]

Owning and driving such a taxi for a living conferred social status on a young Ghanaian man, and could attract jealous mischief. Given the high cost of such cars and their importance as a means of earning a living, their owners would do almost anything to prolong the vehicle's working life.[4] In the pursuit of longevity, such cars may be anthropomorphized by their owners, who look upon repair shops as hospitals and who also take cars to their church pastor or *malam* (spiritual teacher) to bless them and protect them from evil forces.

A similar but rather more aesthetic approach to the maintenance of elderly imported cars was demonstrated in Cuba, where a significant proportion of cars were the product of Detroit styling in its pre-1959 heyday. The way they look, even in their sixth decade, remains meaningful and valuable. They may be powered by Russian engines, and their accessories may be entirely non-functioning, yet such dilapidation is appreciated as a patina that reflects not only the car's long and noble life of service, but also the history of the island of Cuba since the 1950s. Although they serve a practical purpose, mainly as taxis, they have become historic attractions and are part of the crumbling but picturesque fabric of Havana. Their appearance, perhaps more than their use-value, secures their importance in the growing tourist culture of post-Soviet Cuba.

The chrome and fins of such cars have been maintained within the limits of what is possible under a 50-year trade embargo with the West. But as with the Peugeot 504 in Ghana, their simple, pre-silicon technology has enabled local mechanics without sophisticated equipment or tools to adapt available resources to keep

them running and to hold their rusting bodies together. By the turn of the millennium, they had become so embedded in the national culture that the Castro government saw fit to dedicate a series of postage stamps, '*Autos Antiguos*' ('Old Cars'), to them in recognition of their significance.

The extension of the lifespan of superannuated production cars by individuals in the main motoring nations grew as a hobby, rather than a necessity, as soon as mass-produced cars were old enough to become interesting, or when certain preferred models – such as 1950 Mercurys or the Ford Taunus TC – became affordable to prospective customizers. This was a new folk art of the automotive age. The growth in popularity of hot-rodding and customizing reflected a democratization of the personalized coachcraft and high performance that had belonged mainly to the rich in the first 40 years of motoring. Customizing also reflected the pride of amateurs who knew their way around a machine shop and had the skill to

Oozing charm, a very well cared for pink-and-gold 1953 Chevrolet on duty as an airport taxi in Havana, 2010.

transform engines, transmissions, suspensions, sheet metal and upholstery to achieve a unique vision of their perfect car and to express their personal taste through extravagant body shapes, sumptuous interiors and richly decorated paintwork.

Among hobbyists, there is also a tendency to treat their cars as works in progress. Many remain unfinished or in a perpetual state of flux. Some are stripped to bare metal and allowed to rust even when they are in regular use. Salvaged body panels in their original paint colours are commonly inserted into a compatible shell in any condition or colour. Interiors often await their tuck-and-roll upholstery or new instruments over the long term. Most such cars eventually meet their end on the scrap heap, although that fate may have been postponed for several years.

The customizing trend known as Rat Look makes patina and incompleteness into aesthetic features. It can be applied to souped-up Rat Rods, new model cars or old bangers to convey a steampunk image.

Since the 1970s this subcultural approach to prolonging the life of an old vehicle has spawned a customizing trend known as Rat Look or Rat Rodding, which turns patina and incompleteness into aesthetic features, while also introducing the latest high-performance mechanics and conspicuously expensive wheels, in contrast to a general air of neglect. 'Mother Nature painted this car', said one Rat Rod customizer in the television series *Sin City Motors* of the nicely patinated raw material with which he was working.[5] Interiors of Rat Look cars are typically spartan or left intentionally unfinished, with hessian or other rough materials for upholstery and a distinctive lack of creature comforts.

A subgenre known as Nu-Rat couples the rough and the smooth. Late model cars, stripped of external handles, badges or any other ornament, may be lowered or subtly 'improved', highly polished and treated to an expensive set of wheels, but they will be fitted with at least one major body panel that has been intentionally rusted or rust-painted to simulate the genuine patina found on old, dilapidated cars. They typically sport old-fashioned roof racks laden with antique steamer trunks, creating a steampunk look. Building them employs the traditional craft practice of trial and error combined with highly developed skills, including design.

Like the 'make do and mend' motorists of Ghana and Cuba, customizers in more prosperous car cultures can extend indefinitely the commercially and industrially predetermined lifespan of the automobile, usually dictated by the system of planned obsolescence. Cars, which in the normal order of things should have been scrapped or have found their way into a 'junk' sculpture, are rescued and their status elevated. They become distinctive, expressive and seemingly eternal cultural totems in affluent societies, sacred necessities in poorer ones.[6] This is the antithesis of disposability.

Collectors and collections

While most custom cars were created to be driven and seen in such events as London's Chelsea Cruise (which began in the 1970s), some devotees have created car collections that focus on exhibiting customized or one-off vehicles, such as so-called 'show cars' built for films. Many are open to the public in countries or regions where customizing has its own history and flavour. The London Motor Museum, for example, holds over 100 vehicles and demonstrates a particular British-West Indian taste for unique or distinctive American and European cars, ranging from a hot-rod Ford Model B Roadster of 1932 to a brace of wildly restyled low riders. The museum features links between cars, sport, fashion and music, with special emphasis on the black urban entertainment industry, which borrows vehicles from the collection for use in videos and staged events. The involvement of celebrities from the worlds of

A Cadillac Deville low-rider, c. 1980, with continental kit and a 'trunk full of funk' on display at the London Motor Museum, reflecting a transatlantic link between popular music culture and car customizing.

pop music and international football conveys a sense of the cars as part of a broad multi-ethnic and intercontinental taste culture.

The North American custom-car world is celebrated at Darryl Starbird's National Rod & Custom Car Hall of Fame Museum in Oklahoma. The museum shows a rotating selection of cars built by many of the most prominent professional customizers, including Starbird himself, who has been active since the early 1950s. The collection claims a unique place among car museums by preserving and showing exclusively hot rods and custom cars designed, styled and built by the pioneers and greatest names in customizing, alongside a large display of related ephemera. Starbird also led the formation of the National Rod and Custom Association in 1975, and managed the International Specialty Car Association before founding his museum, lending custom cars and hot rods legitimacy as a field for collecting, conservation, exhibition and study as well as popular appreciation.

The London Motor Museum collection includes many well-known cars from films and television, including the yellow 1970s Reliant Regal three-wheel van featured in the much-loved BBC comedy series *Only Fools and Horses*.

While Starbird's museum was purpose-built for the display of cars, the Guggenheim Museum in New York, designed by Frank Lloyd Wright and opened in 1959, was constructed to display Solomon R. Guggenheim's collection of modern art. However, it quickly became apparent to curators that rectangular paintings or traditional sculpture did not sit comfortably on the sloping floor of the museum's spiral ramp or on its curving walls. When a new wing was eventually added to the building, allowing paintings and sculptures to be displayed in conventional galleries, the spiral ramp and the vessel of space it enclosed were liberated for more unorthodox installations. Wright would feel proud to have provided for the avant-garde, experimental art that sits so comfortably in his museum decades after his death.

The Guggenheim's retrospective of the work of John Chamberlain, *Choices* (2012), made such use of the rotunda, where the artist's automotive sculptures appeared completely at home. In the setting

Ron Courtney, who worked in an Oregon body shop, used chopping, channeling, sectioning and shaving to modify the chunky proportions of his 1951 Ford, restyled as the X51 with enormous upswept tail fins. It was widely published and has been exhibited at the Petersen Automotive Museum, founded by the publisher of *Motor Trend, Hot Rod, Rod and Custom* and many other motor-themed magazines.

of the Guggenheim spiral, that architectural symbol of everything futuristic, Chamberlain's works had an elegiac quality that raised them above the car-crash clichés they sometimes evoke. As they sat on the museum's garage-like ramp, they suggested the future of the car as an object of speculation, provocation and veneration far beyond its usefulness as *the* foremost twentieth-century transport machine.

Chinese automotive history is, throughout, a story of privilege, and so it is not surprising that what was considered to be the first car imported to China was exhibited for more than a century in the Imperial Summer Palace, near Beijing. There, in the Hall of Jade Billows, amid a small collection of royal conveyances, was displayed the Duryea phaeton of about 1903, presented as a gift to Dowager Empress Cixi by the powerful general Yuan Shikai. Although the empress was said not to have used it because the seating arrangement forced her to face the driver's back, a breach of Imperial protocol, the car is significant in China's motoring history.

In 2011 Cixi's Duryea was moved to the new Beijing Auto Museum, China's first government-funded public museum for cars, which displays about 80 historic vehicles imported to or made in China. The collection is divided into sections including concept cars, technical innovations and vintage automobiles. Among its most significant objects is a limousine presented to Mao Zedong by Joseph Stalin during Mao's first state visit outside China, shortly after he came to power in 1949. The armoured bullet- and bomb-proof ZIL-110 was built in small numbers for top Soviet officials between 1947 and 1958, based very closely on the Packard Super Eight of 1942, and its elite status was signalled by the Packard-style radiator grille bearing an 18-carat-gold emblem decorated with rubies.

By bringing together cars from the Imperial household and the Communist hierarchy, the Beijing Auto Museum demonstrated the government's recognition of the increasing importance of the car in Chinese life, and its determination to enshrine the historical remnants of Chinese motoring in a politically sanctioned public venue, removed from the elite confines of both the Imperial palaces and the seat of Communist government, the Zhongnanhai.[7]

Built in 1893, about a decade before Cixi's phaeton, the first American Duryea motor car was kept in storage from 1894 until 1920. In that year it was acquired by Inglis Moore Uppercu, a New York Cadillac distributor and founder of the Aeromarine Plane and Motor Company, who had worked for the Duryea company in its early years and recognized the importance of their first car in American industrial history. That vehicle was the prototype for the initial output of the Duryea Motor Wagon Company, which built thirteen examples in 1896, making it the first American manufacturer to build and sell a batch of identical cars. In 1920 Uppercu donated the car to the Smithsonian National Museum of American History; it is now one of the oldest motorized road vehicles in the transportation collection and one of inestimable value in the history of the car.[8]

An original example of that first batch of Duryea Runabouts from 1896 also entered the collection of the Henry Ford Museum in Dearborn, Michigan, contributing to Ford's own idealized image of American invention and industry. This collection of buildings, objects and ephemera, including the Wright Brothers' bicycle shop and Thomas Edison's laboratory, was gathered initially by Ford himself, and presented its artefacts as a homage to rural and small-town America perfected by mechanics, and particularly by the car. Ford offered a nostalgic insight into his collection in his autobiography:

On May 3, 1921, the Ford Motor Company turned out Car No. 5,000,000. It is out in my museum along with the gasoline buggy that I began work on thirty years before and which ran satisfactorily along in the spring of 1893. I was running it when the bobolinks [a type of bird] came to Dearborn and they always come on April 2nd.[9]

Ford's autobiography is infused with such homely details, echoing the wistful passages at the beginning of Booth Tarkington's novel *The Magnificent Ambersons* (1918), filmed in 1942 by Orson Welles, which portrayed a small-town culture killed by the coming of the car and the growth of its industry. Ford's seasonal reference conjured, in particular, the film's depiction of a jolly party of early motorists venturing along a snow-covered country lane in a monumentally tall horseless carriage, noisy and smelly but portrayed nevertheless as a charming, handmade toy, as yet untainted by the deleterious effect of industrial production. As they tooled along, the carefree party sang a popular comic song, 'The Man Who Broke the Bank at Monte Carlo' – music, motoring and money linked from the very beginning.

During the twentieth century, many nations celebrated their early automotive pasts and developed motoring museums to display their

The Henry Ford Museum in Detroit presents the history of the automobile in a variety of cultural and technological contexts, highlighting the issues and problems surrounding the car today as well as its undoubted achievements.

contributions to that inalienable human right, personal mobility. Like the Ford museum, the Danish Technical Museum in Helsingør exhibited that country's earliest cars, such as the Hammelvogn, a one-of-a-kind ICE vehicle built in 1888 in Copenhagen, said to be the oldest 'original' automobile still capable of being driven. Thus, the car's distinction was less to do with its design innovation than with the assertion that it had been kept in working order.[10] Arguably, that superlative historical position of 'first' car resides with the three-wheeled Benz Patent Motorwagen No. 1, which is permanently housed in the transportation centre of the Deutsches Museum in Munich, to which Karl Benz personally donated it in 1906. That provenance confirms the exhibit as possibly the museum world's greatest automotive treasure.

Many other museums around the world exhibit replicas of the Benz Motorwagen. 'See the World's first automobile at the Montana Auto Museum. Now on display in the Visitor Center', shrieks the publicity material for that tourist attraction. Identical cars exhibited in Montana, Dearborn, Nagoya, Frankfurt and collections in other cities around the world were purchased from a batch of fourteen driveable replicas built by the firm of John Bentley Engineering in the UK between 1986 and 1997. They are considered to be the most authentic working copies of the first Benz. Their construction was based on detailed study of the existing original Motorwagen, and the first of ten completed for the centenary of that prototype. One of those replicas, offered for sale in California by the auction house Bonhams as part of its 'Important Sale of Collectors' Motor Cars and Automobilia', went under the hammer for a modest $46,000 (just under £30,000) in 2007.

Despite their limited exchange value, such replicas are valuable even to the most fastidious car and transport museums. The collection of the Daimler-Benz Museum in Stuttgart was formed to trace

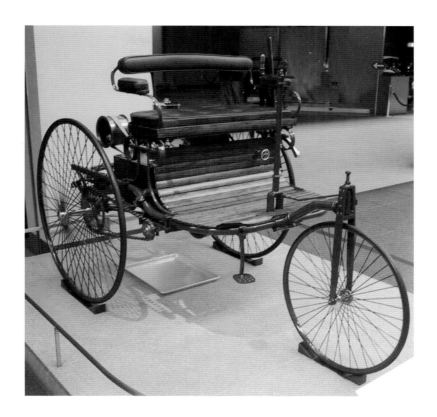

the development of the company's vehicles from 1885 to current models plucked directly from the assembly line. According to the historian William Stobbs,

> the museum is almost unparalleled both in the quality of the vehicles displayed, and the organization of the museum itself. The archives preserve the drawings, facts and photographic material, and a well-informed staff explain (in five languages) the details of engineering from the cars and engines displayed.[11]

A replica of the Benz Motorwagen, built by John Bentley Engineering in the UK, on display in the collection of the Toyota Automobile Museum, Nagoya, Japan.

And within this impeccable setting, a Bentley replica of the Motorwagen found a role in demonstrating to visitors the vehicle in action, its engine sound and even the feel of driving it, while the original could be seen only in static display, protected, like the *Mona Lisa*. Using such techniques, the world's motor museums kept pace with other types of collection that increasingly favoured 'interactive' displays, which generated 'experiences' for their visitors.

Along those lines, the Automobile Driving Museum in Los Angeles houses a collection of mainly American cars ranging from a Model T Ford to 1970s muscle cars, all of which offer visitors the experience of riding in them with museum volunteers driving, describing the controls and providing information about the performance of the cars while they are being experienced. Among many extraordinary vehicles in the collection, it is almost surreal to ride through the quiet boulevards surrounding Los Angeles airport in the silver Packard phaeton given to Joseph Stalin by Franklin D. Roosevelt when they were allies during the Second World War.

By the end of the twentieth century, museums owned and run by large manufacturers followed the global scope of their clientele,

The 1936 Packard touring phaeton, given by President Franklin D. Roosevelt to Joseph Stalin during their brief alliance in the 1940s, is now in the collection of the Automobile Driving Museum in Los Angeles and is frequently used for parades and film appearances as well as giving the museum's visitors an extraordinarily historic ride.

with branches around the world. The Toyota Automobile Museum near Nagoya, Japan, features Toyota vehicles and details of the company's history alongside relevant works of art and documentation, but also gathered a large number of historic vehicles by other makers. They included a replica Benz Motorwagen, American and European vehicles from the era of the horseless carriage, classic sports cars and luxury cars including custom-bodied Duesenbergs and Alfa Romeos. The museum also shows important high-volume production cars, such as the Citroën Type C, an early French 'people's car', and vehicles from Toyota's Japanese competitors, including Nissan and Suzuki. In contrast with the museum in Nagoya, the collection of the Toyota USA Automobile Museum in Torrance, California, contains only Toyota products and company history pertaining to its first US operation, in that local community during the 1960s.

With a collection comprised of cars gathered from many British manufacturers, the Heritage Motor Centre at Gaydon, Warwickshire, represents a uniquely comprehensive history of the British automobile industry. During decades of mergers and takeovers, British Leyland bought up many independent car makers and collected vehicles from each, including early examples saved by the companies that made them, many accompanied by extensive documentation. Those makers included such familiar names as Austin, Land Rover, MG, Morris, Riley, Rover, Standard, Triumph and Wolseley, but also the mostly forgotten Albion and Thornycroft. The resulting collection presents a unique picture of the history of British car manufacturing and motoring culture, and of the ups and downs of the British transport industry in general.

Other important collections reflect the singular vision of their founders. In a restored nineteenth-century woollen mill in Mulhouse, France, the Schlumpf Collection (which was absorbed into the Cité

The original Toyota Toyopet model Crown RS, launched in Japan in 1955, and which introduced Japanese cars to the North American market in 1958, takes pride of place in the Toyota Automobile Museum in Nagoya.

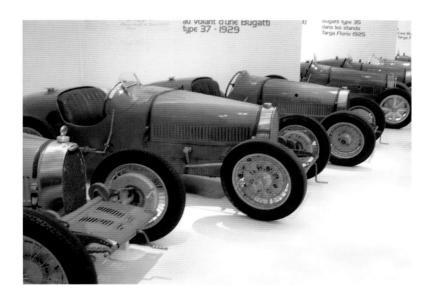

de l'Automobile, France's national motor museum) exhibits nearly 400 of more than 500 meticulously restored European classic cars, including 123 Bugattis, which were acquired obsessively and in great secrecy by the Swiss brothers Hans and Fritz Schlumpf between the end of the Second World War and the early 1970s. The Bugatti collection includes eighteen of Ettore Bugatti's personal cars, including the astounding Bugatti Royale Coupé Napoléon, demonstrating the ambition and impeccable taste of the collectors. The result is the automotive equivalent of fine-art collections brought together personally by such connoisseurs as Samuel Courtauld in London or Isabella Stewart Gardner in Boston. The Schlumpf Collection was acquired by the French state in settlement of debts owed by the brothers, who retreated to exile in Switzerland.

In England, the National Motor Museum at Beaulieu, opened in 1970 by Lord Montague of Beaulieu, was based on the Montague

The Cité de l'Automobile, France's national car museum, holds a collection of more than 500 European classic cars but features the 123 Bugattis acquired obsessively by brothers Hans and Fritz Schlumpf.

Museum, founded in 1952 by the peer's father, a pioneer motorist who championed the car through his position in the House of Lords. This erudite collection is displayed in the extensive grounds of Palace House, the former gatehouse for a Cistercian abbey, and the museum also has a library, a large photographic archive and workshops dedicated to the history of motorized transportation and the car in particular. Lord Montague formed a committee chaired by the architect and connoisseur Sir Hugh Casson to commission a new building, which was designed by the modernist architect Leonard Manasseh and completed in 1964.

Demonstrating the modernity of the museum project, the new complex included a monorail train to conduct visitors around the various attractions on the estate. The collection features a broad range of vehicles including antique motor buses, Formula One racing cars and a collection of vehicles built for British-made James Bond films. Many of the exhibits are in working order and frequently drive the roads within the park. The museum is notable for combining high connoisseurship, research facilities, country-house architecture and gardens, and the atmosphere of a family-orientated theme park. Exhibits, such as the museum's re-creation of a 1930s British garage, dramatize the historical place of the car in British culture.

Entrepreneurs quickly appreciated that automobiles, new or old, attracted crowds to entertainment venues and theme parks, which often feature attention-grabbing vehicles, such as those built as cinema props. Yet epicurean collectors, such as the Schlumpfs, continued to invest their money and energy in highly selective collections driven by personal taste and concentrating on particular manufacturers or special themes, just as connoisseurs of the fine and decorative arts have long been guided by historical period, theme or the work of individual artists. Dealers and collectors watch prices paid at auction for certain vehicles with the same eye to investment as do those interested in the rising values of Picassos or Arts & Crafts furniture. Such sales are also of interest to the general public and to ordinary motoring enthusiasts among them. With only modest hyperbole, the British *Daily Mail* announced in 2012 'The Most Magnificent Rolls-Royce Ever Built':

A 1912 R-R Silver Ghost Double Pullman Limousine, the 'Corgi Silver Ghost', with body by Barker's of Mayfair became the most expensive R-R ever sold at auction (£4,705,500). At the same Bonhams auction, a 1929 'Blower' Bentley single-seater racing car set the highest price ever for a British car at auction, fetching £5,042,000.[12]

Similarly, such acquisitions are carefully curated and interpreted to attribute and contextualize the cars properly within the missions of the institutions that show them.

When in 2011 the Musée des Arts Décoratifs in Paris held an exhibition of seventeen classic cars owned by the clothing designer Ralph Lauren, it called the event *L'Art de l'Automobile. Chefs-d'oeuvre de la collection Ralph Lauren* (*The Art of the Automobile: Masterpieces of the Ralph Lauren Collection*), leaving no doubt that the curators equated the automobile with the grand decorative arts for which the museum is renowned. Its curator, Rodolphe Rapetti, wrote of the exhibition:

Each vehicle is studied in detail, simultaneously on technical, historical and stylistic grounds. Their beauty of line, colours and materials is matched by their mechanical excellence, which results from the quest for efficiency and precision, combined to bring alive a genuine art of the automobile.[13]

In selecting vehicles for the exhibition, Rapetti favoured those cars that demonstrated the same traits as more typical decorative art objects, such as a Fabergé egg or an Ashbee bowl: elegance of line and colour, excellent materials and technical precision. He also chose those with the most impressive provenance. The architect Jean-Michel Wilmotte displayed the cars on white plinths, like traditional sculpture. Ralph Lauren's entire collection, however, reveals his personal taste for the functionalist design aesthetic that is intrinsic to his clothing lines, derived from his interest in sport and the inspiration he takes from the world of work. Lauren is as likely to collect a rare pick-up truck or a Second World War jeep as he is a Ferrari or a Jaguar. Thus those curating cars for particular exhibitions in specific settings may demonstrate different priorities from those collecting them in the first place.

Provenance has always been important to the value and interest of any museum object, and the car is no exception. With collecting come the subjects of authorship, provenance and authenticity, as well as presentation and interpretation. The historian Malcolm Jeal and the restorer Eddie Berrisford are among experts who disclose and resolve problems such as dubious claims to various inventions, including the 'first' petrol-electric hybrid car, contested by Porsche and Pieper, or the identification of the historic Mercedes Grand Prix car of 1914 driven by the legendary Christian Lautenschlager, which was verified only recently through rigorous archaeological research.[14]

By way of illustration, the outline of a complete provenance is given below for a great 1930s classic, the Lancia Astura Tipo 233 Corto, Chassis 33-5313, Cabriolet Aerodinamica with coachwork by Carrozzeria Pininfarina:

Short wheelbase, chassis no. 33-5313, engine type 91 (no. 1171) produced in the summer of 1936 and then delivered to Pininfarina;

coachwork designed by Mario Revelli di Beaumont, Pininfarina four-seat cabriolet, body no. 2511;

exhibited on the Pininfarina stand at the Milan motor show (Fiera Campionaria di Milano, October 1936) and awarded the R.A.C.I. President's Cup (Registro Ancetre Club Italia);

purchased by the Lancia dealer in Genoa (Ghiara & C. SA) and sold to Piero Sanguineti (12 March 1937) and registered: GE 2 2826;

Sanguineti entered the car in the first San Remo concours (Coppa dell' Impero, Concorso d'Eleganza per Automobili, San Remo, 5–6 May 1937);

purchased in late 1937 by Emil Uebel, German Lancia importer/dealer in Berlin-Charlottenburg;

exported to the USA when purchased by pioneer auto collector Barney Pollard in 1947;

purchased from Pollard by former American Lancia Club president Armand Giglio in 1980;

purchased from Giglio by Dragone Classic Cars in 2004;

purchased from Dragone by current owner, the collector Orin Smith, through Vantage Motor Works of North Miami in 2011, for restoration by Vantage;

first exposition after restoration: Pebble Beach Concours d'Elegance, California, 2012.[15]

Resurrection

In the winter of 1970, a young professional couple, Russ and Carla Ricci, bought a 32-ha (65-acre) farm in rural New England as a weekend getaway from their hectic working lives in Boston. But before it could become their idyllic rustic home, the land had to be cleared. It was a car graveyard that had previously belonged to a local junk dealer who had, over a period of 30 years, collected around 100 wrecked or scrapped automobiles. These decaying behemoths were deposited casually on the rolling land with grass, shrubs and trees growing up around and sometimes through them as they slowly settled into the earth, their originally bright paintwork patinated with rust, various parts removed for reuse elsewhere, their once-familiar lines obscured by the crashes they had suffered and by the long process of decomposition.

As a backhoe, bulldozer and crane separated the cars from the land and their carcasses were torn loose from clinging vines, those dormant beasts of the road momentarily regained their animation before final dismemberment, industrial crushing and complete disposal. It was a moment of resurrection for each of those time-ravaged objects, a testament to their persistence and an aerial exhibition of their exotic shapes and the distinctive character of each model: the remains of a 1930s Pierce Arrow limousine, a Studebaker of 1946 on its collapsed roof, a half-crushed turquoise Ford hardtop from 1953, a Volkswagen on its side. That landscape also featured hillocks of tyres, banks of twinkling chrome hubcaps and other dismembered car parts, and a specially allocated sector of the graveyard for children's pedal cars, rusting in the grass alongside their senior brethren.

The project of clearing the Riccis' land was an impressive display of balletic mechanical activity, as the cars swung in mid-air before

being lowered, clunking, roaring and screeching, on to lorries for removal to a recycling facility. Yet this was a mere glimpse of an epic global process of car disposal that has become ever greater in subsequent decades.

The average working life of a car is about thirteen years. We have seen how that typical statistic is extended almost infinitely in cultures where the practical need exists to prolong a car's use, and in the rarefied domains of antique and classic car collections. While old cars were fetishized in such popular British magazines as *Classic Cars* or *Practical Classics* and in the Vermont-based perennial *Hemmings Classic Car*, the specialist interest in driving and preserving old cars is statistically negligible in the face of the global production and disposal of cars.

The design of some cars from the past made their disassembly simple. The Citroën 2CV, for example, was assembled with bolts rather than glue, easing their repair. In the 1990s BMW pioneered

The 65-acre auto junkyard that became a professional couple's weekend retreat in the early 1970s included a special section created by the former owner, a scrap dealer, for toddlers' pedal cars. This automobile junkyard evoked an elegiac atmosphere.

the use of recyclable thermoplastics and experimented with the revival of mechanical connectors to reduce the use of adhesive. They also sought ways of decreasing the number of different materials in their cars to make the separation of parts quicker and easier.[16] Reforms in German law also promoted 'end-of-life vehicle recycling' by requiring its domestic manufacturers to buy back, disassemble and recycle their cars in the domestic market. Throughout the European Union the average weight of recyclable material in a car at the turn of the twenty-first century was about 75 per cent, with the remaining 25 per cent being shredded and sent to landfill. Laws becoming effective in 2015 increased the required rate of material reused and recovered to a minimum of 95 per cent.[17] However, the legal ideal may not correspond with the gritty reality.

During the Cold War, mountains of junked, late-model cars became a symbol of capitalist decadence and of the threadbare premise that planned obsolescence had become during the post-war decades. When Volkswagen was still building its evergreen Beetle in 1971, advertisements by Doyle Dane Bernbach used the image of an American junk-car mountain as a foil to the longevity of the indomitable VW. The tag line was 'Before You Look at Their New Ones, Look at Their Old Ones.' The copy continued: 'Over 13 million Volkswagens are still on the road. And when one drops out, even then it's not always destined to be dropped in a pile. For old Volkswagens have a habit of becoming other things. Like new dune buggies.'[18]

More abstractly, the photographer Edward Burtynsky created a stunning photoessay, 'Oxford Tyre Pile', about one of the world's largest tyre mountains, at Westley, California, while Michael Cory's *Pile* and Michael Shealy's *Tired* also capture the grim beauty of similar tyre dumps in Montana and Colorado. Their images dramatize the extent of the problem resulting from the disposal of the car's most essential component, that with which it meets the road.

Yet the seemingly impossible size of those tyre mountains was only the tip of the iceberg-like problem of car disposal. Estimates suggested that in the early twenty-first century between 2 and 3 billion tyres had accumulated in uncontrolled piles or illegal dumps in the USA alone, and although European statistics were better, national results varied substantially. In Eastern European countries nearly 100 per cent of tyres ended up in landfill, whereas in Scandinavia that percentage was nearly zero. In hot climates prone to brush and forest fires – in the Mediterranean or Central America, for example – tyre mountains present a particular hazard to the environment, since they are difficult to put out once alight. As they burn, they emit toxic fumes and soil pollutants, the effects of which could be aggravated by firefighters' water or foam. Consequently they are often left to smoulder for weeks or months. Even dormant tyre dumps in warm climates can become breeding grounds for disease-carrying mosquitoes, like the urban manure piles in the last days of horse-drawn vehicles.[19]

Michael Cory's photo of a tyre pile in Browning, Montana, conveys the scale of the problem resulting from automobile disposal.

Not surprisingly, the world's largest tyre-recycling industry grew up in the USA, where new markets developed for fuel and products derived from tyres. Those states with the most developed industries for manufacturing products from recycled tyres led the field, and uses for tyres in civil engineering increased, although fuel remained their most important application, particularly in the kilns used for the manufacture of cement.[20] Recycled tyres were also used in the production of shoes, carpet underlay and garden mulch, and in the construction of roads and artificial coastal reefs, although for the latter the question of toxins leeching into the water remains particularly controversial.[21]

Like tyre reclamation, the recycling and crushing of cars began long ago. Ford had a system of disassembly and recycling for old cars that was well established in the era of the Model T. An issue of *Popular Science Monthly* published in November 1930 described the process of recycling in use then at Ford's Dearborn plant. 'Where the Old Car Meets Its End and Starts Life Over Again' took readers on a pictorial tour through the process, beginning in the storage lot from which thousands of worn-out cars were taken for dismantling on a moving conveyor belt, just as they had begun their construction:

EVERYTHING IS SAVED. The horn, ignition, wires, spark plugs, head-lights, floorboards, even the grease, are removed. The floorboards go to a box factory; upholstery to the blacksmiths for aprons. [Then] ITS LIFE IS CRUSHED OUT. Robbed of everything of value, the skeleton of what was once a car is rolled beneath a hydraulic press and crushed into a mass. . . . [At last] A FLAMING FINALE . . . the melting pot into which the car goes. Pig iron comes out.[22]

The article illustrated a 'pancake' crusher, which flattens a car using a large descending steel plate, hydraulically operated. Cars and other scrap metal were also crushed using baling presses, which exerted pressure from several directions and rammed the contents into a box-shaped mould, compressing it into a dense cubic mass, the same process used to create the French sculptor César's various *Compressions*. The dramatic result of the latter process also made it a striking, if impractical, way to dispose of a cinematic murder victim. In the early James Bond film *Goldfinger* (1964), an unsuspecting mobster is killed in a new Lincoln sedan, which is then put through a baling press at a local scrapyard. The resulting cube of crushed metal is hoisted from the machine by an enormous magnet and casually lowered into the back of a waiting pick-up truck for its grisly cargo to be disposed of elsewhere.

While the *Popular Science* photoessay lauded Ford's process for its thrift, the magazine's editors saw the need to comment on the limitations of recycling at the time and on what they themselves were referring to as 'the junk car menace'. In a separate editorial, 'Stopping a Big Waste', they wrote:

> You can't eat iron. . . . Materials become useful only when they have been fabricated into definite shapes; . . . A dress or a suit of clothes may become unwearable because of style changes. An automobile may lose its value for the same reason. . . . In view of these basic facts, the pictures on page 61 are particularly interesting. They show that an earnest effort is being made to salvage the material in discarded automobiles. If such complete salvaging of materials could be applied to all lines [i.e. object types] the effect would be revolutionary.[23]

The surprising aspect of their editorial viewpoint is its familiarity as an expression of wishful thinking sustained over the eight decades since it was written. The main technology and the system for recycling was in operation then, yet design, marketing, economics and emotional, subjective and irrational factors surrounding the car have undermined that common-sense practice of waste-reduction that the canny Henry Ford saw as simple logic and good business practice, while reflecting his innate opposition to the problems of pollution and the depletion of resources caused by his cars.

In addition to his environmentalist ambitions, Ford was typical of the big-business interests that first saw the opportunity to make a profit from recycling scrap, in particular metal, during the First World War. They invested in new machinery and industrial methods to cut the cost of scrappage, and founded an industry, albeit one that became increasingly hampered by the combinations of materials used in the construction of cars. Composites, hybrids and sandwiched material are just a few of the complex new types of flexible, changeable and adaptable materials that came into the manufacturing of cars, other products and buildings in the later twentieth century, and that have created increasing technical challenges for recycling.

Paola Antonelli, curator of the exhibition *Mutant Materials in Contemporary Design* (1995) at the Museum of Modern Art in New York, wrote that within such challenging developments 'recycling is a given . . . An ideal contemporary material is meant to be long-lasting, easily recycled, reusable, non-invasive and more flexible.'[24] Plastics, glass, ceramics and metals now belong to more complex groupings of materials that present designers both with the opportunity to create new forms and with the new challenge of endowing them with durability and extended life while reducing manufacturing energy and material waste.

Such an optimistic view, however, remains at odds with that of political and economic sceptics, who see waste, the conservation of energy and recycling as disruptive to business, a drain on taxpayers, ineffective and costly. And despite the best intentions and global initiatives of the Green Movement, an enormous volume of discarded automotive material still ends up in landfill. One solution has been proposed by advocates of a circular economy, based on the notion 'take, make, recirculate.' Yet such a system will require a change from the economy of infinite growth and universal disposal to one of maintenance, reuse and upgrading. A new genre of self-healing materials will also contribute to the development of such a new model.

During its 125-year reign, the car has become greatly loved as a means of expanding human experience, enriching life and providing pleasure. It was not a fault of the invention that it also became a chief instrument in the industrial exploitation of labour, the greatest consumer of natural resources and the single greatest contributor to pollution and the degradation of both the built environment and the natural world.

That the car has been used for good and ill is indisputable, as is its part in creating beauty of various sorts – through its own image and through the subjects and themes it stimulated in all branches of the arts as well as in the popular imagination. It will not go away, even if the public will to abandon it were widespread, yet any rational assessment of the damage – environmental, psychological, social, political and economic – wrought by its current use must eventually provoke a reappraisal of its fundamental design and employment. Unless the future of that amazing machine incorporates revised types of propulsion that are much more energy efficient and more benign in both production and use, with more appropriate patterns of usage, a reduced automotive footprint (particularly in cities) and a greatly improved lifecycle, the effect will be to blight further all life on the planet, and especially that which the car was purported to improve: human life.

What hope, then, is there for any serious reform of the car's grip on humanity? An answer may lie with two factors in the history of the car that have contributed with such mixed results to its evolution: technology and image. When the car supplanted horse-drawn vehicles, bicycles and the train as the most popular means of getting about during the last century, its glamorous image and promise of increased mobility overturned an established pattern of life and many forms of enterprise and livelihood. Old industries died and new ones replaced them. Just as the irresistible attraction of the tiny Sony Walkman in the late 1970s quickly eliminated the assault of noise caused by the hegemony of the boom box in urban street life, a technical redefinition of the shape, size and systematized technology of the car, made fashionable and globally desirable, could be the most promising means of moving towards a more peaceful, satisfying and successful future regarding getting about over land. And the inexorable trend towards lighter, brainier, smaller products of all types should also provide a clue to future directions in car design.

Recent design competitions offer some ideas. The industry journal *Car Design News* sponsors the annual Interior Motives Design Awards, for which the theme in 2013 was 'the connected car', co-sponsored by Ford and Volkswagen. Applicants were set four challenges: internal and external connectivity, interior layouts for autonomous driving, the multi-purpose interior and the autonomous interior as an immersive, private world. The results showed that such aims could be met within a variety of distinctly new vehicle types.[25]

Similarly, the MIT CityCar project generated several new automotive archetypes tailored to a variety of mobility tasks that could be more appropriately served if individuals took the type of vehicle they need for each journey from a shared car pool. Each vehicle could then be customized for the driver electronically via linked phone or another communication device. Among the resulting archetypes was a series of pod vehicles intended for use on 'the last mile' of a journey made by public transport. Some proposals employed the self-balancing Segway technology developed by Dean Kamen and introduced in 2001.[26] In 2012, with such a principle in mind, the American transport strategist Dan Sturges asked the question:

> Why own a cow when you only want a glass of milk? If you're going to rent a vehicle for just an hour, then rent the right vehicle for your needs. Being stuck with one mode for all trips is a last-century approach to getting around. We're still in this last-century paradigm of automobile monoculture.[27]

Such a scenario suggests that at different times a driver with a long-cherished vintage sports car tucked away in a garage might want a hatchback for a day's shopping at IKEA or a single-seater autonomous tricycle for the frequent hop from home to the railway station. The last two needs could also be met through car-sharing.

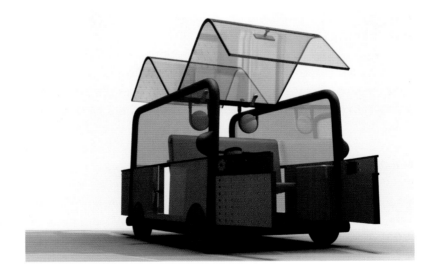

Royal College of Art vehicle-design postgraduate students James Brooks and Richard Bone created The Box to address the 'self-indulgent problems perpetuated by typical car companies', 2011. It is a functionalist answer to personal mobility influenced by Bauhaus design principles.

Sturges worked with students of transportation design at Art Center College of Design in California and with Cleantech Los Angeles to create a transportation think tank modelled on the MIT Media Lab and to promote the concept of more systematized automotive infrastructures. He says: 'Cars are great, but the automobile monoculture we've created is not. Every major urban area today is working to enhance options to car use.'[28]

Even Bill Ford, chairman of the oldest car giant, includes vehicle-sharing as a growing part of his company's business. This view echoes the thoughts of the Canadian designer Bruce Mau, who wrote:

> The car eliminated the problems associated with the horse and buggy and answered the need for personal liberty. But its success brought about a new set of problems. With millions of cars now clogging up the urban landscape in both the developed and developing worlds, the global design challenge is to dream up lighter, smarter and less expensive options.[29]

In 2013 Toyota Design unveiled an attractive addition to the spectrum of automotive type-forms in its traffic-slicing electric three-wheeled cross between a motorcycle and a car, the i-ROAD, engineered by Akihiro Yanaka and designed by Koji Fujita to offer a bike-like thrill for the driver while providing approximately the comfort of a car – just enough vehicle for that last mile of a journey, but cool enough to make it fun. It points one way ahead for either car-sharing or private ownership, primarily in cities.

In 2011 Ford announced a new partnership with America's leading car-sharing organization, Zipcar, to provide about 1,000 Ford cars for use by students at more than 200 university campuses, to train a new generation in the use of shared cars while also attempting to attract them as future customers. Yet dedicated car owners

would find it difficult to embrace new ways of accessing personal transportation. Robin Chase, co-founder of Zipcar, showed how iPhones could transform any car into a taxi, while the green entrepreneurship guru Joel Makower commented:

> Getting people using a 300-lb [136-kg] electric PUMA [Segway pod car] rather than a 6,000-lb [2,700-kg] electric SUV to nip three miles down to the shops to grab papers and coffee is going to have some seriously big environmental and spatial advantages.[30]

Yet it requires innovative design thinking to offer motorists more interesting things to do in a car than drive it by pushing levers, depressing pedals and twirling a wheel while negotiating traffic and avoiding costly or lethal errors.

Small city cars and autonomous vehicles may alarm people who are used to trusting their own skill at the wheel and to depending on

Toyota has consistently led the industry in technological experimentation and implementation. In their i-Road tricycle they introduced a new car typology, combining the thrills and agility of a motorcycle with the comfort of an automobile.

heavy armour to protect them against the foibles of other drivers. Yet with the world's driving population including many new drivers with limited training or experience of the road, accident statistics are once again rising and are predicted to increase rapidly in low- and middle-income countries.[31]

Networked cars can undoubtedly do better. They can be designed so that they will rarely crash; and small, soft city cars can be built so that if they do bump, they will do little harm. Autonomous control is the logical successor to the electric starter, power steering and automatic transmission, all of which were devised more than 70 years ago. Since roughly 90 per cent of accidents are caused by driver error, to remove the driver is virtually to eliminate the accident. Autonomous control should also enhance the motorist's enjoyment of those recent global addictions, 24-hour media and

Michael Velcek's 21st-century iteration of the 20th century's cycle cars and bubble cars is a sophisticated personal mobility device – fully connected, fun to drive and able to drive or park itself, with or without a human on board.

social networks, in addition to offering the potential to refresh those age-old automotive pursuits, romance, food and alcohol. Dashboard dining, perhaps that 'one for the road', and the intimacy of the automotive cabin could be liberated by the elimination of direct responsibility for driving.

Yet a sudden change from manual control to a more passive role as an automotive captain, issuing verbal commands to the vehicle, may be too great a behavioural shift for many driving enthusiasts. Manufacturers and their marketing agents have therefore begun to introduce new features – such as help with parking, automated highway driving and pre-collision braking systems – individually, accustoming motorists to relinquishing manual control gradually. Together with appropriate legislative reform and tailored insurance conditions, those features constitute an autonomous car.

Such an approach to vehicle control is equally applicable to highway cruisers, all-purpose city cars or mobility pods for short hops, although manual control is likely to remain a significant option in

Technology companies are playing an increasing role in the development of future transport solutions. Google's autonomous cars are currently leading the field in testing and promotion.

most types of vehicle, particularly for millions of suburbanites whose typical driving tasks are undemanding and often pleasurable. The private luxury car will undoubtedly remain a status symbol for the gratification of pop stars, oligarchs and sports celebrities, although they may be powered in new ways and wear bodies made of astounding new materials with fantastic science-fiction capabilities. Recent examples are Tesla Motors' prototype autonomous variant of its production electric sedan and BMW's GINA concept with an elastic textile skin replacing sheet metal.

It would sadden many enthusiasts to see cars more than twenty years old, including prized classic models, banned from the streets, as was proposed by the mayor of Paris in 2012. They are, to many observers, a charming feature of the roadscape, offering aesthetic delights and nostalgic pleasures, and they represent the virtues of longevity, creative manufacture, maintenance and genuine involvement of the user. In high-income societies they form an insignificant proportion of transport vehicles, and so contribute a tiny percentage of air pollutants in spite of their relative inefficiency, while in lower-income societies they remain essential tools of personal livelihood. Driving them, riding in them and seeing them move should not become legislative casualties of a new automotive culture.

The coexistence of various modes of transport is not beyond our capabilities, and, in fact, it must become a planning and production priority if we are to develop a more healthy personal transportation culture. Various sorts of significantly different types of car, improved public transport vehicles, bicycles, more sophisticated mobility scooters, recreational vehicles (including owner-driven classics or home-built hot rods) and pedestrians could find their places in a more intelligently organized and equitably shared road space, although current legislative and insurance regulations could prove as resistant to reform as the Victorian Locomotives Act.

The ICE automobile replaced the horse because it was a better means of transportation in every way. Networked communication devices supplanted earlier forms of personal and mass communication because they too better satisfied our wants and offered huge new opportunities for entrepreneurs. Similarly, within the political and economic reality of our time, a revised transportation menu will have to produce something better than the conventional car and the dreary landscape it dominates. It will have to offer significant improvements in comfort and convenience, a more intelligent display of style and image, increased economy of access and operation,

This version of motoring will be around for many years to come – the delicious 1971 Ferrari 365 GTB/4 Daytona Spyder beckons seductively.

higher standards of safety, greater sustainability in production, use and disposal, and, crucially, sufficient economic incentive to satisfy a range of stakeholders, including manufacturers, providers of materials and services, middlemen, governments, banks, insurance companies and users.

The typical car of today is a sophisticated version of an old and increasingly tired idea tied to the fabric of suburban sprawl and outdated notions of fashion and status. The challenge for automotive and transport planners, designers, manufacturers and civic authorities now is to devise more attractive alternatives to the narrowly defined monoculture of ownership and of the narrowly defined twentieth-century car.

References

Preface

1 'What the Automobile Can Do', *Automobile Review*, 1903; see Royal Feltner, *History of Early American Automobile Industry, 1861–1929*, www.earlyamericanautomobiles.com, accessed 12 June 2012.
2 Daniel Miller, ed., *Car Cultures* (Oxford, 2001), p. ix.
3 Mike Featherstone, Nigel Thrift and John Urry, *Automobilities* (London, 2005), pp. 25–6.
4 Miller, ed., *Car Cultures*, p. ix.
5 See also John Keats, *The Insolent Chariots* (New York, 1958).
6 See also David Gartman, 'Tough Guys and Pretty Boys: The Cultural Antagonisms of Engineering and Aesthetics in Automotive History', www.autolife.umd.umich.edu, and Gartman, 'A History of Scholarship on American Automobile Design', annotated bibliography, www.autolife.umd.umich.edu, both accessed 8 August 2012.
7 Brian Ladd, *Autophobia: Love and Hate in the Automotive Age* (Chicago, 2008), pp. 141–5.
8 Kelly Minner, 'Video: Norman Foster Recreates Buckminster Fuller's Dymaxion Car', *Architecture Daily*, 22 March 2011, www.archdaily.com.
9 International Organization of Motor Vehicle Manufacturers (OICA), 2013 production statistics, 2014, www.oica.net.
10 International Organization of Motor Vehicle Manufacturers (OICA), 'Worldometers: Real Time World Statistics', www.worldometers.info, accessed 28 July 2014.
11 Ladd, *Autophobia*, p. 60.
12 Ibid., p. 31.
13 Today's prototype Terrafugia autonomous flying car is a taxi drone for trips of up to 500 miles. As it is remote-controlled, no pilot's licence is required. Bethany Whitfield, 'Terrafugia Announces TF-X Vision Flying Car', *Flying*, 7 May 2013, flyingmag.com.
14 John Thackara, *In the Bubble: Designing in a Complex World* (Cambridge, MA, and London, 2005), p. 87.

1 Design

1 Ralph Turvey, 'Horse Traction in Victorian London', *Journal of Transport History*, XXVI/2 (September 2005), p. 57.
2 Clay McShane and Joel Tarr, 'The Decline of the Urban Horse in American Cities', *Journal of Transport History*, XXIV/2 (September 2003), p. 177.
3 Ibid., pp. 184–5.
4 Henry Ford, *My Life and Work* (Garden City, NY, 1923), p. 23.
5 L.J.K. Setright, *Drive On!: A Social History of the Motor Car* (London, 2003), p. 5.
6 James Flink, *The Automobile Age* (Cambridge, MA, 1990), p. 51.
7 Gerald Silk, *Automobile and Culture* (New York and Los Angeles, 1984), pp. 30–31.
8 Similar laws were passed in Pennsylvania, New York and Vermont during the 1890s in an attempt to curb the use of cars. Ibid., p. 14.
9 See David Hounshell, *From the American System to Mass Production, 1800–1922* (Baltimore, MD, 1985).
10 Malcolm Jeal, 'Mass Confusion: The Beginnings of the Volume-production of Motorcars', *Automotive History Review*, 54 (Autumn 2012), p. 40; author interview with Jeal, chairman of the Society of Automotive Historians in Britain, 7 October 2012.
11 Jeal, 'Mass Confusion'.
12 Huntington Carriage Company used an assembly line as early as 1853 in the production of horse-drawn vehicles. Huntington later used the assembly line for automobile production five years before Olds. See www.earlyamericanautomobiles .com, accessed 8 May 2012.
13 In New York City a male elementary-school teacher with ten years' experience earned $2,100 in 1900, while the national average wage was approximately $450. See www.encyclopedia.com, accessed 5 July 2012. In 1903 the purchase price of a 'good horse and buggy' was around $400, according to *Motor Age*, quoted by James Flink, *America Adopts the Automobile, 1895–1910* (Cambridge, MA, 1970), p. 98.
14 '[United States] State Motor-vehicle Registrations by Year', April 1997, www.fhwa.dot.gov, accessed 5 July 2012. The accuracy of all such early statistics from the USA is limited, principally because of the patchiness of state registration laws up to about 1915. Flink, *America Adopts the Automobile*, pp. 55–62.
15 Census of 1901, www.nationalarchives.gov.uk, accessed 31 May 2012.
16 James M. Laux, 'Some Notes of Entrepreneurship in the Early French Automobile Industry', *French Historical Studies*, III/1 (Spring 1963), pp. 129–34, www.jstor.org.
17 Bruce McCalley, *Model T Ford: The Car That Changed the World* (Iola, WI, 1994), p. 143.

18 Ford, *My Life and Work*, pp. 50–51.

19 Ibid., p. 72.

20 Ibid., pp. 47–63.

21 Sigfried Giedion, *Mechanization Takes Command: A Contribution to Anonymous History* (Oxford, 1979), pp. 79–85, 96–9.

22 Ibid., pp. 115–16.

23 Ford, *My Life and Work*, pp. 79–83.

24 Ibid., p. 56.

25 Royal Feltner, *History of Early American Automobile Industry, 1861–1929*, chapter 1, available at www.earlyamericanautomobiles.com, accessed 4 September 2013.

26 The Curved Dash Oldsmobile is illustrated in Silk, *Automobile and Culture*, title page.

27 Ford, *My Life and Work,* p. 66; see also Flink, *America Adopts the Automobile*, pp. 287–8.

28 Bianca Mugyenyi and Yves Engler, *Stop Signs! Cars and Capitalism on the Road to Economic, Social and Ecological Decay* (Vancouver, 2011), p. 195.

29 Tom McCarthy, *Auto Mania: Cars, Consumers, and the Environment* (New Haven, CT, and London, 2007), pp. 191–2.

30 Frederick Simpich, 'Chemists Make a New World', *National Geographic*, LXXVI/5 (November 1939), p. 606.

31 Quentin R. Skrabec, *The Green Vision of Henry Ford and George Washington Carver: Two Collaborators in the Cause of Clean Industry* (Jefferson, NC, 2013), p. 149.

32 Benson Ford Research Center, 'Soybean Car', www.thehenryford.org, accessed 10 March 2013.

33 William Porter, 'Toledo Wheels: The Design Story of Willys Overland, the Jeep and the Rise of the SUV', in *The Alliance of Art and Industry: Toledo Designs for a Modern America*, ed. Dennis Doordan (Toledo, OH, 2002), pp. 178–9.

34 US Department of Energy, *Transport Energy Data Book*, Edition 30, 25 June 2011, Table 4.15, http://cta.ornl.gov, accessed 8 July 2012.

35 Skrabec, *Green Vision*, p. 102.

36 Borealis Trade Description, www.borealisgroup.com, accessed 8 July 2012.

37 'Greased Lightning', music and lyrics by Jim Jacobs and Warren Casey, *Grease*, 1971.

38 Setright, *Drive On!*, p. 327.

39 Ibid., p. 328.

40 'Automobiles Complete Long Endurance Run', *New York Times*, 15 November 1910, reprinted in Royal Feltner, *History of Early American Automobile Industry 1861–1929*, chapter 14, available at www.earlyamericanautomobiles.com, accessed 3 June 2012.

41 Gijs Morn, *The Electric Vehicle, Technology and Expectations in the Automobile Age* (Baltimore, MD, 2004), p. 13.

42 Ernst Dickmanns, keynote speech, Fourth Conference on Artificial General Intelligence, Mountain View, California, 3–6 August 2011, available at www.youtube.com.

43 William Mitchell, Christopher Borroni-Bird and Lawrence Burns, *Reinventing the Automobile: Personal Urban Mobility for the 21st Century* (Cambridge, MA, 2010), pp. 2–7.

44 Mugyenyi and Engler, *Stop Signs!*, pp. 146–7.

45 Alfred P. Sloan, *My Years with General Motors* (London, 1965), p. 229.

46 US Department of Transportation, Highway Statistics 2004, www.fhwa.dot.gov, accessed 19 July 2012.

47 Tony Swan, 'To Shift for Oneself, or Not? It's Not Really a Question', *Car and Driver*, July 2012, www.caranddriver.com.

48 Setright, *Drive On!*, pp. 262–5.

49 Tony Swan, 'Toyota Revitalizes Its Bestseller's Core Qualities', *Car and Driver*, September 2011, www.caranddriver.com.

50 Reyner Banham, *The Architecture of the Well-tempered Environment* (London, 1969), pp. 11–17.

51 Susan Lambert, *Form Follows Function?* (London, 1993), p. 6.

52 Bryan Wert, 'Dynamics of Car Seat Design', *Illumin*, VII/1 (Autumn 2005), n.pag.

53 For a detailed cinematic interrogation of the interior of the Thunderbird of 1958, see *Mean Streets* (1973), directed by Martin Scorsese.

54 Wert, 'Dynamics of Car Seat Design'.

55 Quoted in Stephen Bayley, *Sex, Drink and Fast Cars: The Creation and Consumption of Images* (London, 1986), p. 78.

56 In 1965 there were 47,089 fatalities on American roads, according to US government statistics; see 'Motor Vehicle Traffic Fatalities and Fatality Rate: 1899–2003', available at www.saferoads.org, accessed 17 July 2012.

57 Ralph Nader, *Unsafe at Any Speed: The Designed-in Dangers of the American Automobile* (New York, 1965), chapter 4.

58 'Safety', *Consumer Reports*, XXIII/4 (April 1958), p. 194.

59 Gregory Votolato, *Transport Design: A Travel History* (London, 2007), pp. 84–6.

60 World Health Organization, 'Injuries, Traffic', www.who.int, accessed 2 October 2014.

61 Quoted in Robert N. Charette, 'This Car Runs on Code', *IEEE Spectrum*, 1 February 2009, www.spectrum.ieee.org.

62 See C. Edson Armi, *The Art of American Automobile Design* (University Park, PA, 1990); also Stephen Bayley, *Harley Earl and the Dream Machine* (London, 1983), Andrew Nahum, *Alec Issigonis* (London, 1988) and Penny Sparke, *A Century of Car Design* (London, 2002).

63 Quoted in Armi, *The Art of American Automobile Design*, p. 217.

64 Ibid., p. 27.

65 Quoted ibid., p. 200.

66 Quoted ibid.

67 Ibid., pp. 247–53.
68 David Gartman, 'A History of Scholarship on American Automobile Design', www.autolife.umd.umich.edu, accessed 8 August 2012.
69 Nina Baker, 'Women Car Designers and Designing Cars for Women: The Arrol Galloway and the Volvo YCC', Women's History Network conference, 'Moving Dangerously: Women and Travel, 1850–1950', University of Newcastle, 13–14 April 2012, www.womenshistorynetwork.org.
70 Cynthia Charwick-Bland (tutor in Vehicle Design, Royal College of Art, London), conversation and correspondence with the author, 26 April 2014.
71 Mike Hanlon, 'The Courreges ZOOOP EV', 9 July 2006, www.gizmag.com.

2 Driver

1 F. Scott Fitzgerald, *The Cruise of the Rolling Junk* [1924] (London, 2011), p. 33; Sinclair Lewis, *Babbitt* [1922] (New York, 1998), p. 32.
2 Author meeting with BMW research team, Royal College of Art, London, 21 March 2014.
3 Beverly Rae Kimes, *The Star and the Laurel: The Centennial History of Daimler, Mercedes, and Benz, 1886–1986* (Montvale, NJ, 1986), pp. 42–3.
4 Julie Wosk, *Women and the Machine: Representations from the Spinning Wheel to the Electronic Age* (New York, 2001), pp. 137–40.
5 Ibid.
6 Steven E. Alford and Suzanne Ferriss, *Motorcycle* (London, 2007), pp. 102, 105–6.
7 Gertrude Stein, *The Autobiography of Alice B. Toklas* [1933] (New York, 1961), pp. 168–77.
8 James Flink, *America Adopts the Automobile, 1895–1910* (Cambridge, MA, 1970), pp. 68–9.
9 Wosk, *Women and the Machine*, p. 125.
10 Floyd Clymer, *Motor Scrapbook No. 4* (Los Angeles, CA, 1952), p. 39.
11 Ibid., p. 109.
12 Alfred P. Sloan, *My Years with General Motors* (London, 1965), p. 264.
13 Bianca Mugyenyi and Yves Engler, *Stop Signs! Cars and Capitalism on the Road to Economic, Social and Ecological Decay* (Vancouver, 2011), p. 166.
14 Henry Ford, *My Life and Work* (Garden City, NY, 1923), p. 11.
15 David Gartman, *Auto Opium: A Social History of American Automobile Design* (London and New York, 1994), pp. 73–7.
16 Sonja Windhager et al., 'Face to Face: The Perceptions of Automotive Designs', *Human Nature*, XIX (November–December 2008).
17 Ilya Ehrenburg, *The Life of the Automobile* [1929] (London, 1985), p. 33.
18 Ibid., p. 27.
19 Kenneth Grahame, *The Wind in the Willows* [1908], available at www.etext.virginia.edu/toc/modeng/public/GraWind.html, pp. 138–9, accessed 28 June 2012.

20 Filippo Tommaso Marinetti, 'The Foundation and Manifesto of Futurism' [1909], in Charles Harrison and Paul Wood, eds, *Art in Theory, 1900-2000: An Anthology of Changing Ideas* (Oxford, 2003), p. 147.

21 The car may have been a Packard, depending on the source. Lotte Eisner, *F. W. Murnau* (Berkeley, CA, 1973), p. 222. See also Kenneth Anger, *Hollywood Babylon* (Paris, 1959).

22 Depending on the source, the car was a Type 35 or Type 47 Bugatti, or an Amilcar.

23 Arthur Drexler and Philip Johnson, *8 Automobiles* (Museum of Modern Art, New York, 1951).

24 Stephen Bayley, *Sex, Drink and Fast Cars: The Creation and Consumption of Images* (London, 1986), p. 77.

25 Dan Quinlan, Royal College of Art project for a city car with expressed honeycomb storage battery, 2014. Clive Birch, ed., *Royal College of Art Vehicle Design 2014* (Buckingham, 2014).

26 Lewis, *Babbitt*, pp. 38–9.

27 Quoted in Daniel Miller, ed., *Car Cultures* (Oxford, 2001), p. 185.

28 Marshall McLuhan, *Understanding Media: The Extensions of Man* (New York, 1964), chapter 22.

29 Lynn Sloman, *Car Sick: Solutions for Our Car-addicted Culture* (Totnes, Devon, 2006), pp. 56–9.

30 Ibid., p. 146.

31 Ibid., p. 155.

32 Ibid., p. 159.

33 Daniel Sperling and Deborah Gordon, *Two Billion Cars: Driving Toward Sustainability* (Oxford, 2009), pp. 236–7.

34 Chris Bangle, 'Great Cars Are Great Art', TED Talk, February 2002, transcribed by Jenny Zurawell, www.ted.com.

35 Adam Setter, 'Glitch', Royal College of Art thesis project, 2012, available at www.greencardesign.com.

3 Image

1 Roland Barthes, *Mythologies* [1955], trans. Annette Lavers (London, 1986), p. 88.

2 Quoted in Charles Harrison and Paul Wood, *Art in Theory, 1900-2000: An Anthology of Changing Ideas* (Oxford, 2003), p. 147.

3 Quoted in Gerald Silk, *Automobile and Culture* (New York and Los Angeles, 1984), p. 79.

4 Arthur Rimbaud, 'The Drunken Boat' [1871], www.mag4.net, accessed 10 January 2009.

5 Quoted in Silk, *Automobile and Culture*, p. 75.

6 Judith Hoos Fox, ed., 'Inside Cars', special edn of *2wice*, V/2 (2001), p. 62.

7 Ant Farm, *Automerica: A Trip down US Highways* (New York, 1976), p. 124.

8 John Beardsley, *Earthworks and Beyond: Contemporary Art in the Landscape* (New York, 1984), p. 31.

9 Deborah Allen, 'Design Review: Cars '55', *Industrial Design*, February 1955, and quoted in Reyner Banham, 'Detroit Tin Re-visited', in *Design 1900–1960: Studies in Design and Popular Culture of the 20th Century*, ed. T. Faulkner (Newcastle upon Tyne, 1976), pp. 130–31.

10 Jack Kerouac, *On the Road* (New York, 1957), chapter 6.

11 See Bart H. Vanderveen, ed., *American Cars of the 1930s* (London, 1971), and other publications of the Olyslager Auto Library, whose American Cars series include many examples of US car chassis fitted with European coachbuilt bodies, particularly those made in Germany, Britain and the Netherlands.

12 Ghislaine Bouchet, *Le Cheval à Paris de 1850 à 1914* (Paris and Geneva, 1993), p. 144. See also Jean-Louis Libourel, *Voitures hippomobiles: vocabulaire typologique et technique* (Paris, 2005).

13 Paul C. Wilson, *Chrome Dreams: Automobile Styling since 1893* (Radnor, PA, 1976), p. 133.

14 Floyd Clymer, *Floyd Clymer's Historical Motor Scrapbook, Number Four* (Los Angeles, 1947) p. 142.

15 Victor Papanek, *The Green Imperative: Ecology and Ethics in Design and Architecture* (London, 1995), p. 65.

16 Daniel Miller, ed., *Car Cultures* (Oxford, 2001), p. 24.

17 Tom Wolfe, *The Kandy-kolored Tangerine-flake Streamline Baby* (London, 1966), pp. 67–74.

18 John Brenneman, 'An Architect Looks at Customizing', *Motor Life*, December 1957, p. 18.

19 Wolfe, *Kandy-kolored*, pp. 82–3.

20 Ibid., p. 94.

21 James Harithas, reprinted from Maurice Robert, James Haritha and Claire Poole, *Art Cars: Revolutionary Movement* (Houston, TX, 1997), www.artcarmuseum.com, accessed 14 March 2013.

22 Of 28 custom cars entered in *Motor Life* magazine's annual 'Custom Cars of the Year' contest in 1958, thirteen were designed and built by their owners. 'The Winning Custom of the Year', *Motor Life*, VIII/3 (October 1958), pp. 38–43.

23 Gregory Votolato, *Transport Design: A Travel History* (London, 2007), pp. 202–17.

24 Ruth Brandon, *Automobile: How the Car Changed Life* (London, 2002), p. 243.

25 Packard Motors, Packard Thirty brochure (Detroit, MI, 1908), www.oldcarbrochures. com, accessed 16 August 2012.

26 Wilson, *Chrome Dreams*, pp. 128–9. Wilson presents the often-repeated 'catastrophe' version of this story, stating that 'Buick's share of the market fell to less than half of what it was the year before.' Actual Buick production figures and ranking for the years 1928–32 were respectively 221,758 (6th), 196,104 (6th), 181,743 (3rd), 138,965 (3rd) and 56,790 (5th).

27 Quoted in Silk, *Automobile and Culture*, p. 219.

28 Kenneth Frampton, *Modern Architecture, 1851–1945* (New York, 1983), p. 204.

29 Quoted in Adrian Forty, 'Of Cars, Clothes and Carpets: Design Metaphors in Architectural Thought: The First Banham Memorial Lecture', *Journal of Design History*, II/1 (1989), pp. 1–14.

30 Henry Ford, *My Life and Work* (Garden City, NY, 1923) p. 56.

31 National Motor Vehicle Company, 'National Motor Cars 1915' (Indianapolis, IN, 1915), www.oldcarbrochures.com, accessed 18 December 2012.

32 Forty, 'Of Cars, Clothes and Carpets', p. 12.

33 Ibid., pp. 7–8.

34 Advertised prices for 1926: Ford Touring $290; Chevrolet Touring $510.

35 'Museum to Open First Exhibition Anywhere of Automobiles Selected for Design', www.moma.org, accessed 20 August 2012.

36 Komenda also designed the bodies for the pre-war Auto Union and post-war Cisitalia Grand Prix cars.

37 Votolato, *Transport Design*, pp. 80–81; L.K.J. Setright, *Drive On!: A Social History of the Motorcar* (London, 2003), pp. 93, 173.

38 Barthes, *Mythologies*, pp. 96–7.

39 Paul Wilson discussed in detail GM's aggressive 'battering-ram' look, which took automotive expressionism to its logical extreme, with particular reference to the Buick of 1950–51, in *Chrome Dreams*, p. 201.

40 Lotus Elite (designed by Ron Hickman; 1962), MGB roadster of 1963 (engineered by Syd Enever, styled by Don Hayter), MGB GT coupé of 1967 (styled by Pininfarina), Mazda MX5 Miata of 1989 (original Mazda design team: Tom Matano, Mark Jordan, Wu Huang Chin, Norman Garrett and Koichi Hayashi), Mercedes SLK series roadsters (series 1 designed by Murat Günak; 1996).

41 Floyd Clymer, *Floyd Clymer's Historical Motor Scrapbook, Number Four* (Los Angeles, 1947), pp. 56, 65, 79.

42 Sinclair Lewis, *Babbitt* [1922] (New York, 1998), p. 123.

43 Vance Packard, *The Hidden Persuaders* (London, 1971), pp. 128–9.

44 Heon Stevenson, *American Automobile Advertising, 1930–1980: An Illustrated History* (London, 2008), p. 228.

45 Quoted ibid.

46 See Penny Sparke, *As Long as It's Pink: The Sexual Politics of Taste* (Halifax, Nova Scotia, 2010).

4 Road

1 Ilya Ehrenburg, *The Life of the Automobile* [1929] (London, 1985), p. 19.

2 Ibid., pp. 20–21.

3 Celia Fremlin, War Factory, Mass Observation, 1943, quoted in Caleb Crain, 'History of the Assembly Line from Below', www.steamthing.com, 6 November 2006.

4 Henry Ford, *My Life and Work* (Garden City, NY, 1923), p. 105.

5 Ibid., p. 103.

6 Quoted in Gerald Silk, *Automobile and Culture* (New York and Los Angeles, 1984), pp. 102–4.

7 David Gartman, *Auto Opium: A Social History of American Automobile Design* (London and New York, 1994), p. 212.

8 Joseph P. Cabadas, *River Rouge: Ford's Industrial Colossus* (St Paul, MN, 2004), p. 21.

9 Gillian Darley, *Factory* (London, 2003) pp. 82–92.

10 Ibid., pp. 84–6.

11 H. G. Wells, *Experiment in Autobiography: Discoveries and Conclusions of a Very Ordinary Brain (Since 1866)* (London, 1934), p. 543.

12 Octave Mirbeau, *Sketches of a Journey: La 628-E8* (London, 1989), pp. 86–8.

13 Ibid., p. 48.

14 F. Scott Fitzgerald, *The Cruise of the Rolling Junk* [1924] (London, 2011), p. 81.

15 Ibid., p. 60.

16 Peter Hessler, *Country Driving: A Chinese Road Trip* (New York, 2010), p. 57.

17 Erin Baker, 'Driven: Renault Twizy', *The Telegraph*, 26 September 2012, www.telegraph.co.uk.

18 Reyner Banham, 'Detroit Tin Re-visited', in T. Faulkner, ed., *Design 1900–1960: Studies in Design and Popular Culture of the 20th Century* (Newcastle upon Tyne, 1976), p. 120.

19 Roland Barthes, 'The New Citroën', in *Mythologies* (London, 1986), pp. 88–90.

20 Malcolm Bobbitt, *Citroën DS* (Dorchester, 2005), p. 58.

21 Mike Featherstone, Nigel Thrift and John Urry, *Automobilities* (London, 2005), p. 189.

22 Dennis Sharp, *A Visual History of Twentieth Century Architecture* (Greenwich, CT, 1972), p. 26.

23 Shannon Sanders McDonald, 'Cars, Parking and Sustainability', annual forum of the Transport Research Forum, Tampa, Florida, 2012, available at www.trforum.org.

24 Quoted in Shannon Sanders McDonald, 'The Parking Garage as the Undocumented Search for Modernism', ACSA International Conference, Mexico City, 2005, available at www.academia.edu.

25 Sharp, *Visual History*, p. 258.

26 Edgar Kaufmann, ed., *Frank Lloyd Wright: An American Architecture* (New York, 1955), pp. 205–8.

27 Thierry Koskas, International Website of Renault Group, Environment, www.renault.com, 2012.

28 Sharp, *Visual History*, p. 99.

29 Richard Gutman, *American Diner* (New York, n.d.), p. 36.

30 Walter Dorwin Teague, *Design This Day: The Technique of Order in the Machine Age* (New York, 1940).

31 Claudette Stager and Martha A. Carver, eds, *Looking beyond the Highway: Dixie Roads and Culture* (Knoxville, TN, 2006), p. 187.

32 Francesco Gatti, 'Drive-in Automobile Museum | 3GATTI', http://plusmood.com, accessed 31 December 2012.

33 According to designer Peter Stephens, the cycle car movement 'grew out of early socialist cycle clubs and remained a left wing manifestation', congruent with ideals of the Progressive Movement in North America in the early twentieth century. Peter Stephens, correspondence with the author, 28 April 2015.

34 Donald Hoffmann, *Frank Lloyd Wright's Robie House: The Illustrated Story of an Architectural Masterpiece* (New York, 1984), pp. 5–6.

35 Daniel Carson Bruechert, 'Frank Lloyd Wright and the Automobile: Designs for Automobility', Masters diss., University of Georgia, 2006, p. 18.

36 Ibid., p. 20.

37 Quoted in Donald C. Shoup, 'The High Cost of Free Parking', *Journal of Planning Education and Research*, XVII (1997), pp. 3–20.

38 Ibid.

39 Alison Lurie, *The Nowhere City* [1965] (New York, 1986), pp. 7, 232.

40 Peter Engelhard, 'Making Room for Beetle: Volkswagen's Impact on the German Motor Industry', *Automotive History Review*, LIV (Autumn 2012), p. 14.

41 Andrés Duany et al., 'Charter of the New Urbanism', North American Congress for New Urbanism, www.cnu.org, 2011.

5 Chaos

1 Malcolm Jeal, 'Facts Spoil a Bloody Tale: The 1903 Paris–Madrid Race', *Aspects of Motoring History* (2005), p. 32.

2 John L. Matthews, dir., *Madness on Wheels: Rallying's Craziest Years*, BBC4 television, broadcast 3 April 2012.

3 Quoted in Charles Harrison and Paul Wood, *Art in Theory, 1900–2000: An Anthology of Changing Ideas* (Oxford, 2003), p. 147.

4 Gaston Bachelard, *The Poetics of Space* (Boston, MA, 1994), pp. 38–46.

5 Ibid.

6 Peter Stearns, *American Fear: The Causes and Consequences of High Anxiety* (New York, 2006), n.pag.

7 Peter Wells, 'The Suitability of Offroad Vehicles for Urban Environments', *Offroad Cars, Onroad Menace: 4×4s in the City*, www.greenpeace.org.uk, 2006.

8 Quoted in David R. Williams, 'The Apollo Lunar Roving Vehicle', http://nssdc.gsfc.nasa.gov, 15 November 2005.

9 John Heskett, 'The Desire for the New: The Context of Brooks Stevens' Career', in *Industrial Strength Design: How Brooks Stevens Shaped Your World*, ed. Glenn Adamson (Cambridge, MA, 2003), p. 5.

10 Adamson, *Industrial Strength Design*, pp. 92–6. Willys Overland staff designer Robert Andrews contested the authorship of the Jeep Station Wagon, which was developed from a Stevens sketch by Andrews and Art Kibiger. See also William Porter, 'Toledo Wheels: The Design Story of Willys Overland, the Jeep and the Rise of the SUV', in *The Alliance of Art and Industry: Toledo Designs for a Modern America*, ed. Dennis Doordan (Toledo, OH, 2002), pp. 109–27.

11 E. Bartholomew, *Early Armoured Cars* (Princes Risborough, Bucks, 1988), pp. 3–5.

12 'Automobile Fighting Engines for Russia', *Popular Mechanics*, VIII/4 (April 1906), p. 413.

13 Ibid.

14 Bartholomew, *Early Armoured Cars*, p. 6.

15 Canadian War Artist Suzanne Steele in conversation with the author, Oxford University, 5 and 6 September 2014. Correspondence with the author, 30 October 2014.

16 S. Steele, 'War Poems', *Journal of Military and Strategic Studies*, North America, 12 November 2009, www.jmss.org., accessed 30 October 2014.

17 'Nuit Dramatique au Quartier Latin', *Le Monde*, 13 May 1968, http://lemonde.fr.

18 Quoted in Ken Knabb, *Situationist International Anthology* (Berkeley, CA, 2006), pp. 69–70. 'Positions situationnistes sur la circulation' originally appeared in *Internationale Situationniste*, 3 (December 1959), www.bopsecrets.org, accessed 21 January 2013.

19 Quoted in Knabb, *Situationist International Anthology*.

20 Edwin J. Sanow, *Ford Police Cars: 1932–1997* (Osceola, WI, 1997), p. 14.

21 Paul Clinton, 'The World's Last Ford Crown Vic Police Interceptor', *Police: The Law Enforcement Magazine*, 12 June 2012, www.policemag.com.

22 Peter Wollen, 'Mappings: Situationists and/or Conceptualists', in *Rewriting Conceptual Art*, ed. Michael Newman and Jon Bird (London, 1999), p. 32.

23 Michèle Bernstein, *Potlatch 911, 1731*, August 1954. *Potlatch* was the 'information bulletin of the French Section of the Lettrist International'. Twenty-seven issues were published between 1954 and 1957. Contributors included Guy Debord and Bernstein (his wife), founders of the Situationist International. Christian Nolle, 'Books of Warfare: The Collaboration between Guy Debord and Asger Jorn from 1957–1959', www.virose.pt, accessed 7 December 2012.

24 Geremie R. Barmé, 'Engines of Revolution: Car Cultures in China', in *Autopia: Cars and Culture*, ed. Peter Wollen and Joe Kerr (London, 2002), p. 184.

25 Ibid., p. 185.

26 Ibid.

27 Classified advertisements, *Washington Herald*, 19 February 1913, p. 11, http://chroniclingamerica.loc.gov.

28 Adam Millard-Ball, *Car-Sharing: Where and How It Succeeds* (Washington, DC, 2005), pp. 2–5.
29 Clive Birch, ed., *Royal College of Art: Vehicle Design 2012* (Buckingham, 2012), pp. 80–81.

6 Afterlife

1 'Special Notices', *The Horseless Age* (4 April 1900), p. 27.
2 *San Francisco Call*, classified advertisements, 19 February 1913, p. 12, chroniclingamerica.loc.gov. See also James Flink, *America Adopts the Automobile, 1895–1910* (Cambridge, MA, 1970), pp. 255–6.
3 Daniel Miller, ed., *Car Cultures* (Oxford, 2001), pp. 157–8.
4 Ibid., pp. 160–61.
5 *Sin City Motors* is a series owned in the UK by UKTV and BBC Worldwide television. It is set in the workshops of a Las Vegas-based Rat Rod builder. See dave.uktv.co.uk, accessed 11 November 2014.
6 Author interview with Professor Peter Stevens, Royal College of Art, 19 March 2014.
7 Zhongnanhai, the headquarters for the Communist Party of China, is also used as a metonym for the Chinese leadership, just as the term 'White House' can refer to the US President.
8 Smithsonian Institution, http://amhistory.si.edu, accessed 24 February 2013.
9 Henry Ford, *My Life and Work* (Garden City, NY, 1923), p. 19.
10 Thomas Dickson, *Dansk Design* (London, 2006), p. 402.
11 William Stobbs, *Motor Museums of Europe* (London, 1983), p. 67.
12 'The Most Magnificent Rolls-Royce Ever Built', *Daily Mail*, 5 July 2012, p. 13.
13 Rodolphe Rapetti, *L'art de l'automobile: Chefs-d'œuvre de la collection Ralph Lauren* (Paris, 2011), author's translation.
14 Malcolm Jeal, 'A Tangled Web', and Eddie Berrisford, 'The 1914 Grand Prix Mercedes', Society of Automotive Historians in Britain, autumn seminar, Sir Henry Royce Memorial Foundation, Paulerspury, Northamptonshire, 7 October 2012.
15 Malcolm Jeal, 'The History of a Lancia Astura', *Society of Automotive Historians Journal*, 258 (September/October 2012), pp. 6–9.
16 Victor Papanek, *The Green Imperative: Ecology and Ethics in Design and Architecture* (London, 1995), p. 238.
17 N. Kanari, J.-L. Pineau and S. Shallari, 'End-of-life Vehicle Recycling in the European Union', *Journal of Minerals, Metals and Materials*, LV/8 (August 2003), www.tms.org.
18 Doyle Dane Bernbach, Volkswagen advertisement, *Life*, 24 September 1971, pp. 56–7.
19 Kurt Reschner, 'Scrap Tyre Recycling: A Summary of Prevalent Disposal and Recycling Methods, Berlin, Germany', 2008, www.entire-engineering.de.

20 CRiSiL, 'Tire Recycling Industry: A Global View', www.irevna.com, accessed 2 March 2013.
21 Hester Lacey, 'Tread Carefully: Recycling Tyres', *The Independent*, 29 June 2006, www.independent.co.uk.
22 'Where the Old Car Meets Its End and Starts Life Over Again', *Popular Science Monthly*, CXVII/5 (November 1930), p. 61.
23 See Quentin R. Skrabec, *The Green Vision of Henry Ford and George Washington Carver: Two Collaborators in the Cause of Clean Industry* (Jefferson, NC, 2013); editorial, *Popular Science Monthly*, CXVII/5 (November 1930), p. 76.
24 Paola Antonelli, *Mutant Materials in Contemporary Design* (New York, 1995), pp. 17–18.
25 Interior Motives Design Awards 2013, *Car Design News*, www.interiormotivesawards.com, accessed 30 April 2013.
26 William Mitchell, Chris Borroni-Bird and Lawrence Burns, *Reinventing the Automobile: Personal Urban Mobility for the 21st Century* (Cambridge, MA, 2010), pp. 72–7.
27 Martin C. Pedersen, 'Q&A: Dan Sturges', *Metropolis*, 22 October 2012, www.metropolismag.com.
28 Quoted in Bruce Mau and the Institute without Boundaries, *Massive Change* (London, 2004), p. 53.
29 Ibid., p. 49.
30 Quoted in Joel Simpson, 'The Future of the Urban Car? It's a "PUMA" say GM and Segway', *Re*Move* blog, Movement Design Bureau, 2009, www.movementbureau.blogs.com.
31 Mau, *Massive Change*, p. 48.

Select Bibliography

Amado, A., *Voiture Minimum: Le Corbusier and the Automobile* (Cambridge, MA, 2011)

Ant Farm, *Automerica: A Trip down US Highways* (New York, 1976)

Armi, C. E., *The Art of American Automobile Design: The Profession and Personalities* (University Park, PA, 1990)

Bachelard, G., *The Poetics of Space* (Boston, MA, 1994)

Banham, R., 'Detroit Tin Re-visited', in T. Faulkner, ed., *Design 1900–1960: Studies in Design and Popular Culture of the 20th Century* (Newcastle upon Tyne, 1976)

Barthes, R., *Mythologies* [1955], trans. Annette Lavers (London, 1986)

Bartholomew, E., *Early Armoured Cars* (Princes Risborough, Bucks, 1988)

Bayley, S., *Sex, Drink and Fast Cars: The Creation and Consumption of Images* (London, 1986)

Bobbitt, M., *Citroën DS* (Dorchester, 2005)

Cabadas, J., *River Rouge: Ford's Industrial Colossus* (St Paul, MN, 2004)

Clymer, F., *Floyd Clymer's Historical Motor Scrapbook, Number Four* (Los Angeles, 1947)

Darley, G., *Factory* (London, 2003)

Drexler, A., and P. Johnson, *8 Automobiles* (New York, 1951)

Ehrenburg, I., *The Life of the Automobile* [1929] (London, 1985)

Featherstone, M., N. Thrift and J. Urry, *Automobilities* (London, 2005)

Flink, J., *America Adopts the Automobile, 1895–1910* (Cambridge, MA, 1970)

–, *The Automobile Age* (Cambridge, MA, 1990)

Ford, H., *My Life and Work* (Garden City, NY, 1923)

Fox, J. H., ed., 'Inside Cars', special edn of *2wice*, V/2 (2001)

Gartman, D., *Auto Opium: A Social History of American Automobile Design* (London and New York, 1994)

Giedion, S., *Mechanization Takes Command: A Contribution to Anonymous History* (Oxford, 1979)

Giucci, G., *The Cultural Life of the Automobile: Roads to Modernity* (Austin, TX, 2012)

Gutman, R., and E. Kaufman, *American Diner* (New York, n.d.)

Heskett, J., 'The Desire for the New: The Context of Brooks Stevens' Career', in
    G. Adamson, ed., *Industrial Strength Design: How Brooks Stevens Shaped Your
    World* (Cambridge, MA, 2003)
Hessler, P., *Country Driving: A Chinese Road Trip* (New York, 2010)
Hoffmann, D., *Frank Lloyd Wright's Robie House: The Illustrated Story of an
    Architectural Masterpiece* (Mineola, NY, 1984)
Hounshell, D., *From the American System to Mass Production, 1800–1932*
    (Baltimore, MD, 1985)
Jeal, M. J., ed., 'Facts Spoil a Bloody Tale: The 1903 Paris–Madrid Race', *Aspects of
    Motoring History* (2005, reprinted 2012)
–, 'The History of the Lancia Astura', *Society of Automotive Historians Journal*, 258
    (September–October 2012)
Keats, J., *The Insolent Chariots* (New York, 1958)
Kerr, J., and P. Wollen, eds, *Autopia: Cars and Culture* (London, 2002)
Kimes, B. R., *The Star and the Laurel: The Centennial History of Daimler, Mercedes,
    and Benz, 1886–1986* (Montvale, NJ, 1986)
Ladd, B., *Autophobia: Love and Hate in the Automotive Age* (Chicago, 2008)
McCalley, B., *Model T Ford: The Car That Changed the World* (Iola, WI, 1994)
McCarthy, T., *Auto Mania: Cars, Consumers, and the Environment* (New Haven, CT,
    and London, 2007)
Marinetti, F. T., 'The Foundation Manifesto of Futurism' [1909], in C. Harrison and
    P. Wood, *Art in Theory, 1900–2000: An Anthology of Changing Ideas* (Oxford,
    2003)
Mau, B., and Institute without Boundaries, *Massive Change* (London, 2004)
Millard-Ball, A., *Car-sharing: Where and How It Succeeds* (Washington, DC, 2005)
Miller, D., ed., *Car Cultures* (Oxford, 2001)
Mirbeau, O., *Sketches of a Journey: La 628-E8* (London, 1989)
Mitchell, W., C. Borroni-Bird and L. Burns, *Reinventing the Automobile: Personal
    Urban Mobility for the 21st Century* (Cambridge, MA, 2010)
Mugyenyi, B., and Y. Engler, *Stop Signs! Cars and Capitalism on the Road to
    Economic, Social and Ecological Decay* (Vancouver, 2011)
Nader, R., *Unsafe at Any Speed: The Designed-in Dangers of the American
    Automobile* (New York, 1965)
Packard, V., *The Hidden Persuaders* (London, 1971)
Papanek, V., *The Green Imperative: Ecology and Ethics in Design and Architecture*
    (London, 1995)
Porter, W., 'Toledo Wheels: The Design Story of Willys Overland, the Jeep and the
    Rise of the SUV', in D. Doordan, ed., *The Alliance of Art and Industry: Toledo
    Designs for a Modern America* (Toledo, OH, 2002)
Rapetti, R., *L'art de l'automobile: Chefs-d'œuvre de la collection Ralph Lauren*
    (Paris, 2011)
Rubinyi, K., *The Car in 2035: Mobility Planning for the Near Future*
    (Los Angeles, 2013)

Sanow, E. J., *Ford Police Cars: 1932–1997* (Osceola, WI, 1997)

Science Museum, *Fiat, 1899–1989: An Italian Industrial Revolution* (Milan, 1988)

Seiler, C., *Republic of Drivers: A Cultural History of Automobility in America* (Chicago and London, 2008)

Setright, L.J.K., *Drive On! A Social History of the Motor Car* (London, 2003)

Silk, G., *Automobile and Culture* (New York and Los Angeles, 1984)

Skrabec, Q. R., *The Green Vision of Henry Ford and George Washington Carver: Two Collaborators in the Cause of Clean Industry* (Jefferson, NC, 2013)

Sloan, A. P., *My Years with General Motors* (London, 1965)

Sloman, L., *Car Sick: Solutions for our Car-addicted Culture* (Totnes, Devon, 2006)

Sparke, P., *A Century of Car Design* (London, 2002)

Sperling, D., and D. Gordon, *Two Billion Cars: Driving toward Sustainability* (Oxford, 2009)

Stager, C., and M. Carver, eds, *Looking beyond the Highway: Dixie Roads and Culture* (Knoxville, TN, 2006)

Stearns, P., *American Fear: The Causes and Consequences of High Anxiety* (New York, 2006)

Stevenson, H., *American Automobile Advertising, 1930–1980: An Illustrated History* (London, 2008)

Stobbs, W., *Motor Museums of Europe* (London, 1983)

Thackara, J., *In the Bubble: Designing in a Complex World* (Cambridge, MA, and London, 2005)

Votolato, G., *American Design in the Twentieth Century* (Manchester, 1998)

—, *Transport Design: A Travel History* (London, 2007)

Wilson, P. C., *Chrome Dreams: Automobile Styling since 1893* (Radnor, PA, 1976)

Wolfe, T., *The Kandy-kolored Tangerine-flake Streamline Baby* (London, 1966)

Wollen, P., 'Mappings: Situationists and/or Conceptualists', in M. Newman and J. Bird, ed., *Rewriting Conceptual Art* (London, 1999)

Wosk, J., *Women and the Machine: Representations from the Spinning Wheel to the Electronic Age* (New York, 2001)

Acknowledgements

My acknowledgements begin with my elder brother, the Hon. Arthur Votolato, who taught me at the age of two or thereabouts that a funeral flower car should not be called a Cadillac pickup truck. Posthumously my father, the Hon. Arthur Sr, provided the diary of his honeymoon with my mother during the summer of 1929 in which he recorded every episode of chassis lubrication, oil change and tire repair during a three-month excursion in a new Dodge Victory Six through New England and the province of Quebec in Canada. More recently, my son Max has tirelessly and cheerfully offered up some serious and other thoroughly fantastic automotive information and observations from his usual com - munication headquarters, a Mustang convertible on the 210 Freeway in Los Angeles.

At Reaktion Books, I am grateful to Oliver Keen and Martha Jay for their invaluable design and editorial advice and to Vivian Constantinopulous for giving me the opportunity to vent a lifetime of love, loathing, curiosity and hope for the automobile. Her commentary on my efforts was always sobering, inspiring, amusing and constructive. The producer Sheila Cook enabled me to test my more contentious ideas about the car on a very large audience through her BBC radio series, *Four Thought*. Recently Charlotte Klonk and Franziska Solte of Humboldt University in Berlin created a fascinating context for cross-disciplinary conversations relating the automobile to other modes and systems of transportation in their conference, 'The Moving Interior'. Other university colleagues have also let me loose on their students with lectures and seminars presenting and receiving ideas that found their way into this book. Among them Claire O'Mahony of Kellogg College, Oxford, Anne Massey and Penny Sparke at Kingston University (both contributing significant design history perspectives to the field of transport studies), Jo Banham and Mary LeComte of the Learning Department at the Victoria & Albert Museum, and Joe Kerr at the Royal College of Art in London have been great supporters. Joe has also shared many unique and original stories drawn from his vast experience of automotive and transport history, particularly regarding the lore of Detroit, past and present. Professor Peter Stevens offered unique insights and rare information drawn from a deeply informed designer's perspective.

I also want to offer special thanks to other colleagues in the Critical & Historical Studies and Vehicle Design courses at the RCA. They and the postgraduate students of

Product Design, Innovation Design, Architecture and Service Design have stimulated much of what I tried to express about the bigger issues surrounding the car in our lives today. Because they come from everywhere, they have greatly broadened my geogra - phical perspective on the developing role of the car as it functions in various cultures and in countless individual lives from Asia to the Swiss Alps, the suburbs of Phoenix, rural England and the city where we meet, London.

Over the years during which I have been learning about this huge subject, certain places, events and people stand out as notably helpful. Among the car collections of the world, the following offered particularly valuable information, enlightening con - texts and extraordinary experiences of cars:

Automobile Driving Museum, El Segundo, California
Cité de l'Automobile, Mulhouse, France
DAF Museum, Eindhoven, The Netherlands
The Henry Ford, Dearborn, Michigan
Lars Andersen Museum, Boston, Massachusetts
London Motor Museum, UK
National Motor Museum, Beaulieu, Hampshire, UK
Nethercutt Collection, Los Angeles, California
Petersen Automotive Museum, Los Angeles, California

The Society of Automotive Historians in Britain has been a source of extraordinary information and inspiration through their publications, seminars and stimulating con - versations with members. Among them, Andy Joliffe involved me as a member of the 'team' running his 1904 Oldsmobile, 'Olivia', in the annual London to Brighton Veteran Car Run, which for me is a uniquely revealing insight into late Victorian and early Edwardian motoring and motorcars. Finally, I thank the Design History Society for many opportunities over the years to present papers related to the subject of this book, some of which led to earlier publications and all of which attracted responses from delegates that have been helpful in forming my arguments and ideas. For many more friends, relatives, colleagues, students and acquaintances who sent me articles, links, book titles, pictures, tips on places to visit, rides in their cars and so much more, I can only give a sincere thank you.

Photo Acknowledgements

The author and publishers wish to express their thanks to the below sources of illustrative material and/or permission to reproduce it:

Ad*Access On-Line Project - Ad #R0067 – John W. Hartman Center for Sales, Advertising & Marketing History, Duke University David M. Rubenstein Rare Book & Manuscript Library (http://library.duke.edu/digitalcollections/adaccess): p. 111; AlfvanBeem: p. 96; photo author: pp. 6, 8, 51, 63, 67, 87, 134, 142, 146, 147, 150, 192, 193, 195, 201, 211, 236, 258, 262, 265, 268, 277; from *Autocar Handbook* (London, 1935): p. 61; photo © Bettmann/CORBIS: p. 225; Michael Cory: p. 279; Crittenden Automotive Library: p. 21; © DACS 2015: p. 119; Royal Feltner: p. 198; Art Fitzpatrick (fitz@fitz-art.com): p. 123; Geoffrey Hacker: p. 44; Hirshhorn Museum and Sculpture Garden, Washington, DC: p. 119; Andrew Joliffe: p. 40; Library of Congress, Washington, DC: pp. 11, 31, 32, 33, 39, 56, 71, 95, 102, 173, 174, 176, 184, 191, 199; Library of Congress, Washington, DC (Carol M. Highsmith Archive): p. 122; luc106: p. 153; Colin Millum: p. 108; MPW57: p. 137; NASA: p. 221; Official White House photo by Pete Souza: p. 227 bottom; Royal College of Art: pp. 99, 285, 288; US Air Force photo (photographer Staff Sgt. Jerry Fleshman): p. 227 top; Roger Welch: p. 194; Wolf D.: p. 14.

cliff1066™, the copyright holder of the image on p. 119, Robert Hextall, the copyright holder of the image on p. 52, jurvetson, the copyright holder of the images on pp. 113 and 289, mashleymorgan, the copyright holder of the image on p. 223, Brian Snelson, the copyright holder of the images on pp. 129 and 210, and Terry Whalebone, the copyright holder of the image on p. 94, have published these online under conditions imposed by a Creative Commons Attribution 2.0 Generic license; Rex Gray, the copyright holder of the image on p. 64, has published this image online under conditions imposed by a Creative Commons Attribution-Share Alike 2.0 Generic license; BMW Werk Leipzig, the copyright holder of the images on pp. 165 and 166, have published these images online under conditions imposed by a Creative Commons Attribution-Share Alike 2.0 Germany license; Biso, the copyright holder of the image on p. 72, and Huhu Uet, the copyright holder of the image on p. 17, have published these online under conditions imposed by a Creative Commons Attribution 3.0 Unported license; burts, the copyright holder of the image on p. 45, Chris 73, the copyright holder of the image on p. 267, Martin Falbisoner, the copyright holder of the image on p. 187, Hideki Kimura, the copyright holder of the image on p. 215, Morio, the copyright holder of the images on pp. 270 and 287, Mr.choppers, the copyright holder of the images on pp. 26 and 151, Kärjens Slædebjørg, the copyright holder of the image on p. 271, Spantax, the copyright holder of the image on p. 180, SurfAst, the copyright holder of the image on p. 120, and Xavigivax, the copyright holder of the image on p. 127, have published these online under conditions imposed by a Creative Commons Attribution-Share Alike 3.0 Unported license; and Harry Pot, the copyright holder of the image on p. 214, has published it online under conditions imposed by a Creative Commons Attribution-Share Alike 3.0 Netherlands license.

Readers are free:

> to share – to copy, distribute and transmit these images alone
> to remix – to adapt these images alone

Under the following condition:

> attribution – readers must attribute any image in the manner specified by the author or licensor (but not in any way that suggests that these parties endorse them or their use of the work).

Antony, the copyright holder of the image on p. 261, Isaac Bordas, the copyright holder of the image on p. 217, Martin Brigden, the copyright holder of the image on p. 219, DiamondBack Truck Covers, the copyright holder of the image on p. 19, ehpien, the copyright holder of the image on p. 249, Florian Hardwig, the copyright holder of the image on p. 155 (right), Ludovic Hirlimann, the copyright holder of the image on p. 250, Jurgen, the copyright holder of the image on p. 255, Iker Merodio, the copyright holder of the image on p. 257, Steve Parker, the copyright holder of the image on p. 260 and theopie, the copyright holder of the image on p. 217, have published these online under conditions imposed by a Creative Commons Attribution 2.0 Generic license (*with a specific additional clause relating to technological measures*).

Readers are free:

> to share – to copy, distribute and transmit these images alone
> to remix – to adapt these images alone

Under the following conditions:

> attribution – readers must attribute any image in the manner specified by the author or licensor (but not in any way that suggests that these parties endorse them or their use of the work).
> No additional restrictions — You may not apply legal terms or technological measures that legally restrict others from doing anything the license permits.

Index